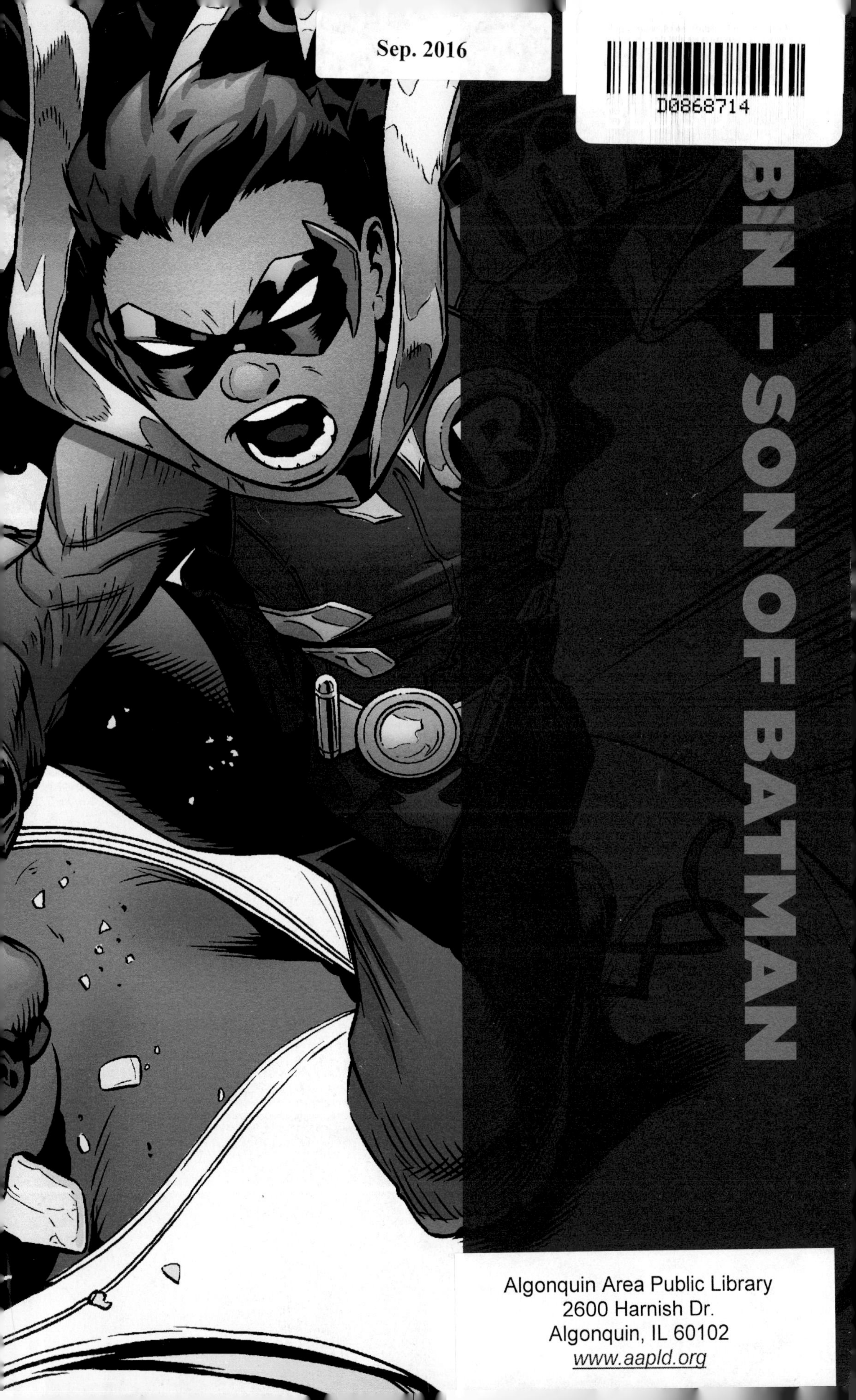
BIN – SON OF BATMAN

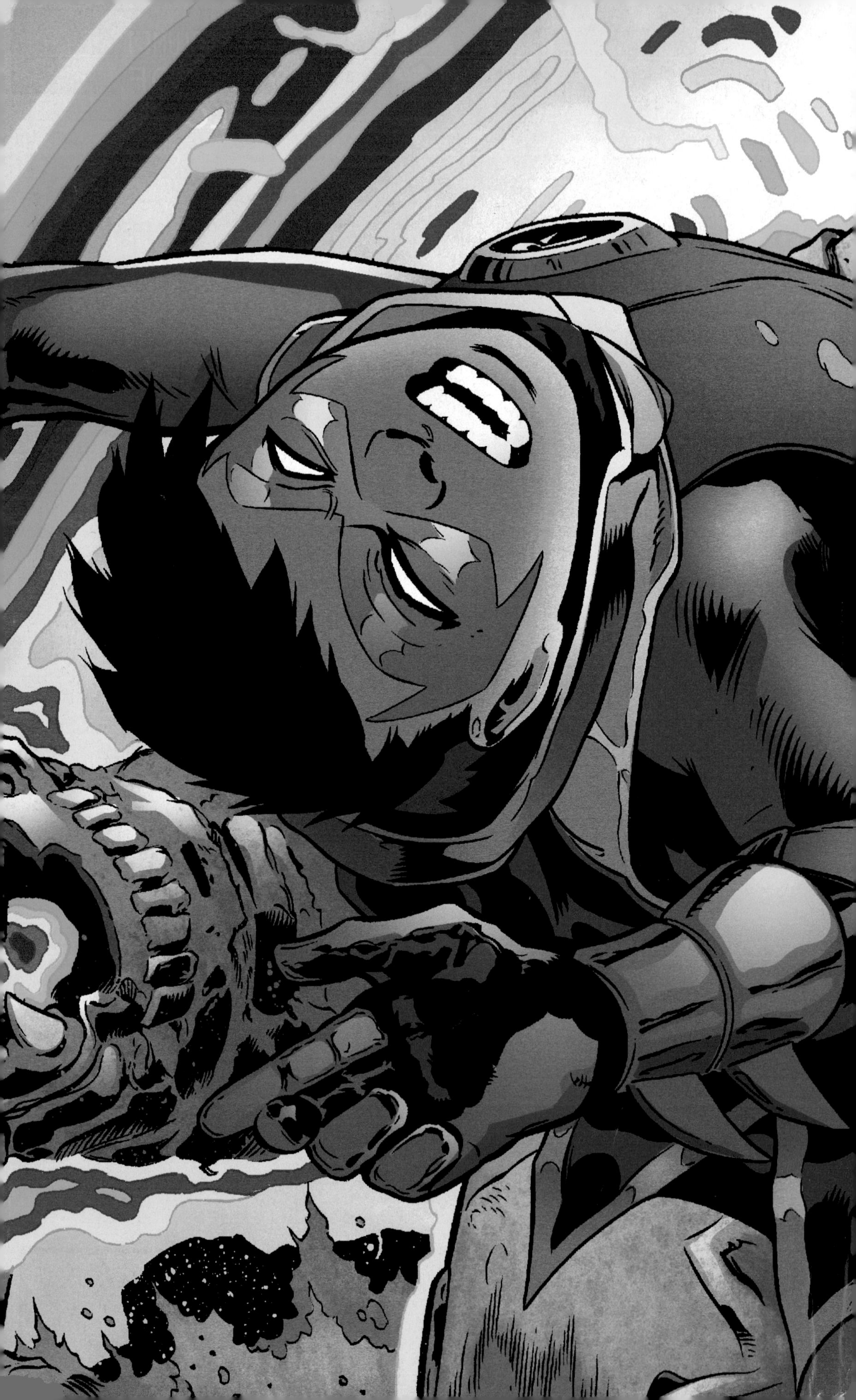

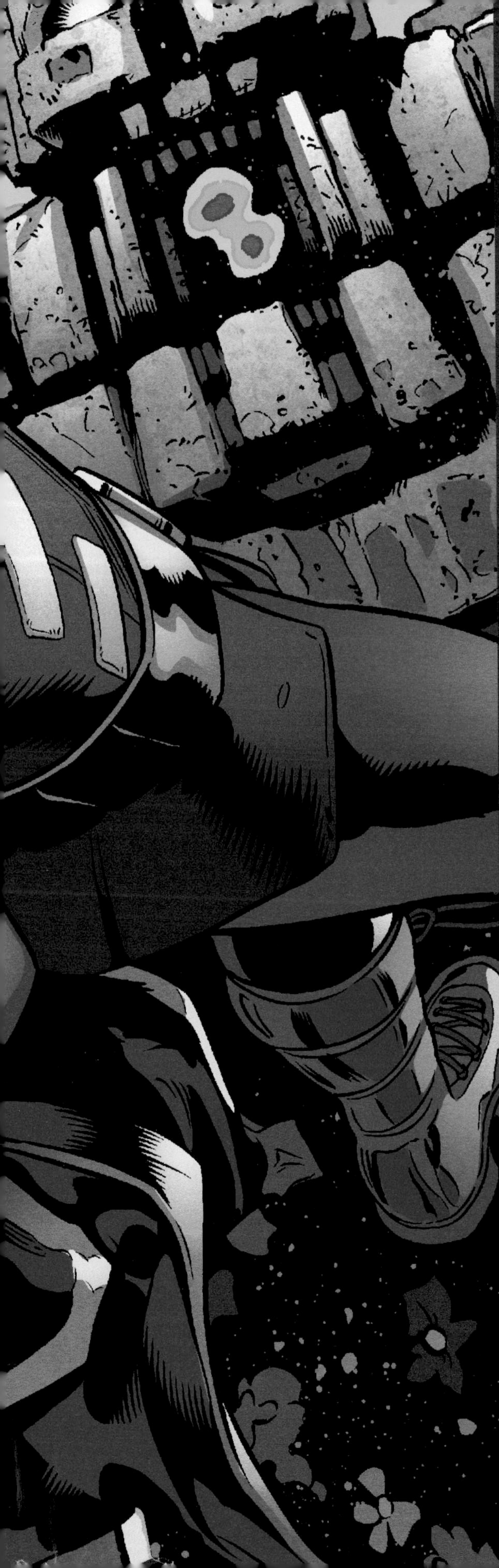

ROBIN – SON OF BATMAN

VOLUME 1
YEAR OF BLOOD

WRITTEN & PENCILLED BY
PATRICK GLEASON

INKS BY
MICK GRAY
TOM NGUYEN

COLOR BY
JOHN KALISZ
JEROMY COX

LETTERS BY
TOM NAPOLITANO
TODD KLEIN

COLLECTION COVER ARTISTS
PATRICK GLEASON,
MICK GRAY & JOHN KALISZ

BATMAN CREATED BY
BOB KANE WITH **BILL FINGER**

DEATHSTROKE CREATED BY
MARV WOLFMAN
& GEORGE PÉREZ

ROBIN: SON OF BATMAN VOLUME 1: YEAR OF BLOOD

Published by DC Comics. Compilation and all new material Copyright © 2016 DC Comics. All Rights Reserved.
Originally published online as ROBIN: SON OF BATMAN SNEAK PEEK and in single magazine form as
ROBIN: SON OF BATMAN 1-6 Copyright © 2015 DC Comics. All Rights Reserved. All characters, their distinctive likenesses
and related elements featured in this publication are trademarks of DC Comics. The stories, characters and incidents featured
in this publication are entirely fictional. DC Comics does not read or accept unsolicited ideas, stories or artwork.

DC Comics, 2900 West Alameda Ave., Burbank, CA 91505
Printed by RR Donnelley, Salem, VA, USA. 8/5/16. First Printing.
ISBN: 978-1-4012-6479-6

Library of Congress Cataloging-in-Publication Data

Names: Gleason, Patrick, author. | Gray, Mick, illustrator. | Nguyen, Tom,
illustrator. | Kalisz, John, illustrator. | Napolitano, Tom, illustrator.
| Klein, Todd, illustrator.
Title: Robin, son of Batman. Volume 1, Year of blood / Patrick Gleason,
writer and penciller ; Mick Gray, Tom Nguyen, inkers ; John Kalisz,
colorist ; Tom Napolitano, Todd Klein, letterers ; Patrick Gleason, Mick
Gray & John Kalisz, collection and series covers.
Other titles: Year of blood
Description: Burbank, CA : DC Comics, [2016] | "Originally published online
as ROBIN: SON OF BATMAN SNEAK PEEK and in single magazine form as ROBIN:
SON OF BATMAN 1-6." | "Batman Created by Bob Kane with Bill Finger." |
"Deathstroke created by Marv Wolfman and George Perez."
Identifiers: LCCN 2015049453 | ISBN 9781401264796
Subjects: LCSH: Graphic novels. | Superhero comic books, strips, etc.
Classification: LCC PN6728.R576 G57 2016 | DDC 741.5/973—dc23
LC record available at http://lccn.loc.gov/2015049453

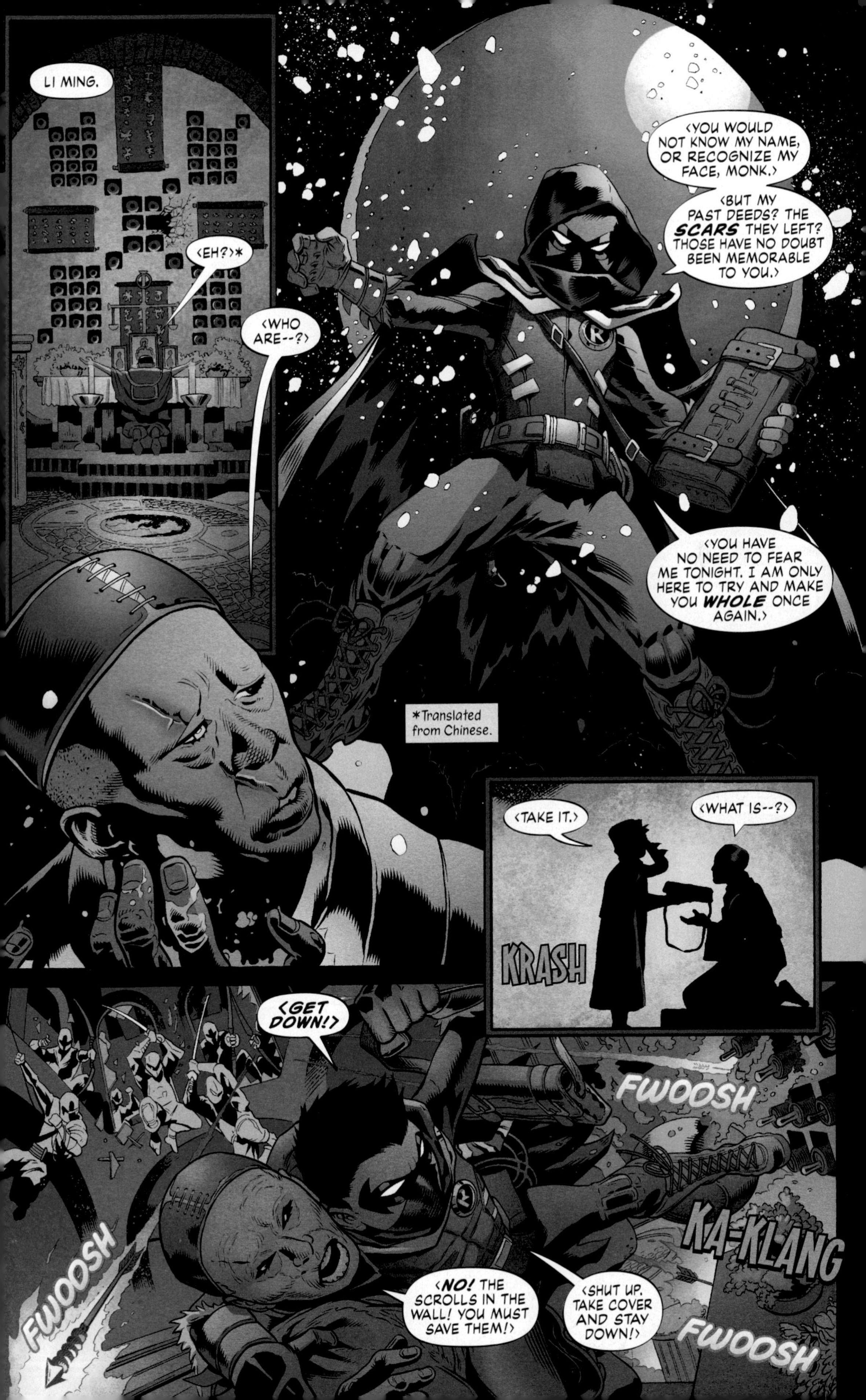
LI MING.
‹EH?›*
‹WHO ARE--?›
‹YOU WOULD NOT KNOW MY NAME, OR RECOGNIZE MY FACE, MONK.›
‹BUT MY PAST DEEDS? THE SCARS THEY LEFT? THOSE HAVE NO DOUBT BEEN MEMORABLE TO YOU.›
‹YOU HAVE NO NEED TO FEAR ME TONIGHT. I AM ONLY HERE TO TRY AND MAKE YOU WHOLE ONCE AGAIN.›
*Translated from Chinese.
‹TAKE IT.›
‹WHAT IS--?›
KRASH
‹GET DOWN!›
FWOOSH
KA-KLANG
FWOOSH
‹NO! THE SCROLLS IN THE WALL! YOU MUST SAVE THEM!›
‹SHUT UP. TAKE COVER AND STAY DOWN!›
FWOOSH

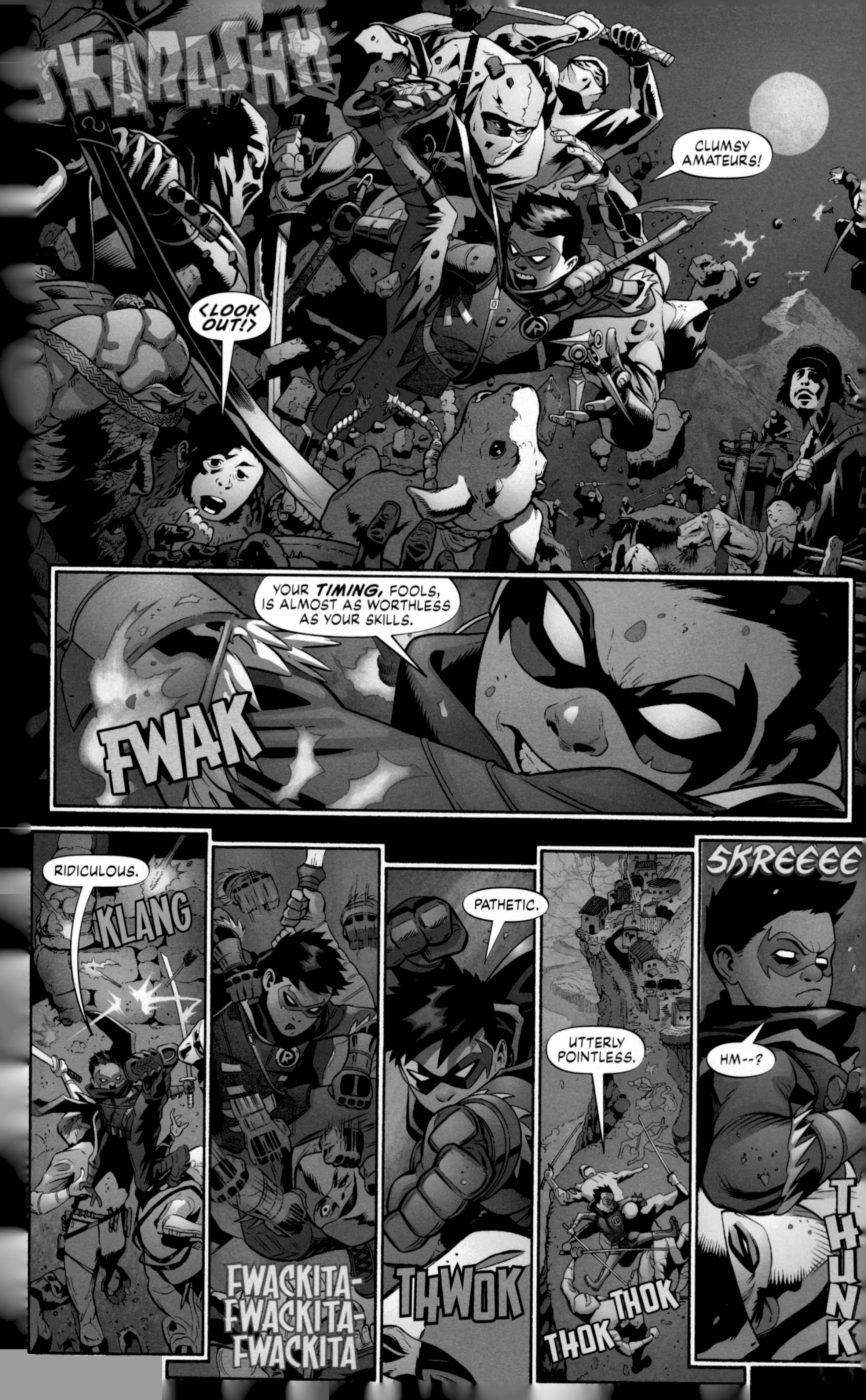
SKARASHH
CLUMSY AMATEURS!
<LOOK OUT!>
YOUR TIMING, FOOLS, IS ALMOST AS WORTHLESS AS YOUR SKILLS.
FWAK
RIDICULOUS.
KLANG
FWACKITA-FWACKITA-FWACKITA
PATHETIC.
THWOK
UTTERLY POINTLESS.
THOK THOK
SKREEEE
HM--?
THUNK

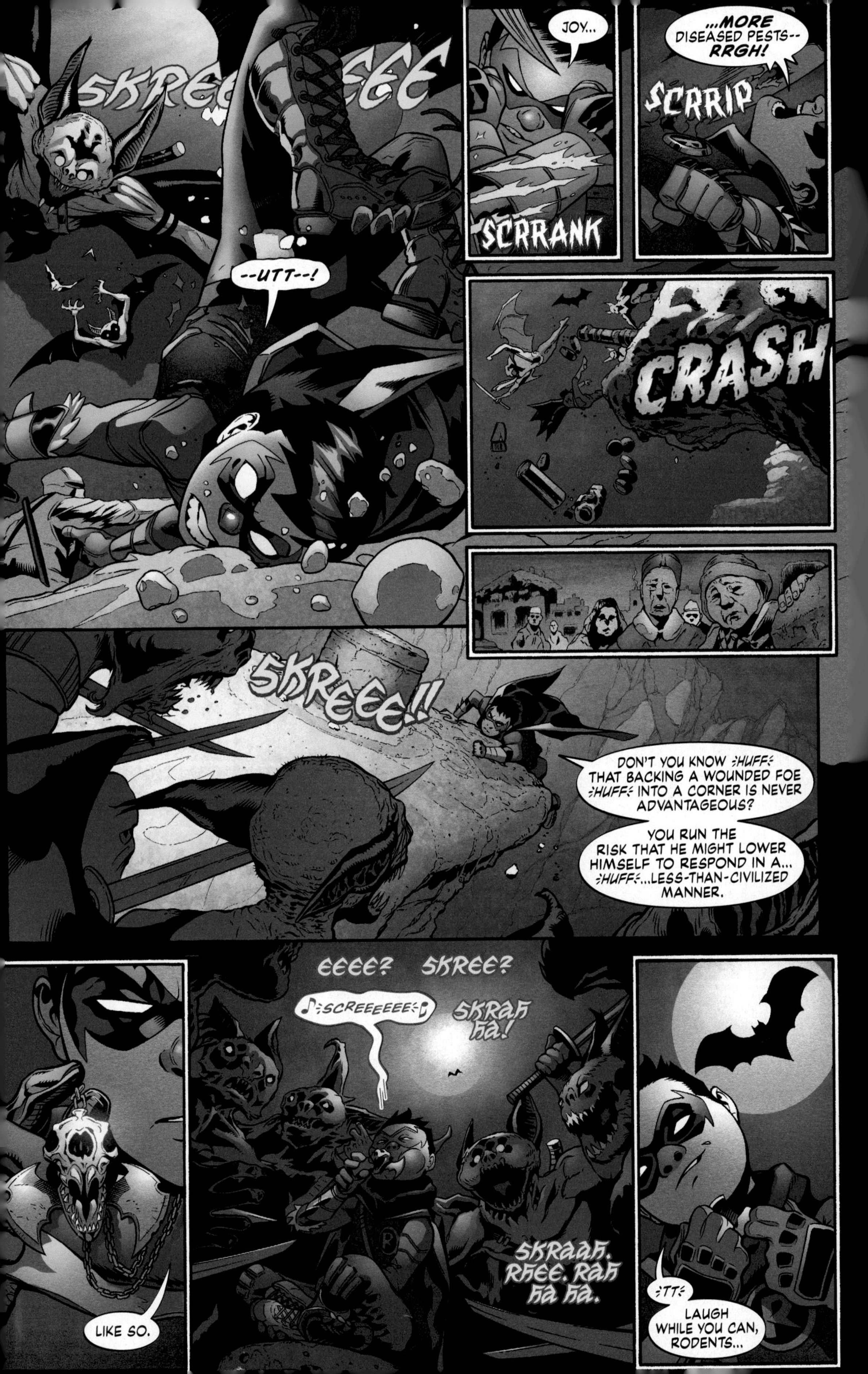
SKREEEEEE
--UTT--!
JOY...
SCRRANK
...MORE DISEASED PESTS-- RRGH!
SCRRIP
CRASH
SKREEE!!
DON'T YOU KNOW ⁝HUFF⁝ THAT BACKING A WOUNDED FOE ⁝HUFF⁝ INTO A CORNER IS NEVER ADVANTAGEOUS?
YOU RUN THE RISK THAT HE MIGHT LOWER HIMSELF TO RESPOND IN A... ⁝HUFF⁝...LESS-THAN-CIVILIZED MANNER.
LIKE SO.
EEEE? SKREE?
♪⁝SCREEEEEEE⁝♪
SKRAH HA!
SKRAAH. RHEE. RAH HA HA.
⁝TT⁝
LAUGH WHILE YOU CAN, RODENTS...

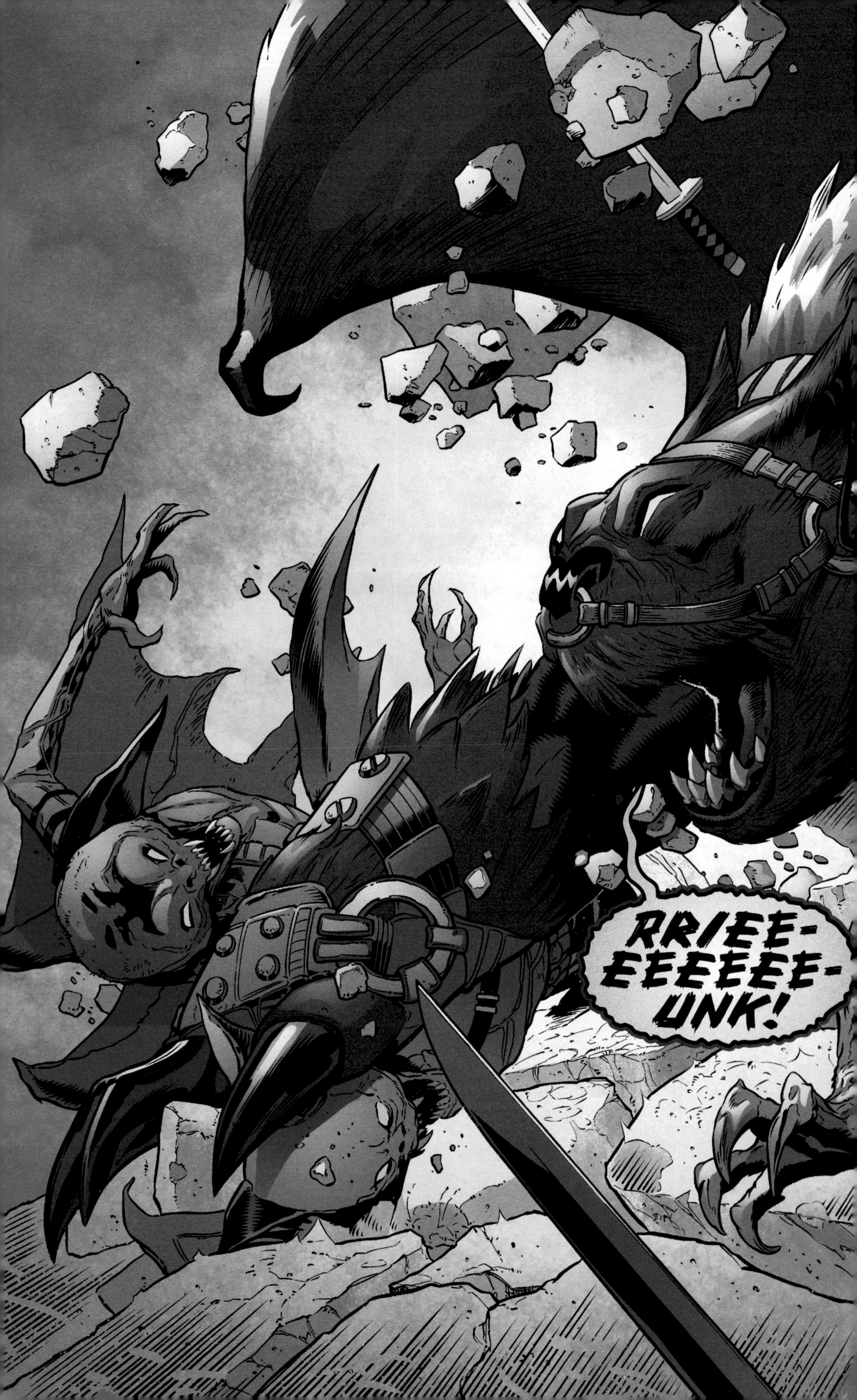
RRIEE-EEEEEE-UNK!

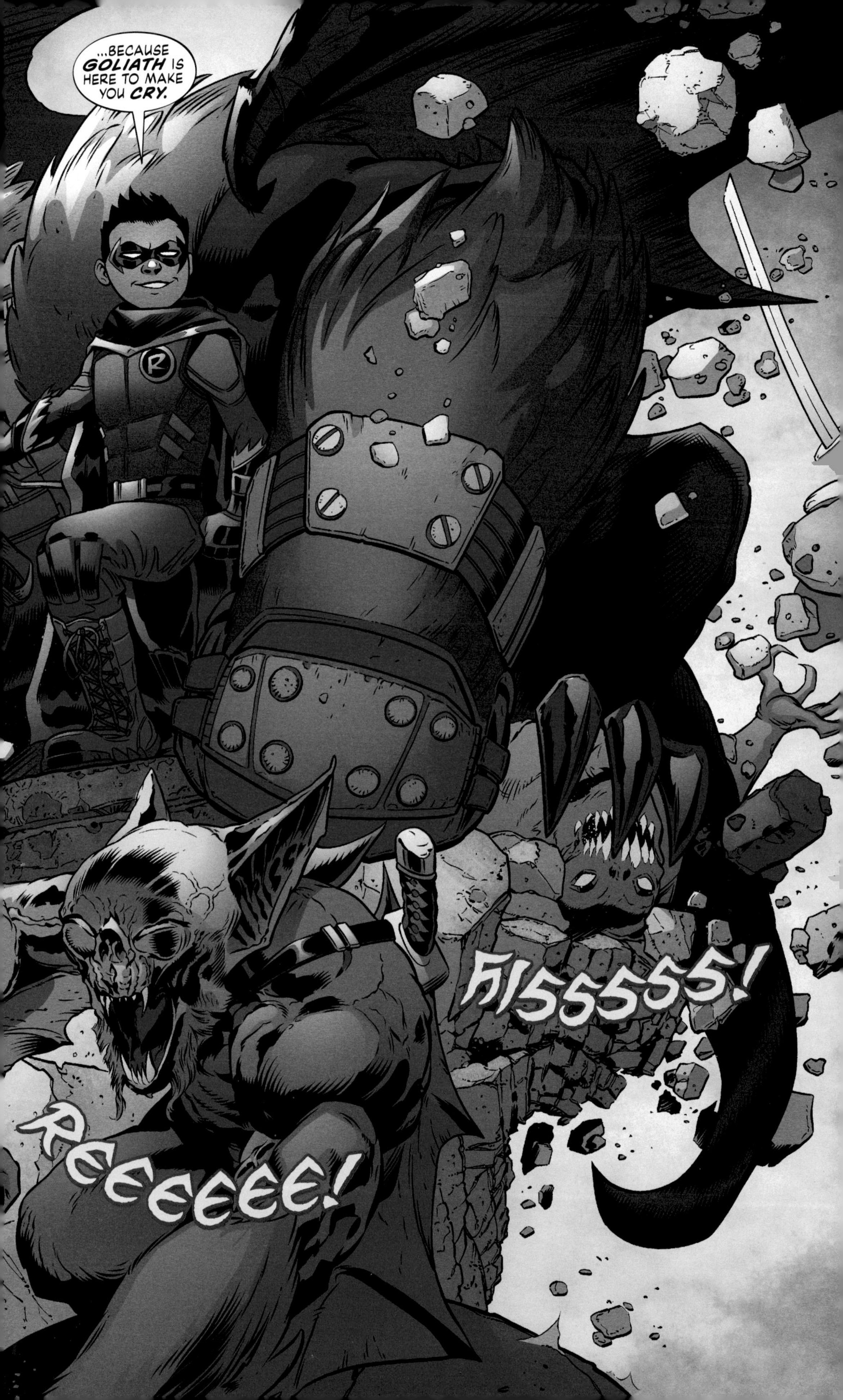
...BECAUSE GOLIATH IS HERE TO MAKE YOU CRY.
HISSSSSS!
REEEEEE!

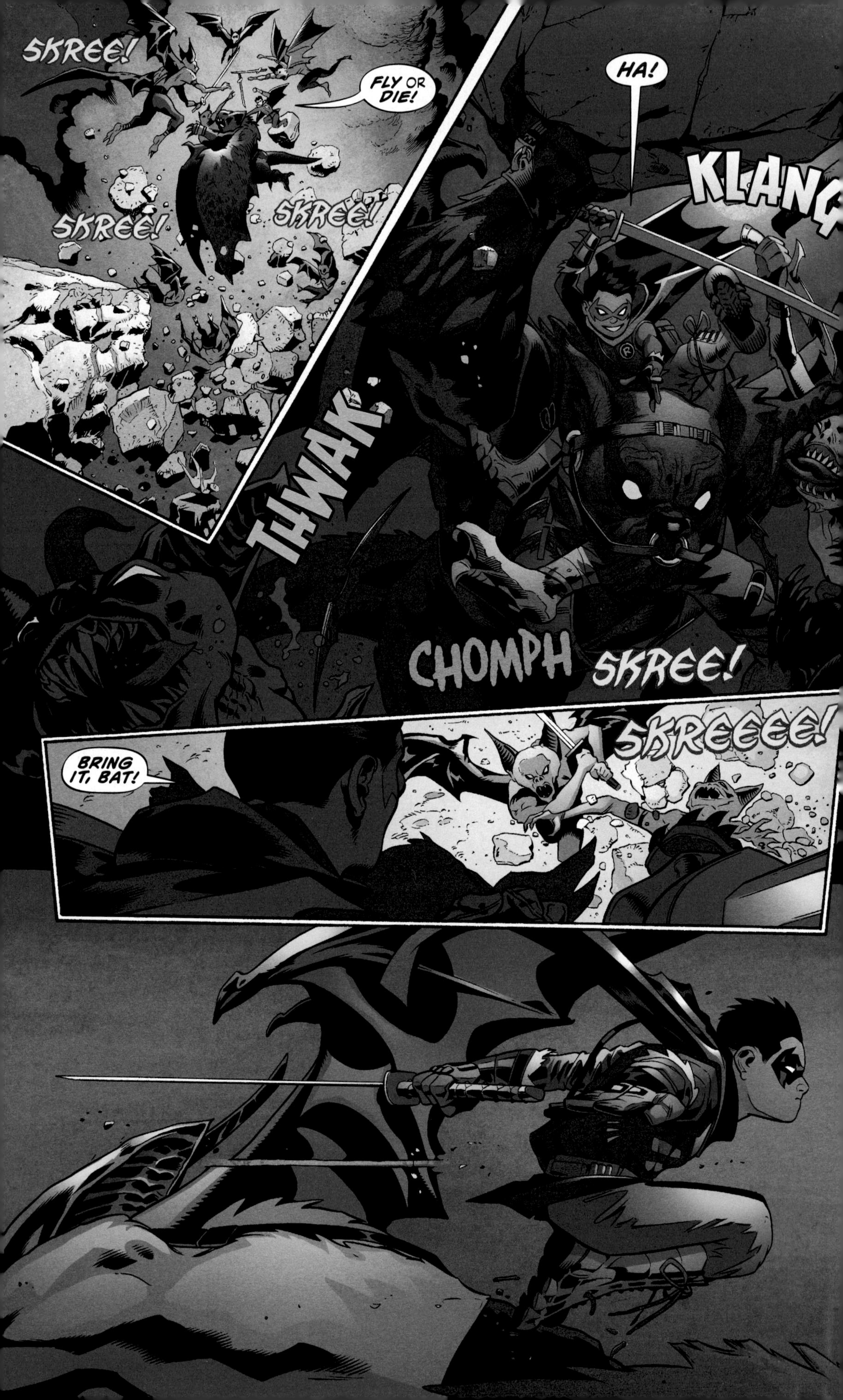
SKREE!
FLY OR DIE!
SKREE!
SKREE!
HA!
KLANG
THWAK
CHOMPH
SKREE!
BRING IT, BAT!
SKREEEE!

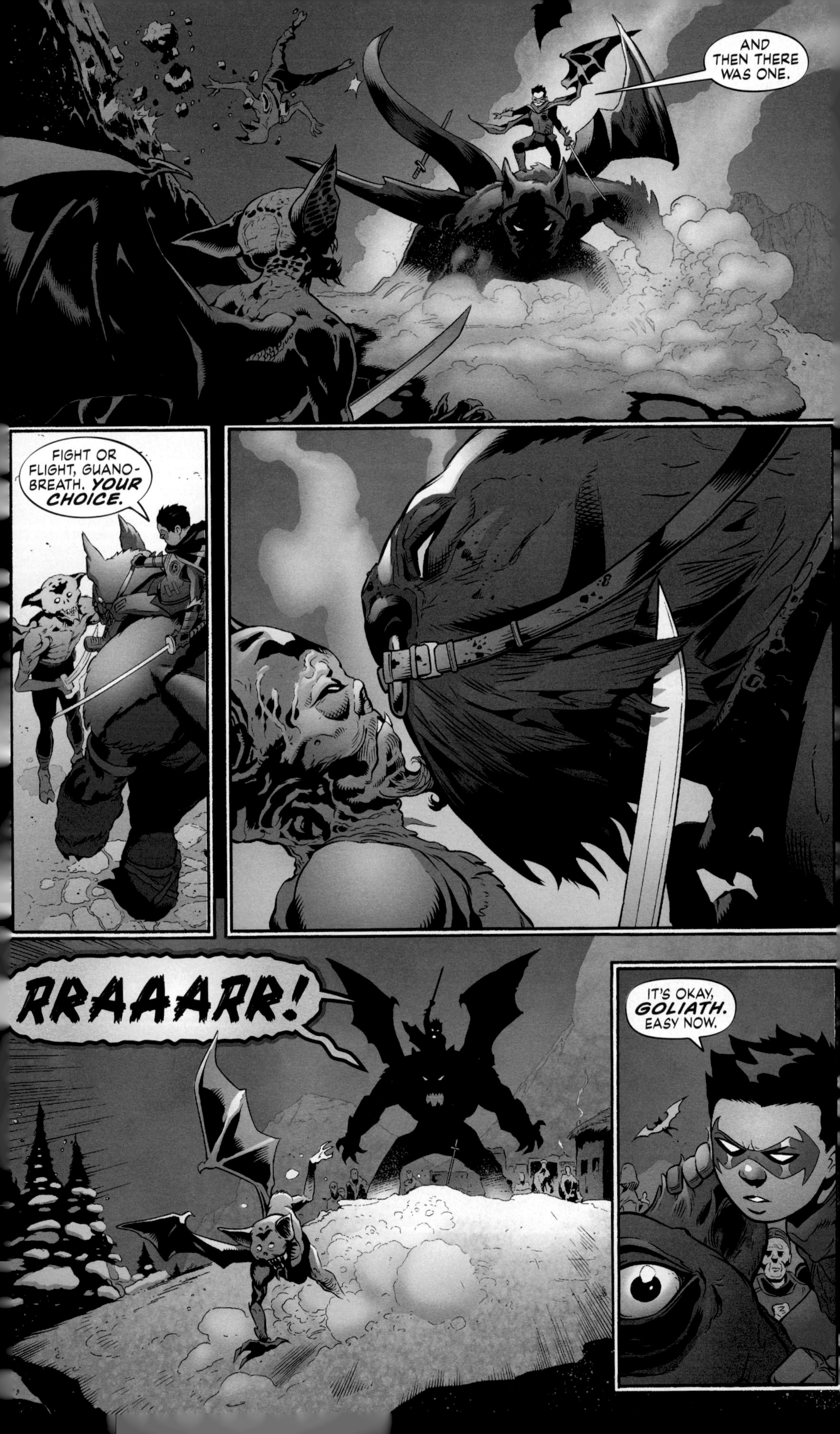
AND THEN THERE WAS ONE.
FIGHT OR FLIGHT, GUANO-BREATH. ***YOUR CHOICE.***
RRAAARR!
IT'S OKAY, ***GOLIATH.*** EASY NOW.

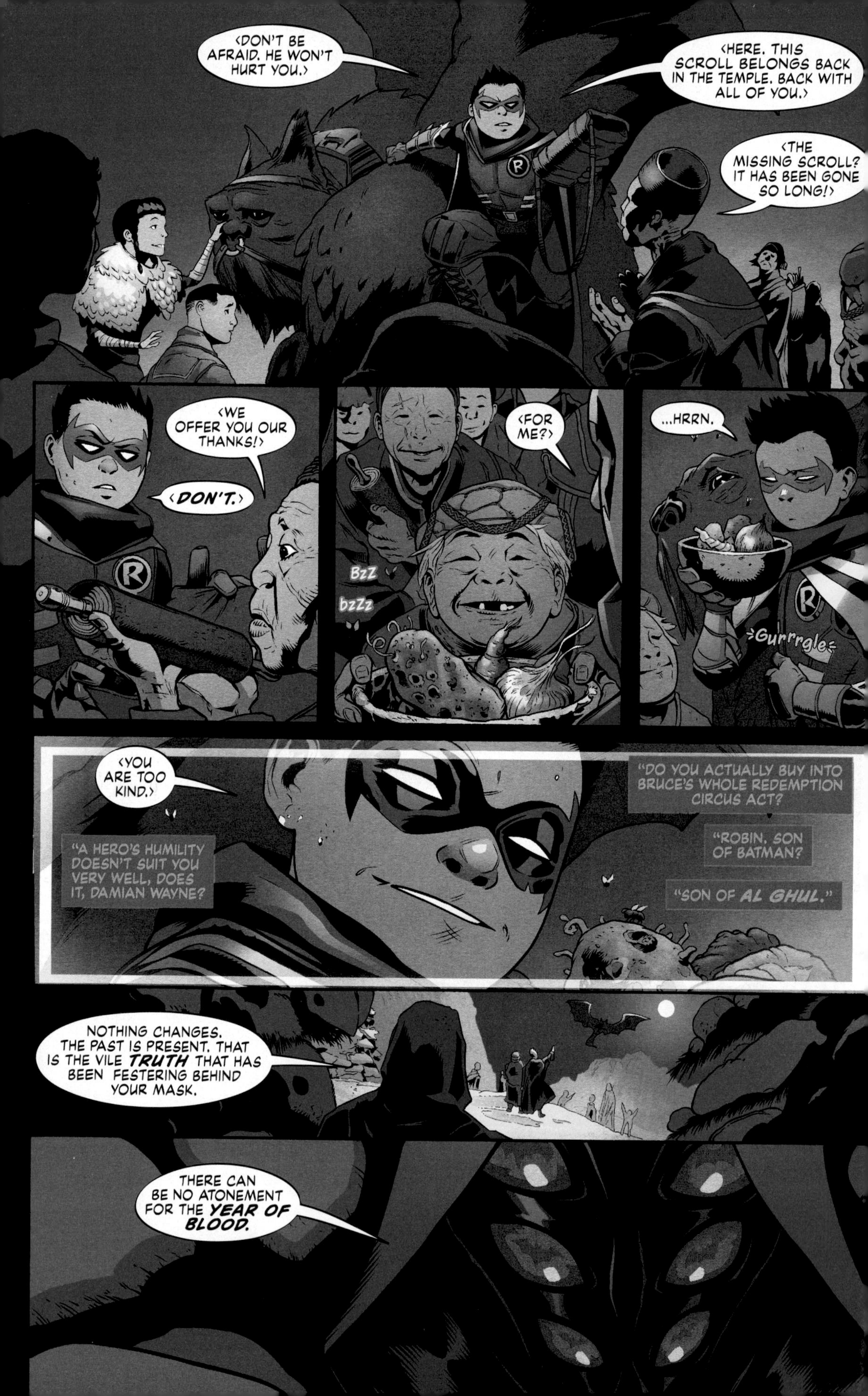
‹DON'T BE AFRAID. HE WON'T HURT YOU.›
‹HERE. THIS SCROLL BELONGS BACK IN THE TEMPLE. BACK WITH ALL OF YOU.›
‹THE MISSING SCROLL? IT HAS BEEN GONE SO LONG!›
‹WE OFFER YOU OUR THANKS!›
‹DON'T.›
‹FOR ME?›
BzZ
bzZz
...HRRN.
Gurrrgle
‹YOU ARE TOO KIND.›
"A HERO'S HUMILITY DOESN'T SUIT YOU VERY WELL, DOES IT, DAMIAN WAYNE?
"DO YOU ACTUALLY BUY INTO BRUCE'S WHOLE REDEMPTION CIRCUS ACT?
"ROBIN, SON OF BATMAN?
"SON OF AL GHUL."
NOTHING CHANGES. THE PAST IS PRESENT. THAT IS THE VILE TRUTH THAT HAS BEEN FESTERING BEHIND YOUR MASK.
THERE CAN BE NO ATONEMENT FOR THE YEAR OF BLOOD.

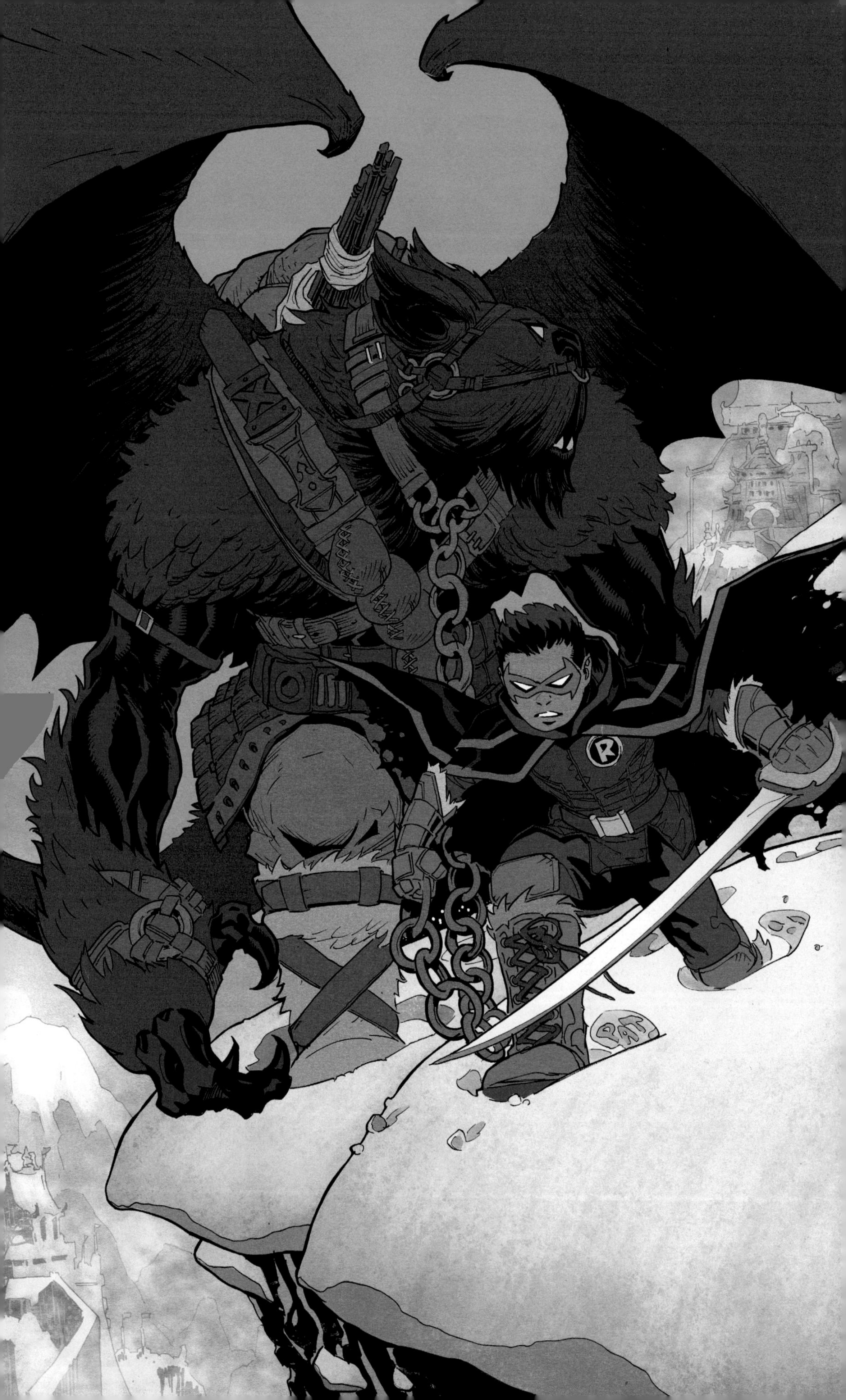

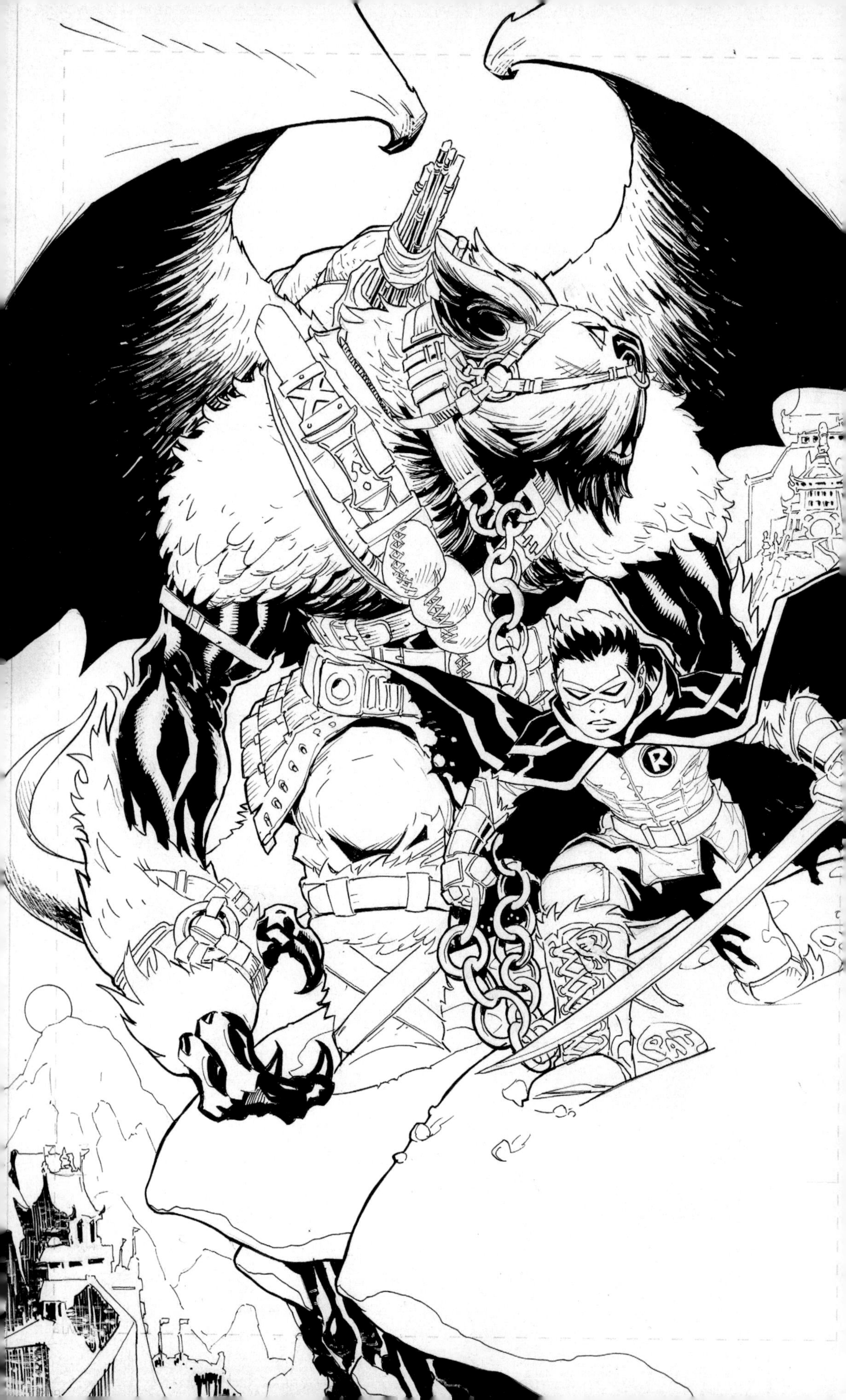

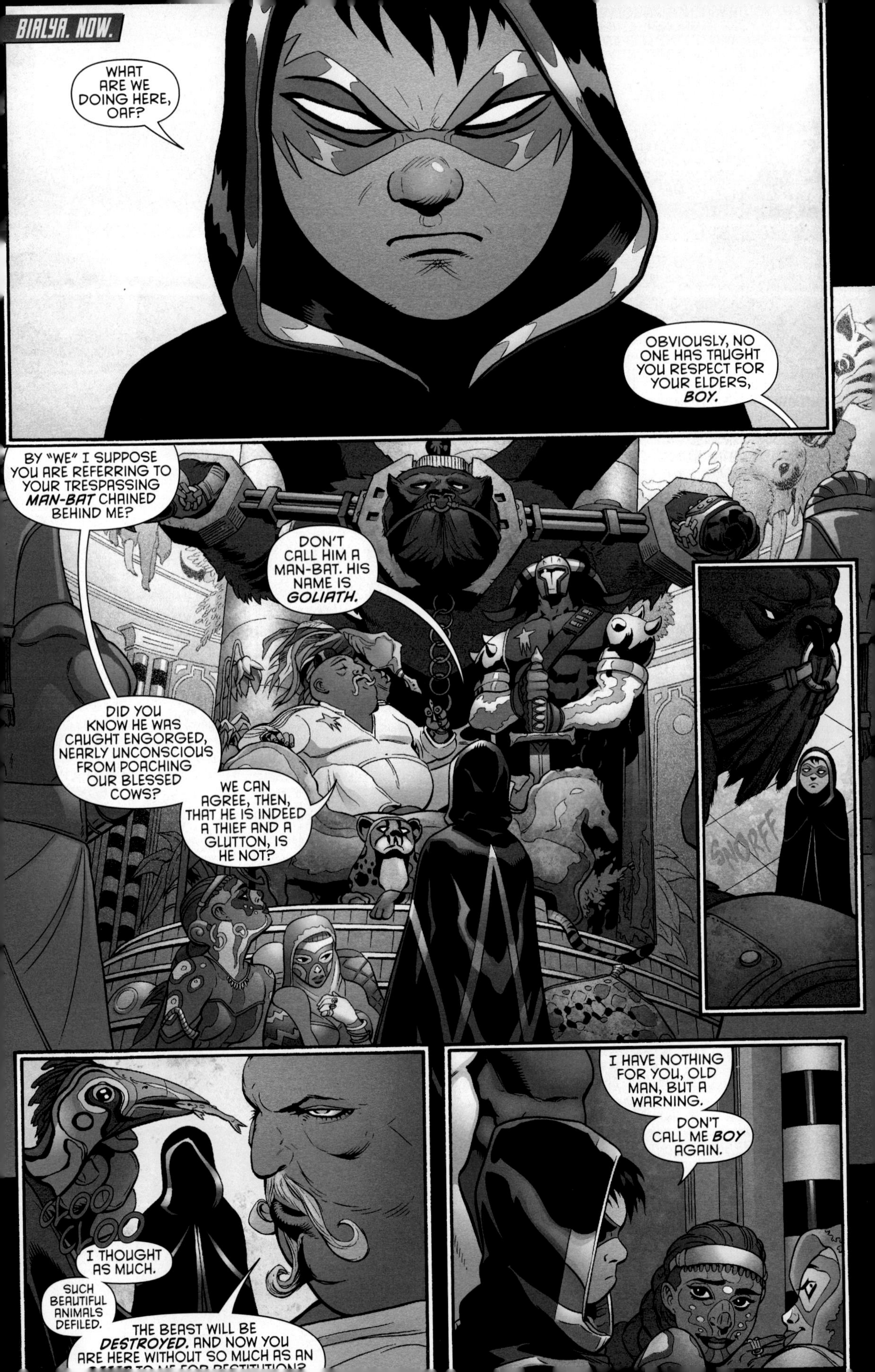
BIALYA. NOW.
WHAT ARE WE DOING HERE, OAF?
OBVIOUSLY, NO ONE HAS TAUGHT YOU RESPECT FOR YOUR ELDERS, BOY.
BY "WE" I SUPPOSE YOU ARE REFERRING TO YOUR TRESPASSING MAN-BAT CHAINED BEHIND ME?
DON'T CALL HIM A MAN-BAT. HIS NAME IS GOLIATH.
DID YOU KNOW HE WAS CAUGHT ENGORGED, NEARLY UNCONSCIOUS FROM POACHING OUR BLESSED COWS?
WE CAN AGREE, THEN, THAT HE IS INDEED A THIEF AND A GLUTTON, IS HE NOT?
SNORFF
I THOUGHT AS MUCH.
SUCH BEAUTIFUL ANIMALS DEFILED.
THE BEAST WILL BE DESTROYED. AND NOW YOU ARE HERE WITHOUT SO MUCH AS AN
I HAVE NOTHING FOR YOU, OLD MAN, BUT A WARNING.
DON'T CALL ME BOY AGAIN.

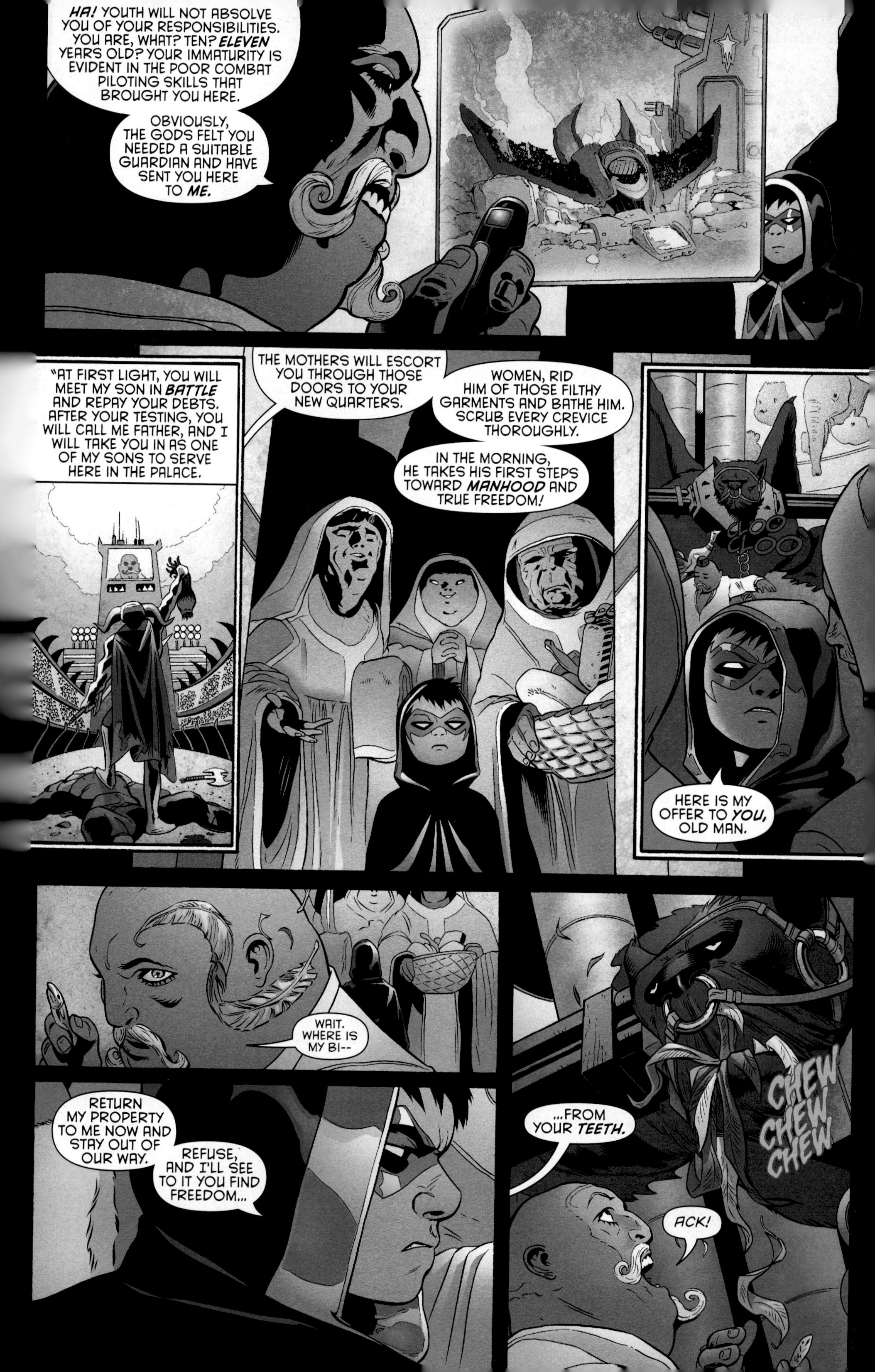

HA! YOUTH WILL NOT ABSOLVE YOU OF YOUR RESPONSIBILITIES. YOU ARE, WHAT? TEN? ELEVEN YEARS OLD? YOUR IMMATURITY IS EVIDENT IN THE POOR COMBAT PILOTING SKILLS THAT BROUGHT YOU HERE.
OBVIOUSLY, THE GODS FELT YOU NEEDED A SUITABLE GUARDIAN AND HAVE SENT YOU HERE TO ME.
"AT FIRST LIGHT, YOU WILL MEET MY SON IN BATTLE AND REPAY YOUR DEBTS. AFTER YOUR TESTING, YOU WILL CALL ME FATHER, AND I WILL TAKE YOU IN AS ONE OF MY SONS TO SERVE HERE IN THE PALACE.
THE MOTHERS WILL ESCORT YOU THROUGH THOSE DOORS TO YOUR NEW QUARTERS.
WOMEN, RID HIM OF THOSE FILTHY GARMENTS AND BATHE HIM. SCRUB EVERY CREVICE THOROUGHLY.
IN THE MORNING, HE TAKES HIS FIRST STEPS TOWARD MANHOOD AND TRUE FREEDOM!
HERE IS MY OFFER TO YOU, OLD MAN.
WAIT. WHERE IS MY BI--
RETURN MY PROPERTY TO ME NOW AND STAY OUT OF OUR WAY.
REFUSE, AND I'LL SEE TO IT YOU FIND FREEDOM...
...FROM YOUR TEETH.
CHEW CHEW CHEW
ACK!

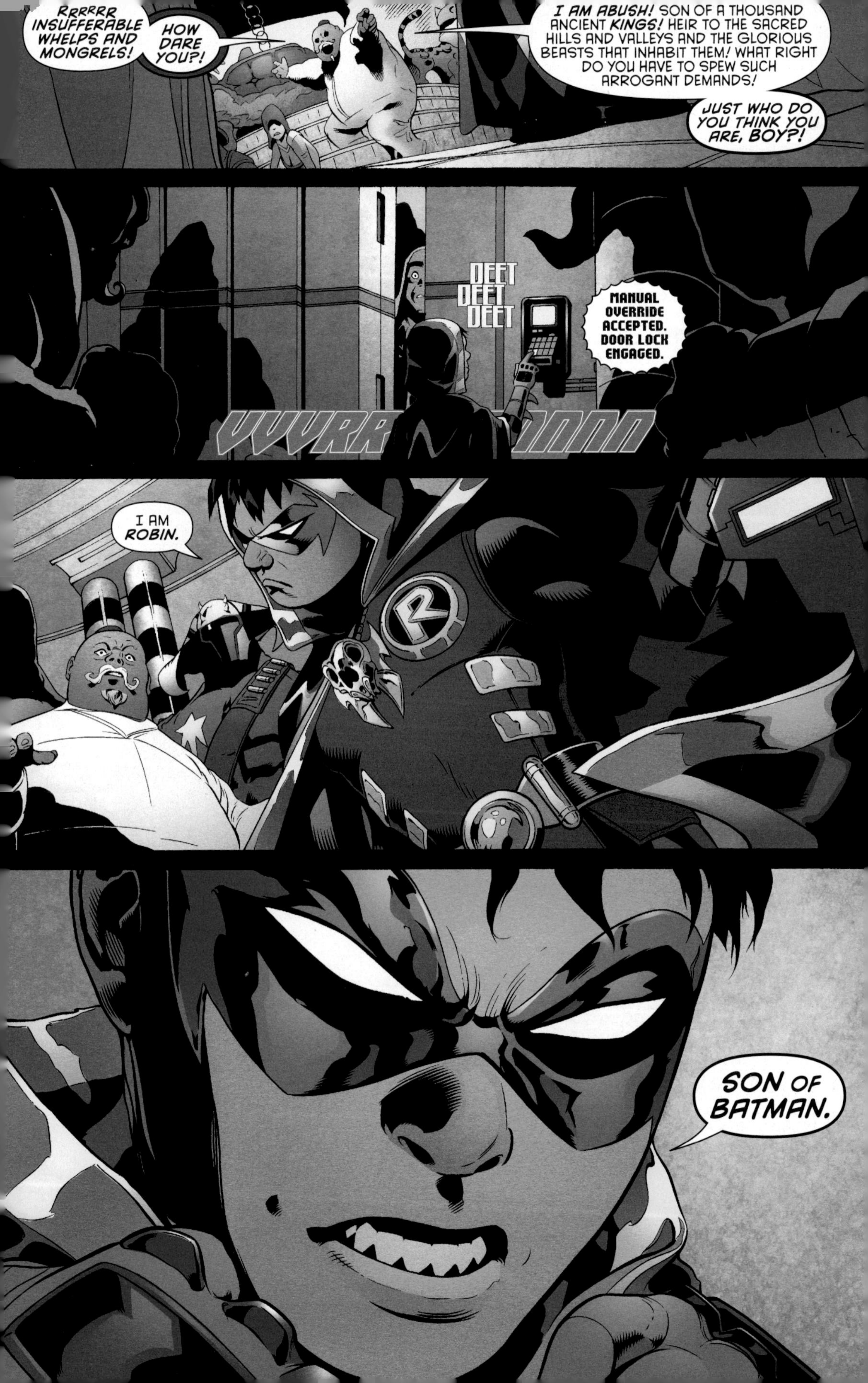
RRRRRR INSUFFERABLE WHELPS AND MONGRELS!
HOW DARE YOU?!
I AM ABUSH! SON OF A THOUSAND ANCIENT KINGS! HEIR TO THE SACRED HILLS AND VALLEYS AND THE GLORIOUS BEASTS THAT INHABIT THEM! WHAT RIGHT DO YOU HAVE TO SPEW SUCH ARROGANT DEMANDS!
JUST WHO DO YOU THINK YOU ARE, BOY?!
DEET DEET DEET
MANUAL OVERRIDE ACCEPTED. DOOR LOCK ENGAGED.
VVVRR
NNNN
I AM ROBIN.
SON OF BATMAN.

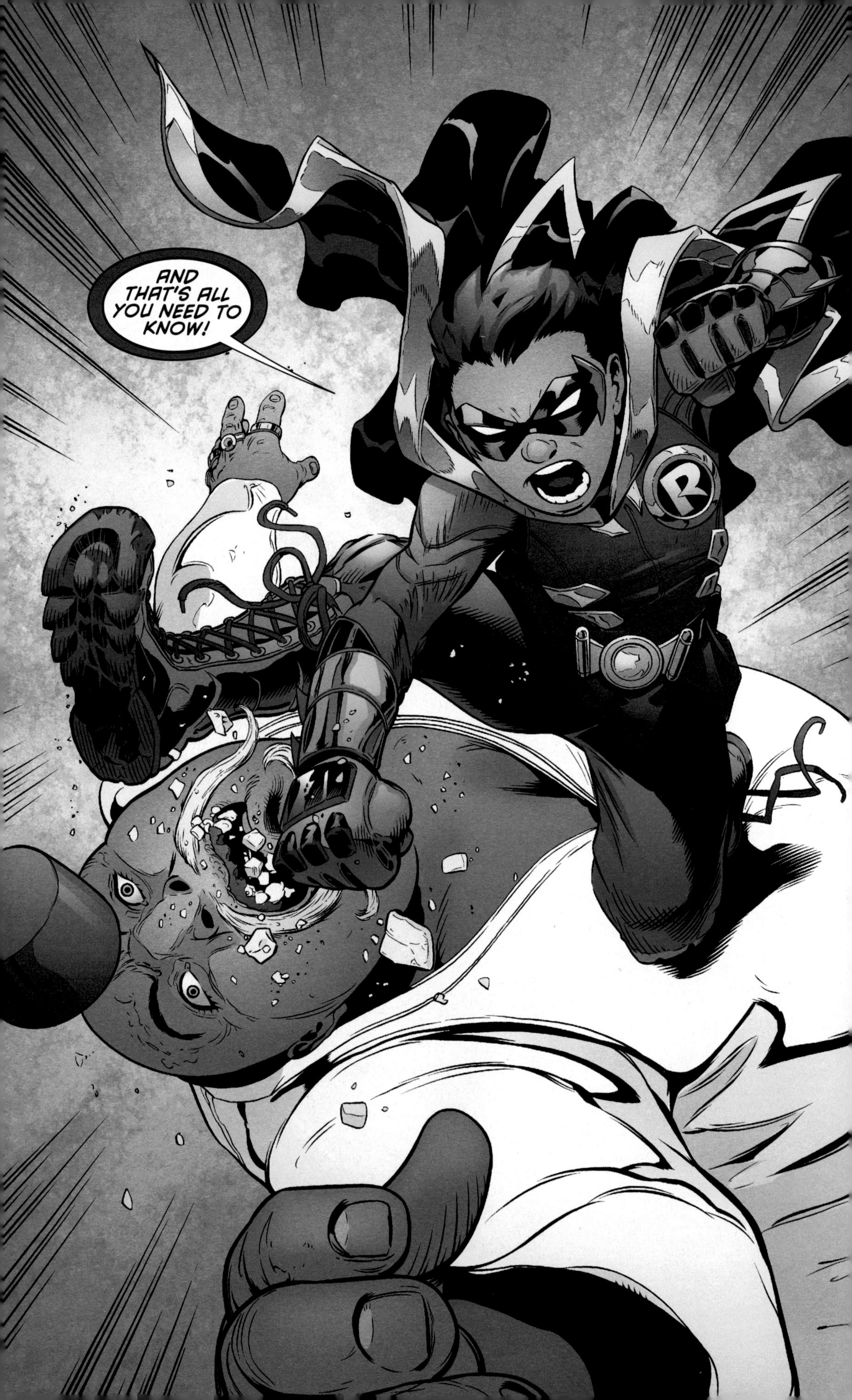
AND THAT'S ALL YOU NEED TO KNOW!

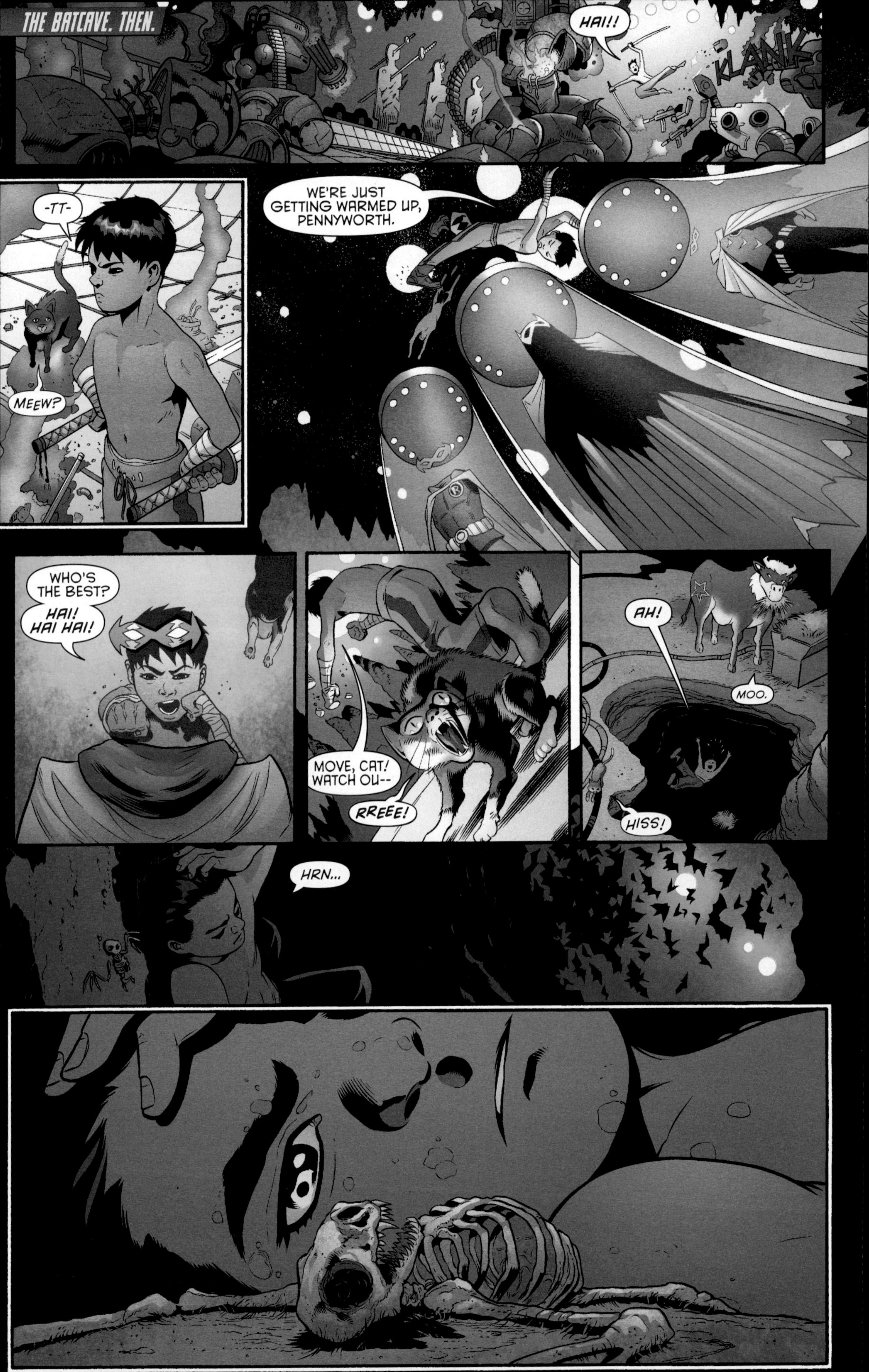
THE BATCAVE. THEN.
HAI!!
KLANK
-TT-
MEEW?
WE'RE JUST GETTING WARMED UP, PENNYWORTH.
WHO'S THE BEST?
HAI! HAI HAI!
MOVE, CAT! WATCH OU--
RREEE!
AH!
MOO.
HISS!
HRN...

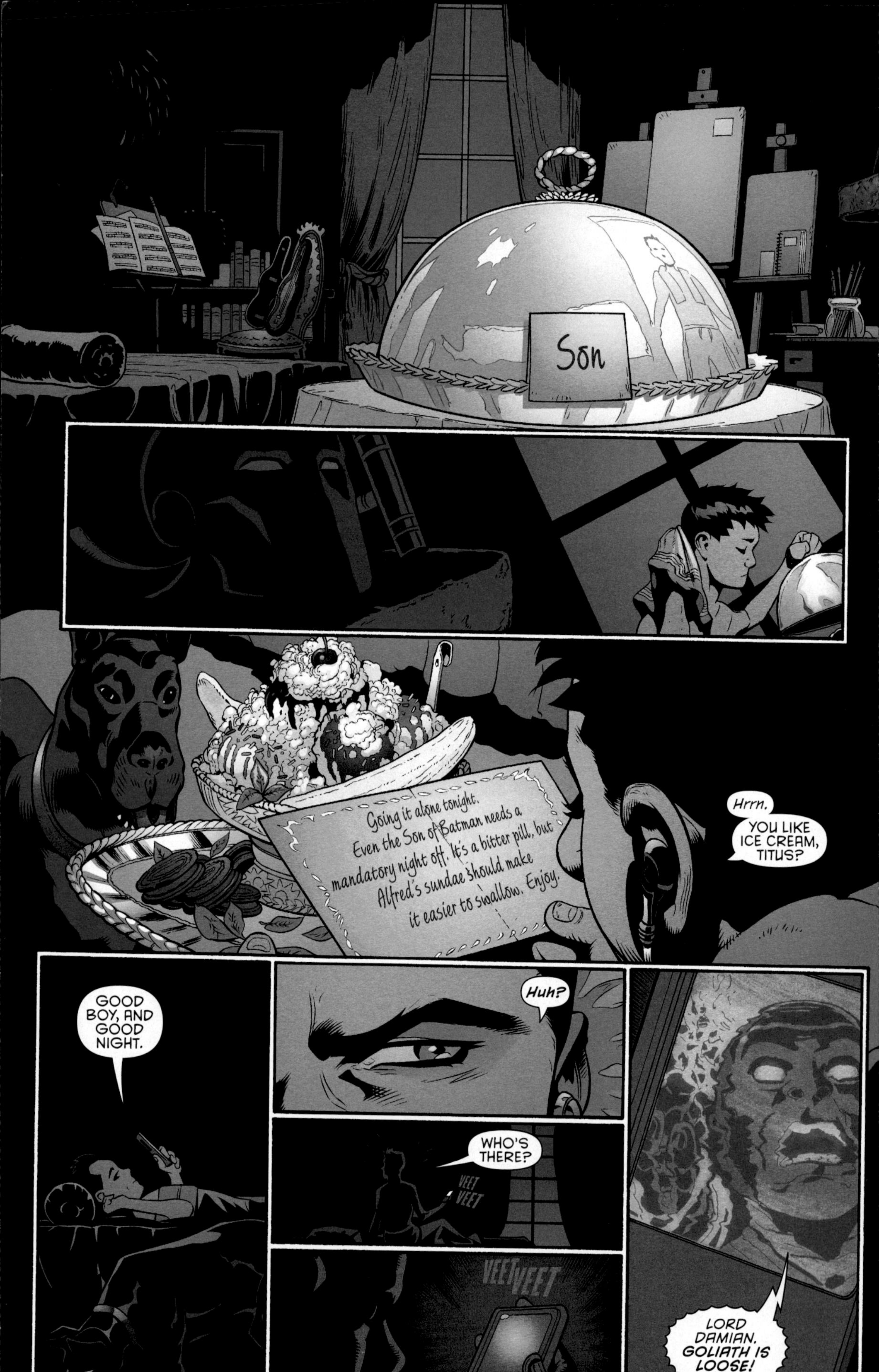
Son
Going it alone tonight. Even the Son of Batman needs a mandatory night off. It's a bitter pill, but Alfred's sundae should make it easier to swallow. Enjoy.
Hrrn.
YOU LIKE ICE CREAM, TITUS?
GOOD BOY, AND GOOD NIGHT.
Huh?
WHO'S THERE?
VEET VEET
VEET VEET
LORD DAMIAN. GOLIATH IS LOOSE!

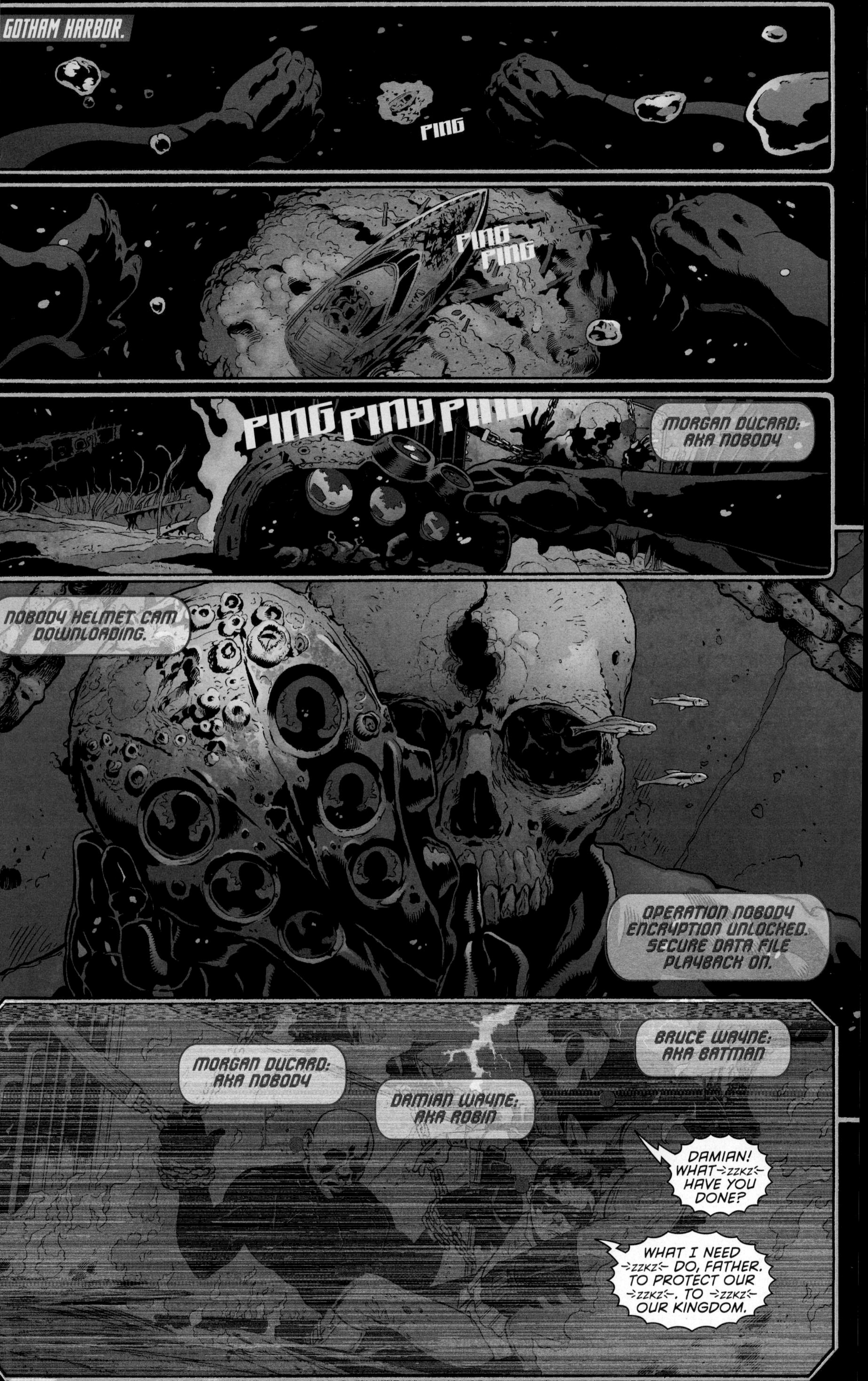
GOTHAM HARBOR.
PING
PING
PING
PING PING PING
MORGAN DUCARD: AKA NOBODY
NOBODY HELMET CAM DOWNLOADING.
OPERATION NOBODY ENCRYPTION UNLOCKED. SECURE DATA FILE PLAYBACK ON.
MORGAN DUCARD: AKA NOBODY
DAMIAN WAYNE: AKA ROBIN
BRUCE WAYNE: AKA BATMAN
DAMIAN! WHAT ~ZZKZ~ HAVE YOU DONE?
WHAT I NEED ~ZZKZ~ DO, FATHER. TO PROTECT OUR ~ZZKZ~. TO ~ZZKZ~ OUR KINGDOM.

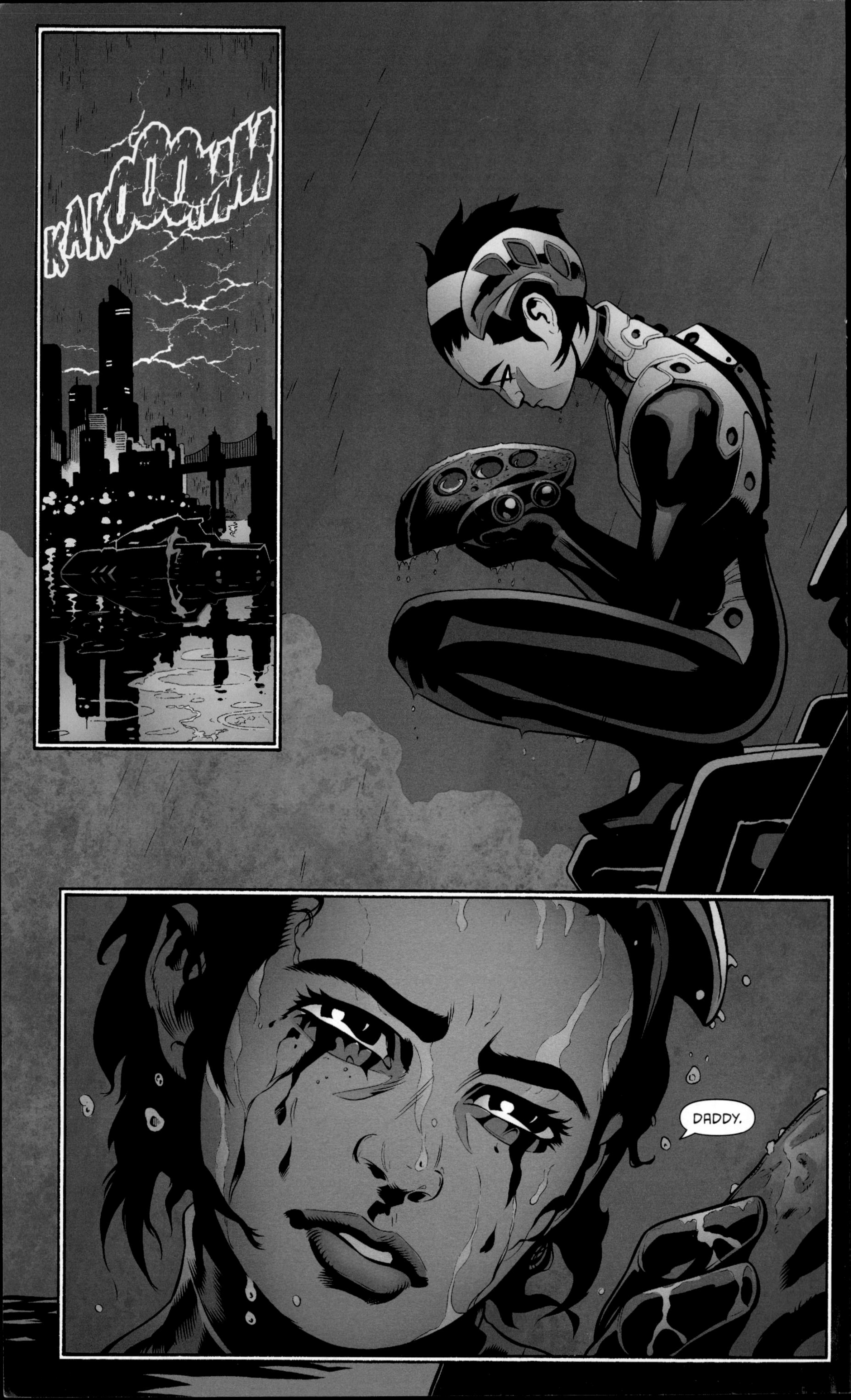
KAKOOOM
DADDY.

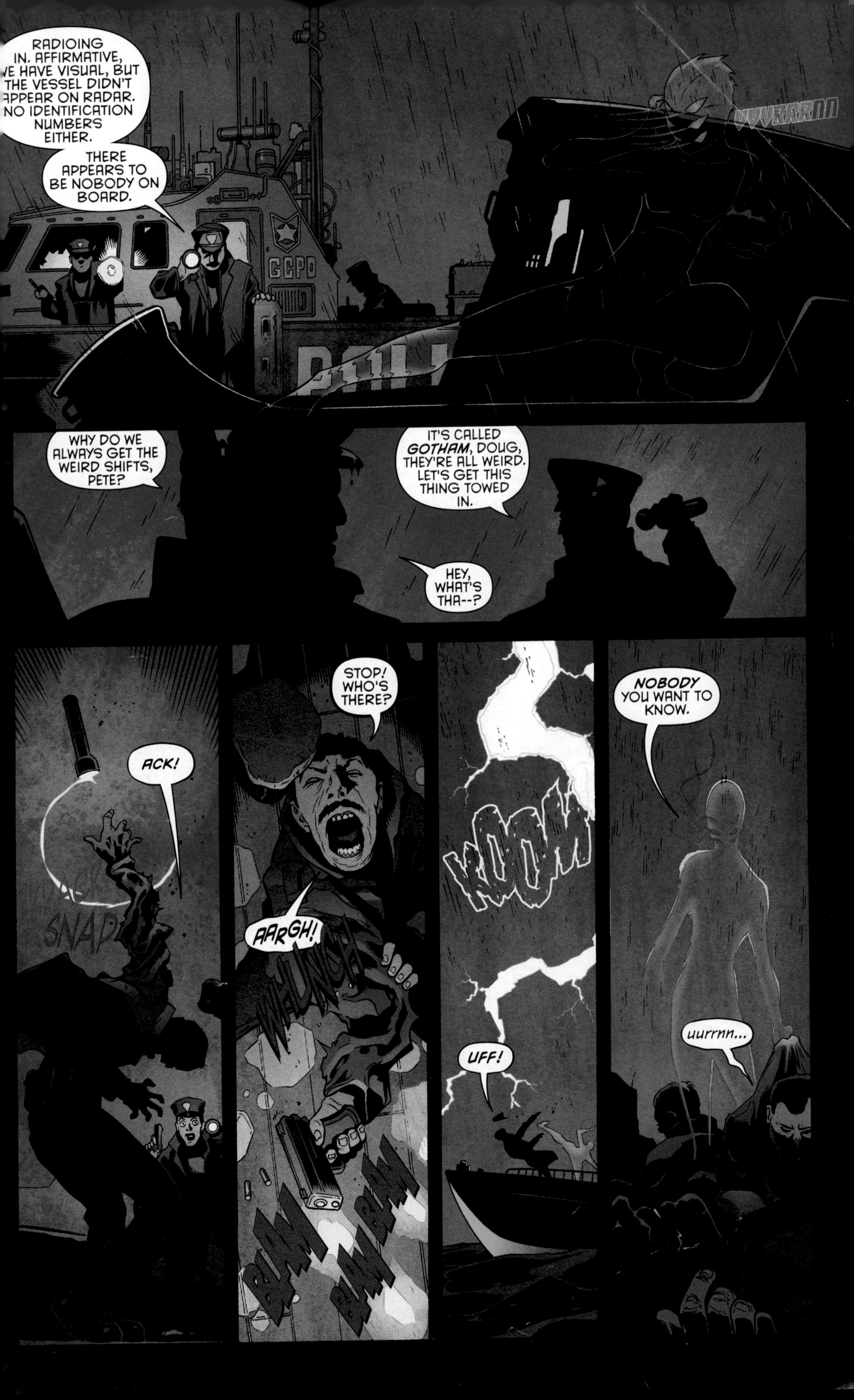
RADIOING IN. AFFIRMATIVE, WE HAVE VISUAL, BUT THE VESSEL DIDN'T APPEAR ON RADAR. NO IDENTIFICATION NUMBERS EITHER.
THERE APPEARS TO BE NOBODY ON BOARD.
VVVRRRNN
GCPD
WHY DO WE ALWAYS GET THE WEIRD SHIFTS, PETE?
IT'S CALLED GOTHAM, DOUG, THEY'RE ALL WEIRD. LET'S GET THIS THING TOWED IN.
HEY, WHAT'S THA--?
ACK!
SNAP
STOP! WHO'S THERE?
AARGH!
WHUNCH
BLAM BLAM
KOOM
UFF!
NOBODY YOU WANT TO KNOW.
uurrnn...

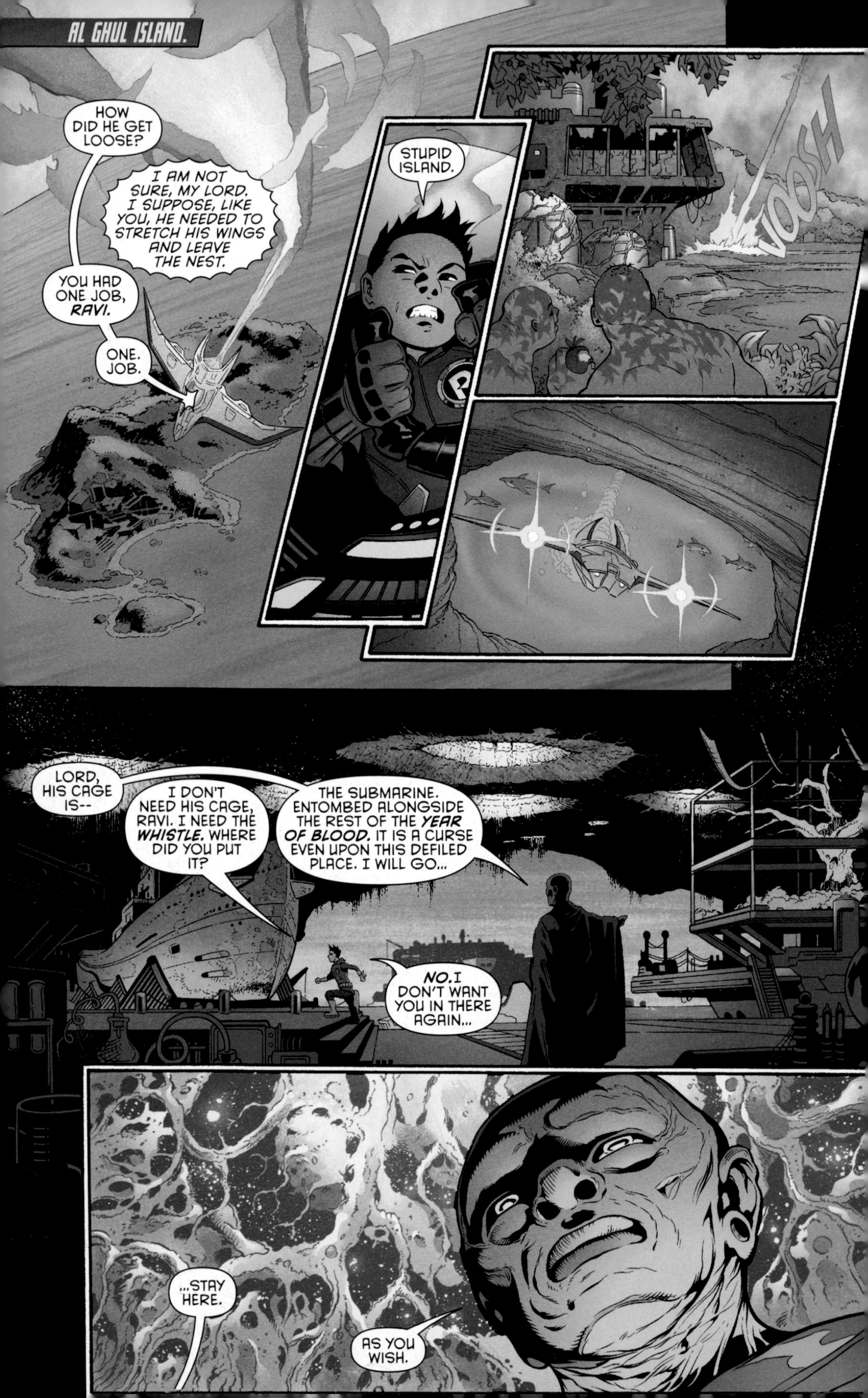
AL GHUL ISLAND.
HOW DID HE GET LOOSE?
I AM NOT SURE, MY LORD. I SUPPOSE, LIKE YOU, HE NEEDED TO STRETCH HIS WINGS AND LEAVE THE NEST.
YOU HAD ONE JOB, RAVI.
ONE. JOB.
STUPID ISLAND.
VOOSH
LORD, HIS CAGE IS--
I DON'T NEED HIS CAGE, RAVI. I NEED THE WHISTLE. WHERE DID YOU PUT IT?
THE SUBMARINE. ENTOMBED ALONGSIDE THE REST OF THE YEAR OF BLOOD. IT IS A CURSE EVEN UPON THIS DEFILED PLACE. I WILL GO...
NO. I DON'T WANT YOU IN THERE AGAIN...
...STAY HERE.
AS YOU WISH.

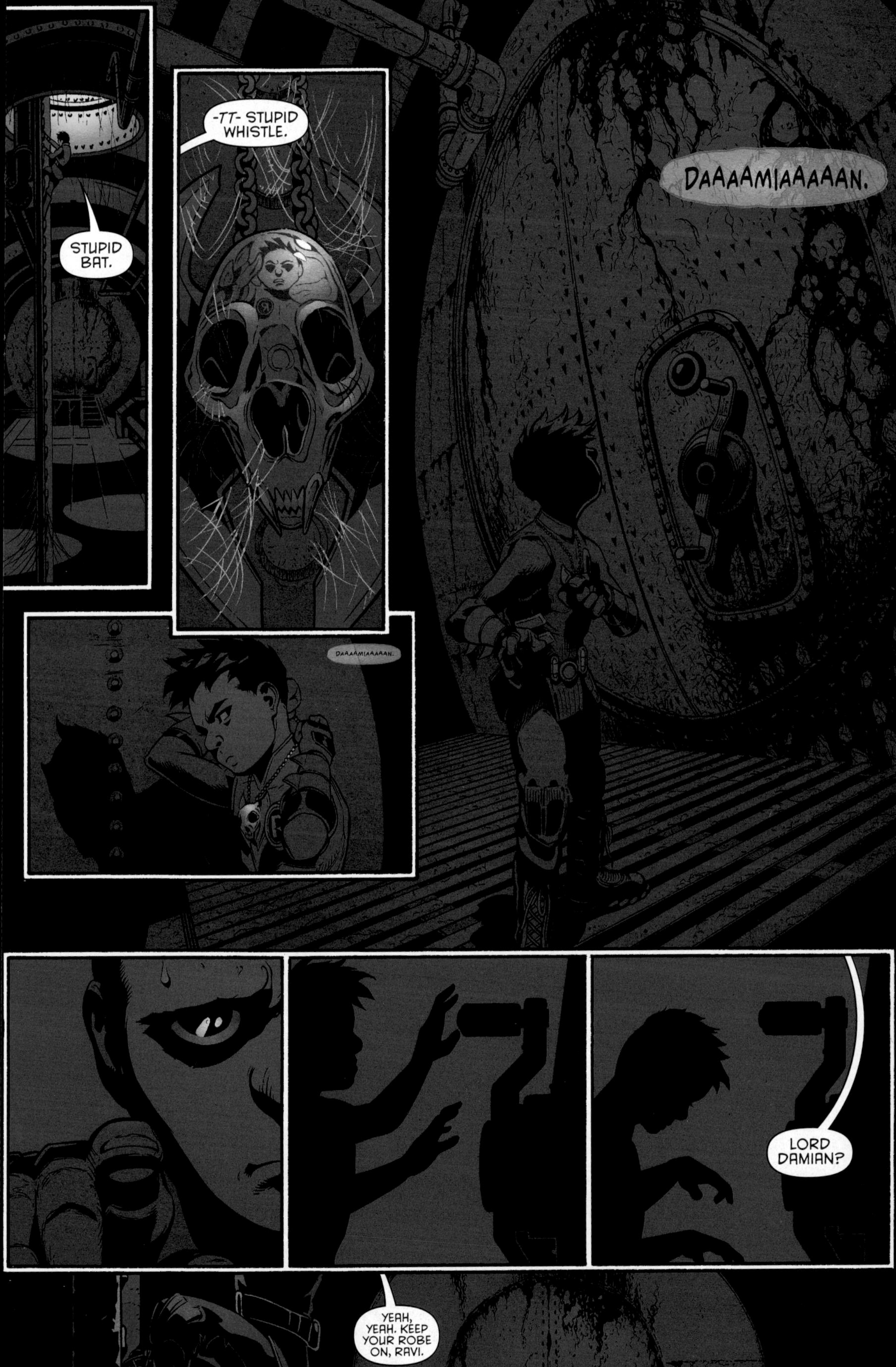
STUPID BAT.
-TT- STUPID WHISTLE.
DAAAAMIAAAAAN.
DAAAAMIAAAAAN.
LORD DAMIAN?
YEAH, YEAH. KEEP YOUR ROBE ON, RAVI.

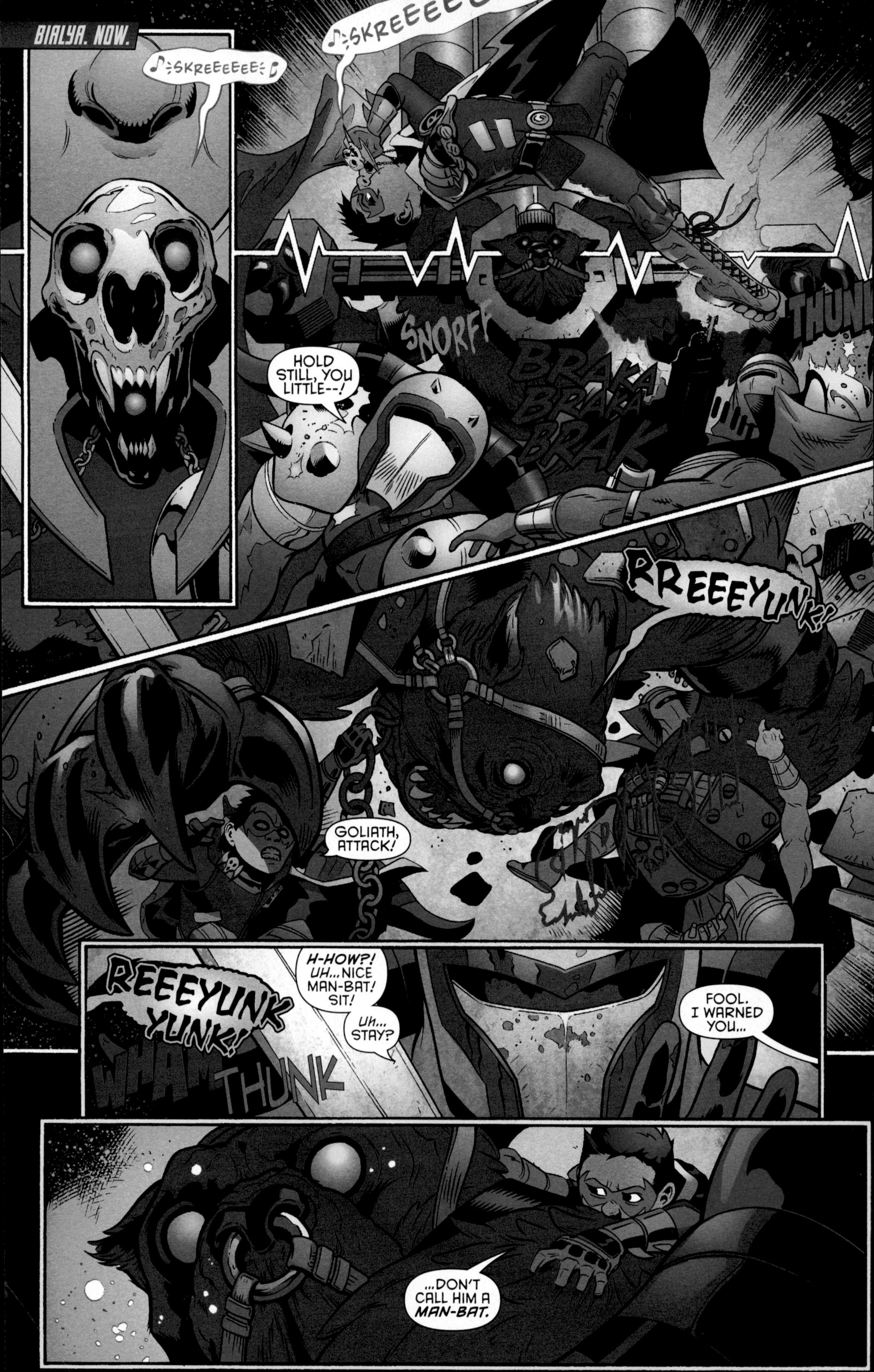
BIALYA. NOW.
SKREEEEEEE
SKREEEEE
SNORFF
HOLD STILL, YOU LITTLE--!
BRAKA BRAKA BRAK
THUNK
RREEEEYUNK!
GOLIATH, ATTACK!
REEEYUNK YUNK!
WHAM THUNK
H-HOW?! UH... NICE MAN-BAT! SIT!
UH... STAY?
FOOL. I WARNED YOU...
...DON'T CALL HIM A MAN-BAT.

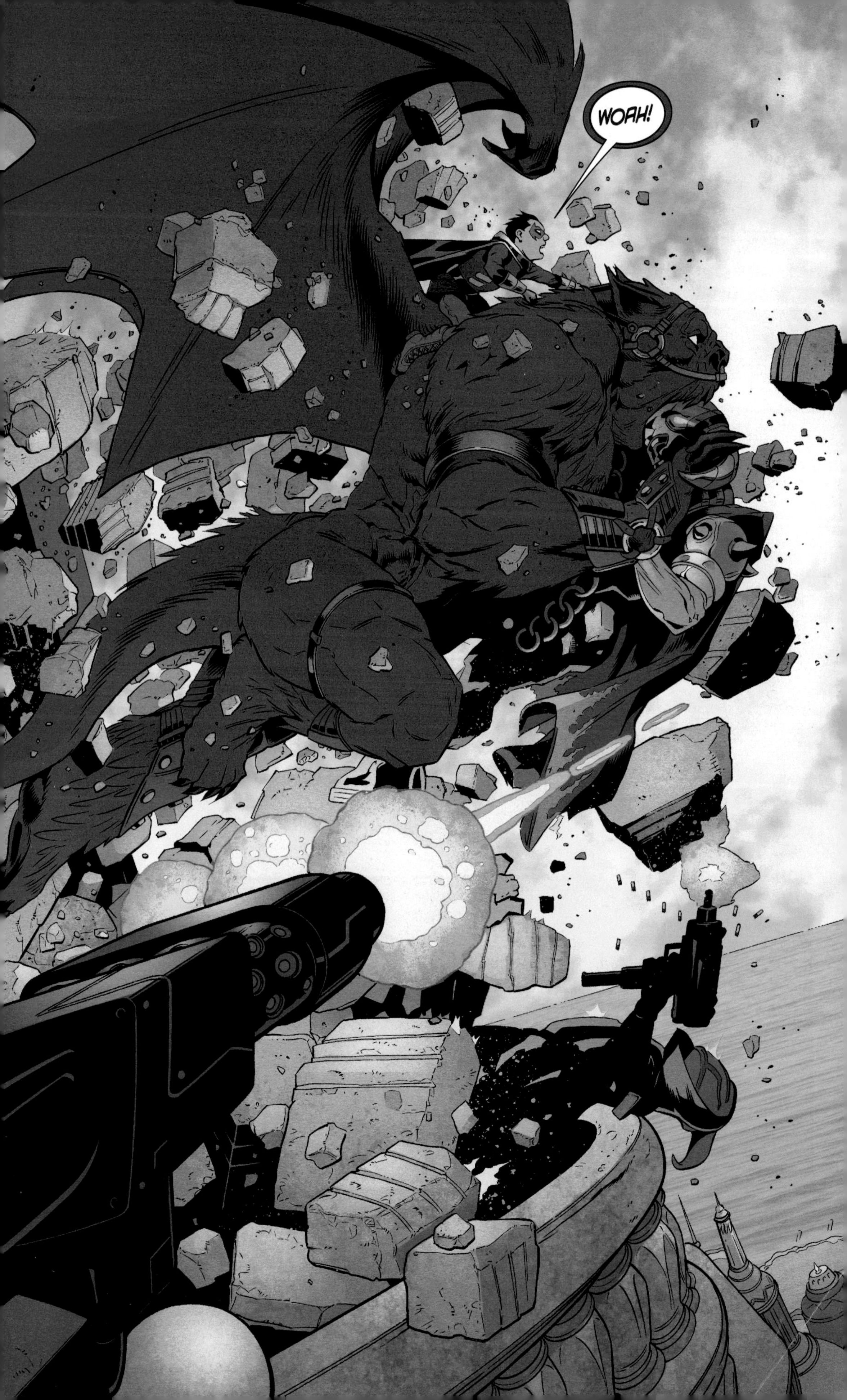
WOAH!

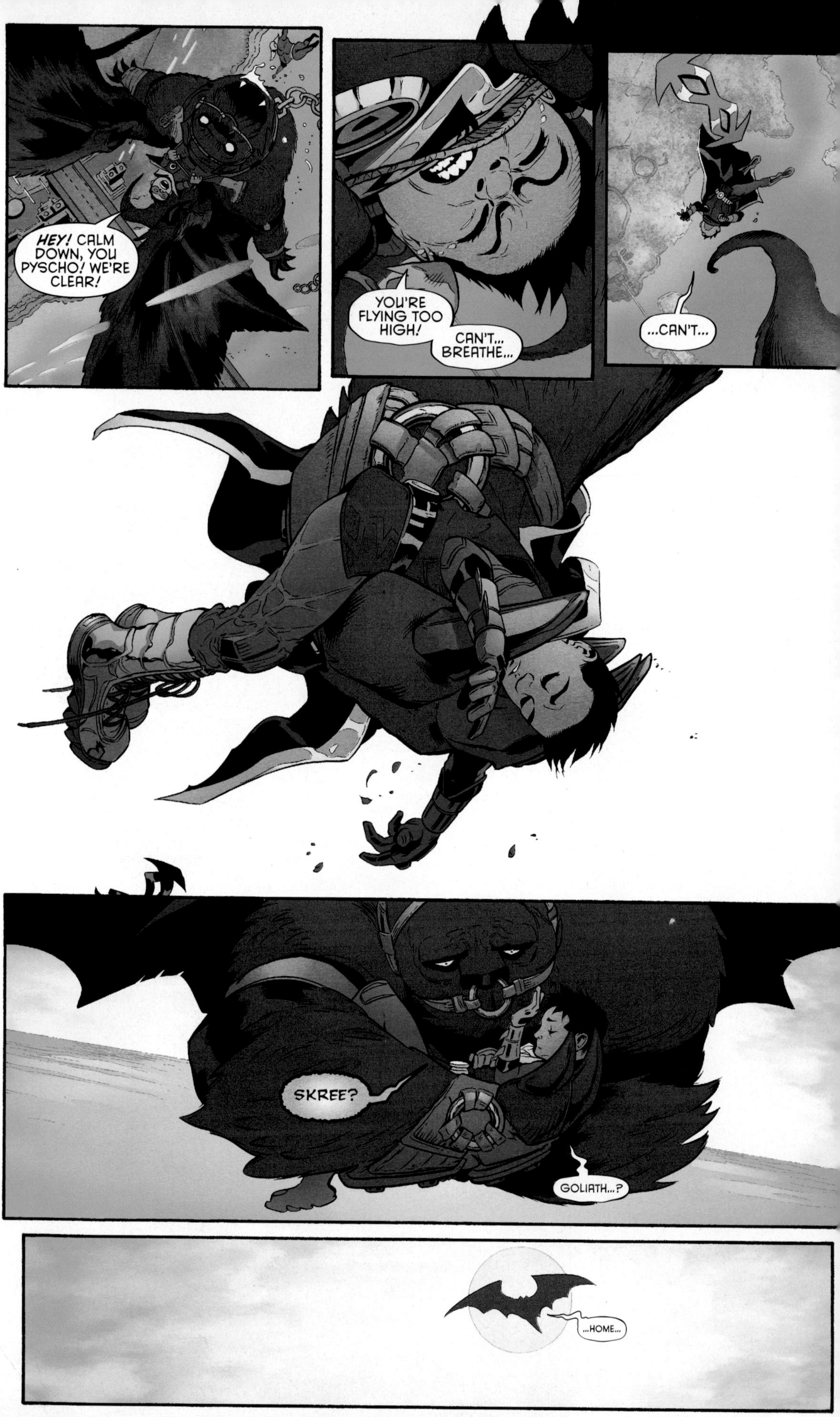
HEY! CALM DOWN, YOU PYSCHO! WE'RE CLEAR!
YOU'RE FLYING TOO HIGH!
CAN'T... BREATHE...
...CAN'T...
SKREE?
GOLIATH...?
...HOME...

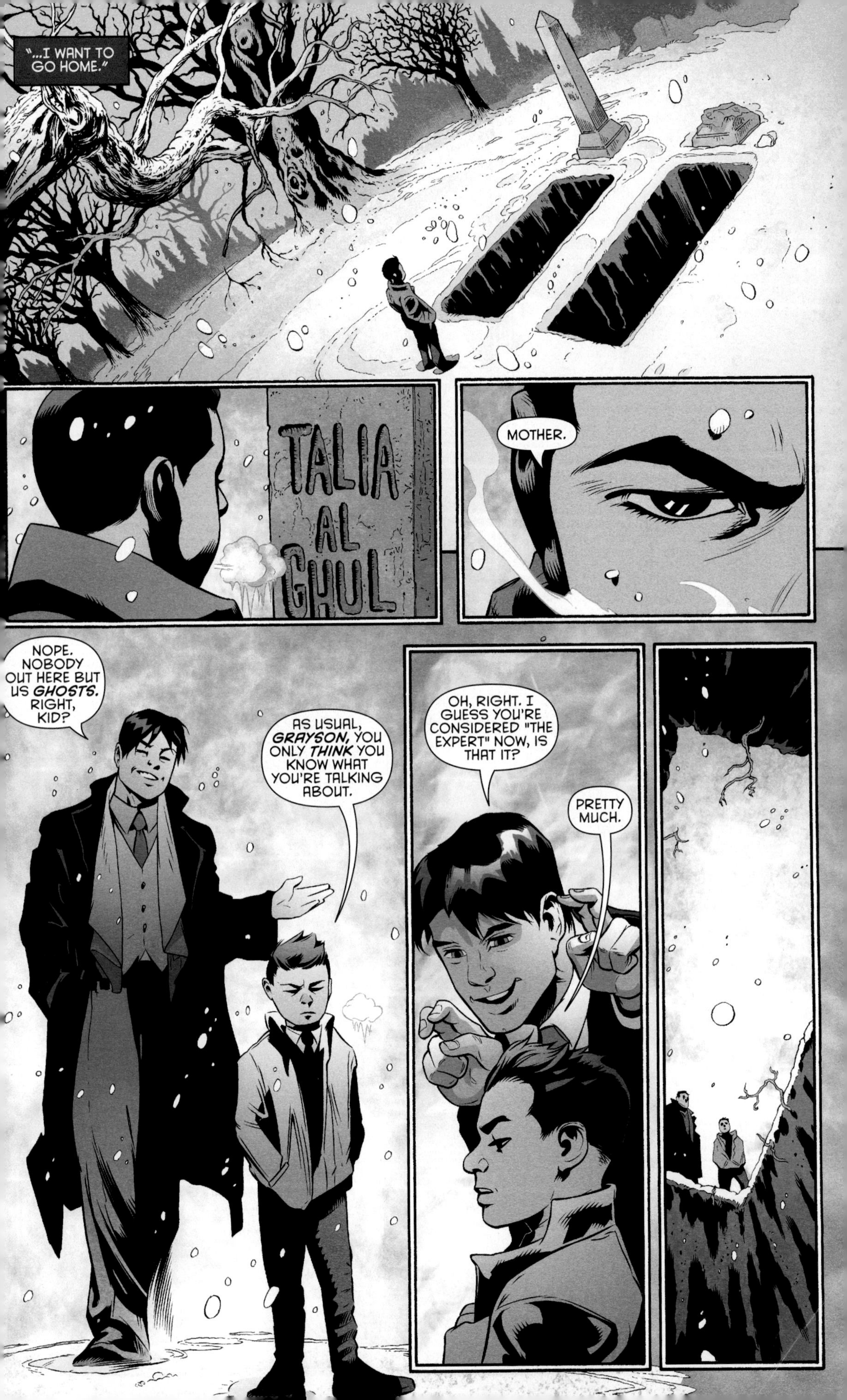
"...I WANT TO GO HOME."
TALIA AL GHUL
MOTHER.
NOPE. NOBODY OUT HERE BUT US GHOSTS. RIGHT, KID?
AS USUAL, GRAYSON, YOU ONLY THINK YOU KNOW WHAT YOU'RE TALKING ABOUT.
OH, RIGHT. I GUESS YOU'RE CONSIDERED "THE EXPERT" NOW, IS THAT IT?
PRETTY MUCH.

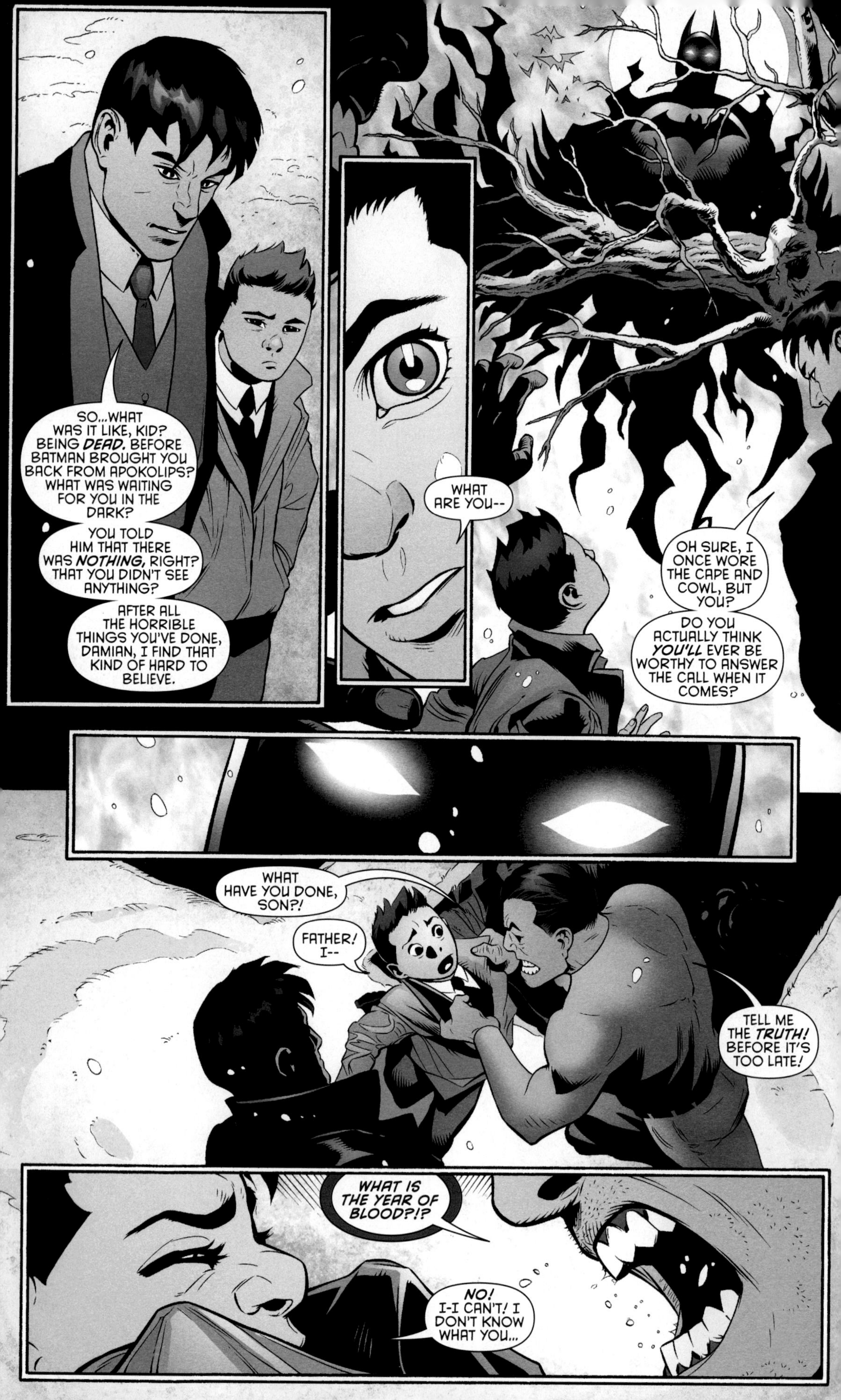
SO...WHAT WAS IT LIKE, KID? BEING DEAD. BEFORE BATMAN BROUGHT YOU BACK FROM APOKOLIPS? WHAT WAS WAITING FOR YOU IN THE DARK?
YOU TOLD HIM THAT THERE WAS NOTHING, RIGHT? THAT YOU DIDN'T SEE ANYTHING?
AFTER ALL THE HORRIBLE THINGS YOU'VE DONE, DAMIAN, I FIND THAT KIND OF HARD TO BELIEVE.
WHAT ARE YOU--
OH SURE, I ONCE WORE THE CAPE AND COWL, BUT YOU?
DO YOU ACTUALLY THINK YOU'LL EVER BE WORTHY TO ANSWER THE CALL WHEN IT COMES?
WHAT HAVE YOU DONE, SON?!
FATHER! I--
TELL ME THE TRUTH! BEFORE IT'S TOO LATE!
WHAT IS THE YEAR OF BLOOD?!?
NO! I-I CAN'T! I DON'T KNOW WHAT YOU...

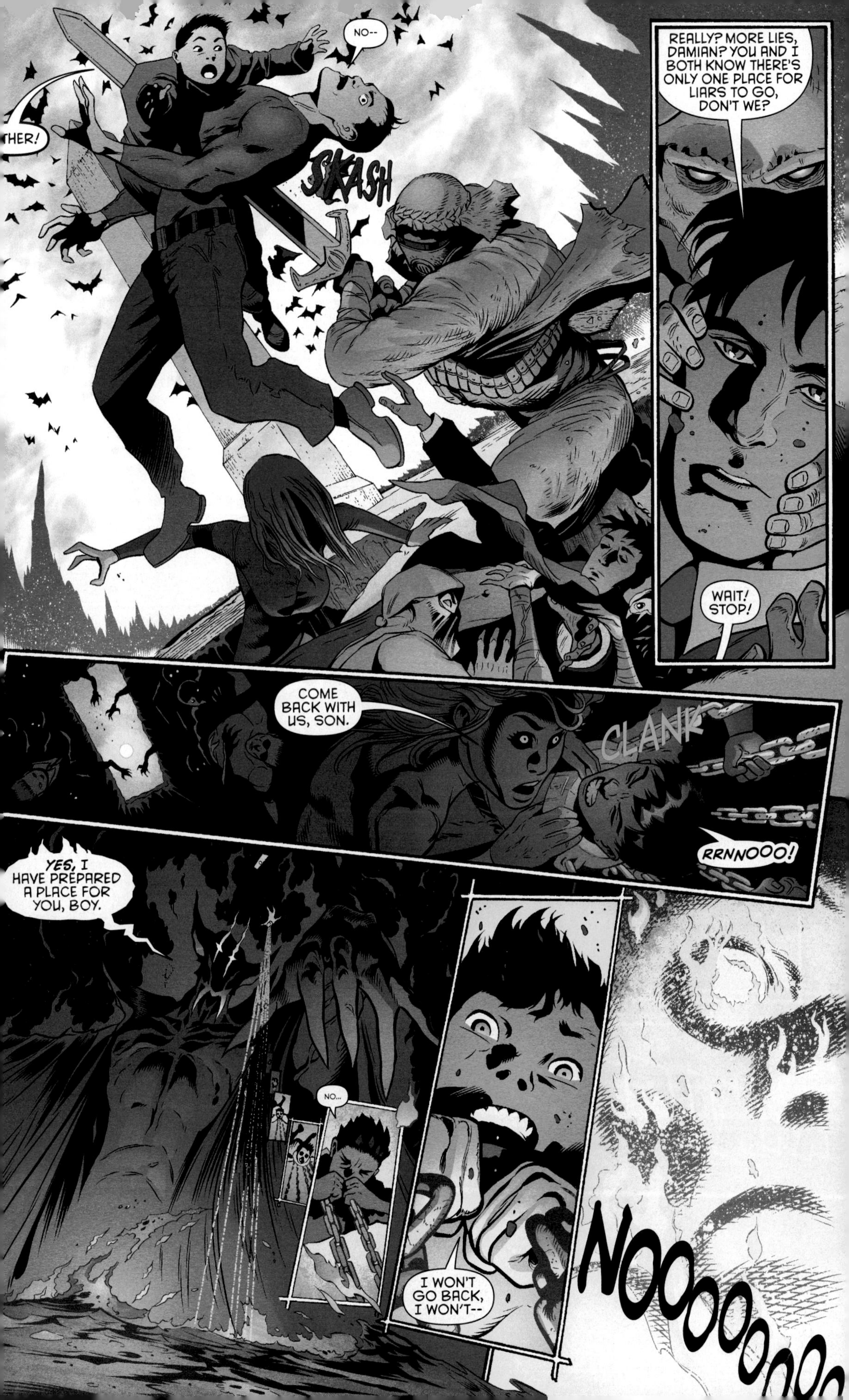

NO--
THER!
SKASH
REALLY? MORE LIES, DAMIAN? YOU AND I BOTH KNOW THERE'S ONLY ONE PLACE FOR LIARS TO GO, DON'T WE?
WAIT! STOP!
COME BACK WITH US, SON.
CLANK
RRNNOOO!
YES, I HAVE PREPARED A PLACE FOR YOU, BOY.
NO...
I WON'T GO BACK, I WON'T--
NOOOOOOOO

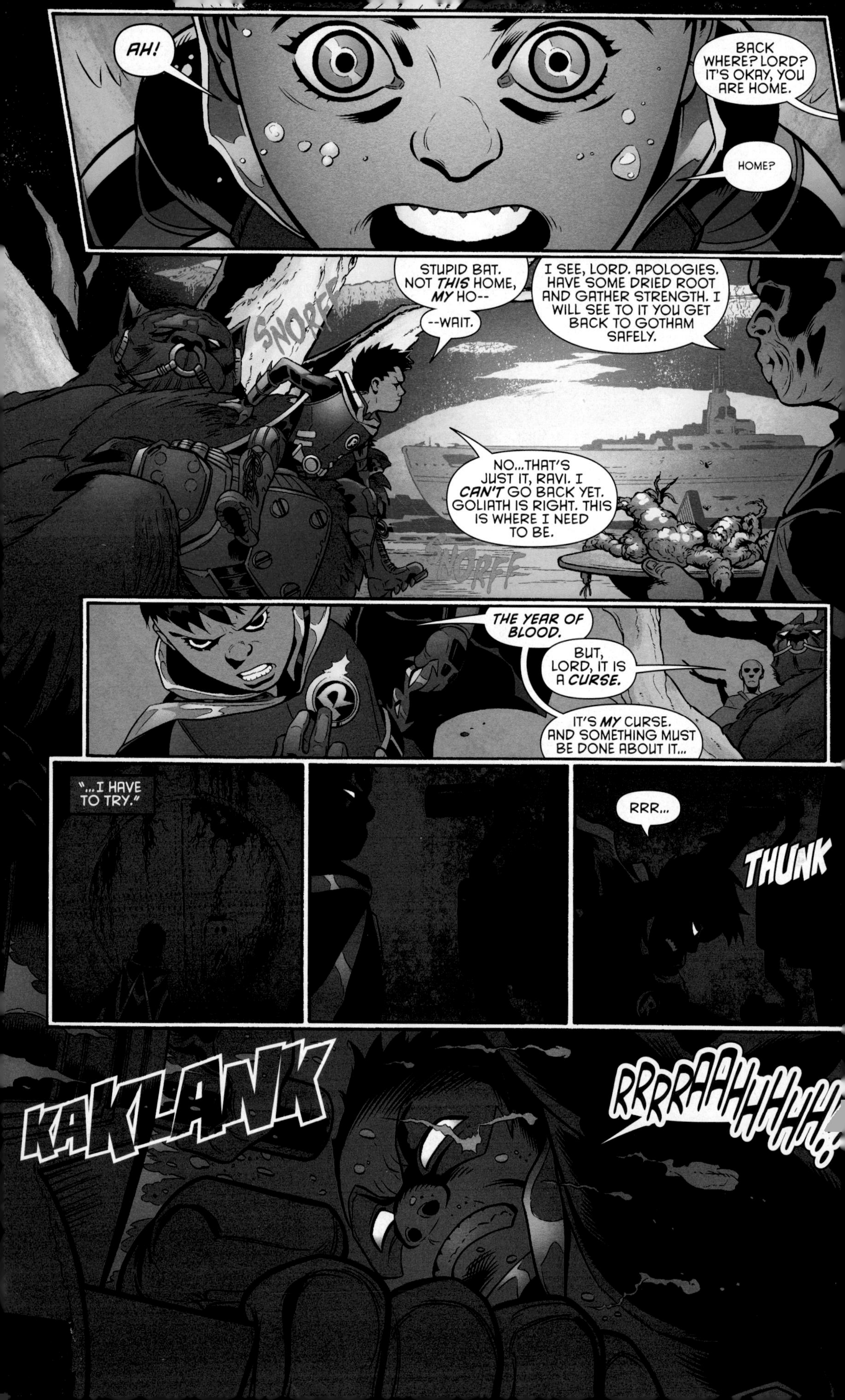
AH!
BACK WHERE? LORD? IT'S OKAY, YOU ARE HOME.
HOME?
STUPID BAT. NOT THIS HOME, MY HO--
--WAIT.
I SEE, LORD. APOLOGIES. HAVE SOME DRIED ROOT AND GATHER STRENGTH. I WILL SEE TO IT YOU GET BACK TO GOTHAM SAFELY.
SNORFF
NO...THAT'S JUST IT, RAVI. I CAN'T GO BACK YET. GOLIATH IS RIGHT. THIS IS WHERE I NEED TO BE.
SNORFF
THE YEAR OF BLOOD.
BUT, LORD, IT IS A CURSE.
IT'S MY CURSE. AND SOMETHING MUST BE DONE ABOUT IT...
"...I HAVE TO TRY."
RRR...
THUNK
KAKLANK
RRRRAAHHHHH!

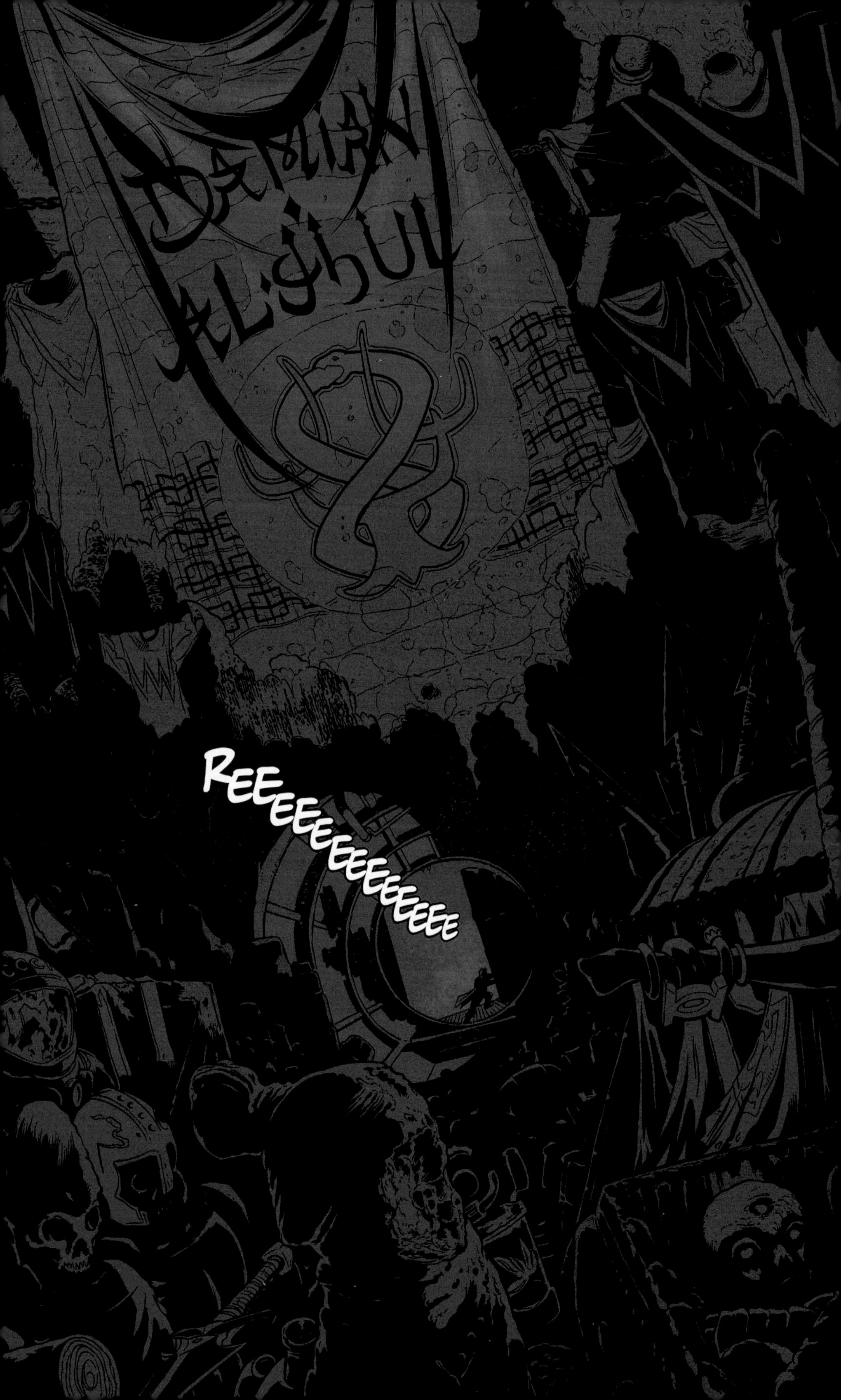
DAMIAN AL GHUL
REEEEEEEEEEEEEE

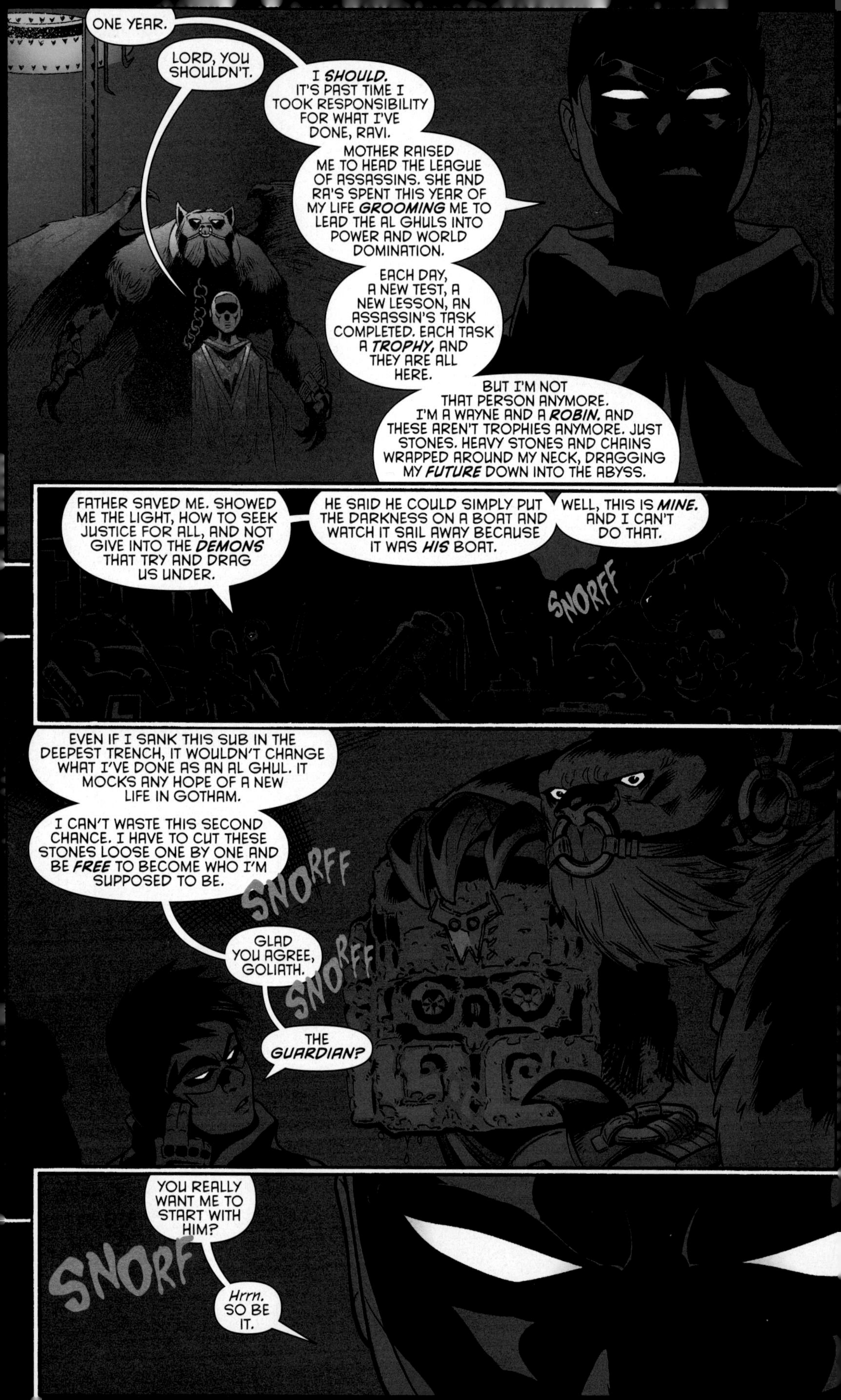
ONE YEAR.
LORD, YOU SHOULDN'T.
I SHOULD. IT'S PAST TIME I TOOK RESPONSIBILITY FOR WHAT I'VE DONE, RAVI.
MOTHER RAISED ME TO HEAD THE LEAGUE OF ASSASSINS. SHE AND RA'S SPENT THIS YEAR OF MY LIFE GROOMING ME TO LEAD THE AL GHULS INTO POWER AND WORLD DOMINATION.
EACH DAY, A NEW TEST, A NEW LESSON, AN ASSASSIN'S TASK COMPLETED. EACH TASK A TROPHY, AND THEY ARE ALL HERE.
BUT I'M NOT THAT PERSON ANYMORE. I'M A WAYNE AND A ROBIN. AND THESE AREN'T TROPHIES ANYMORE. JUST STONES. HEAVY STONES AND CHAINS WRAPPED AROUND MY NECK, DRAGGING MY FUTURE DOWN INTO THE ABYSS.
FATHER SAVED ME. SHOWED ME THE LIGHT, HOW TO SEEK JUSTICE FOR ALL, AND NOT GIVE INTO THE DEMONS THAT TRY AND DRAG US UNDER.
HE SAID HE COULD SIMPLY PUT THE DARKNESS ON A BOAT AND WATCH IT SAIL AWAY BECAUSE IT WAS HIS BOAT.
WELL, THIS IS MINE. AND I CAN'T DO THAT.
SNORFF
EVEN IF I SANK THIS SUB IN THE DEEPEST TRENCH, IT WOULDN'T CHANGE WHAT I'VE DONE AS AN AL GHUL. IT MOCKS ANY HOPE OF A NEW LIFE IN GOTHAM.
I CAN'T WASTE THIS SECOND CHANCE. I HAVE TO CUT THESE STONES LOOSE ONE BY ONE AND BE FREE TO BECOME WHO I'M SUPPOSED TO BE.
SNORFF
GLAD YOU AGREE, GOLIATH.
SNORFF
THE GUARDIAN?
YOU REALLY WANT ME TO START WITH HIM?
SNORF
Hrrn. SO BE IT.

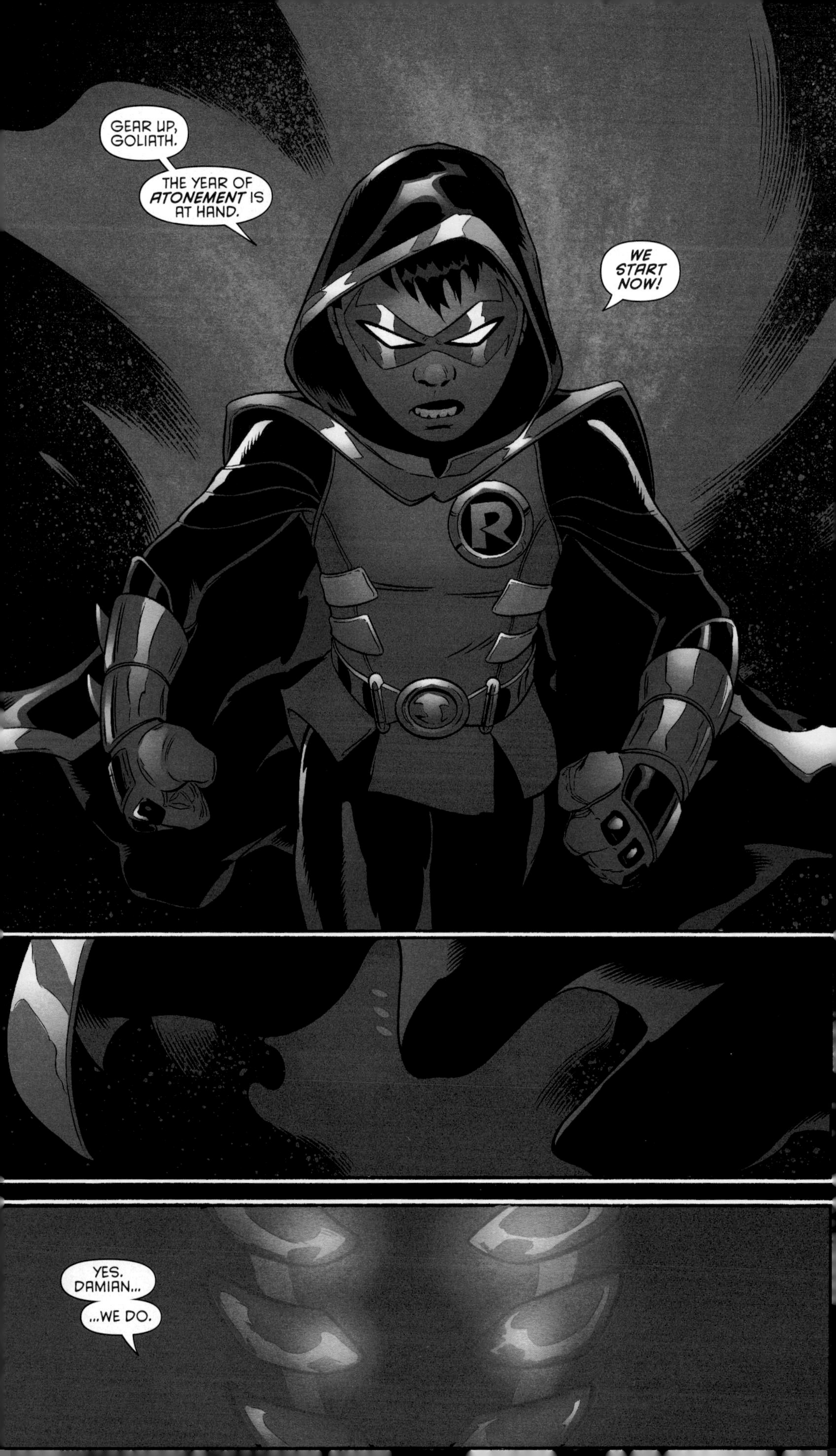
GEAR UP, GOLIATH.
THE YEAR OF *ATONEMENT* IS AT HAND.
WE START NOW!
YES. DAMIAN...
...WE DO.

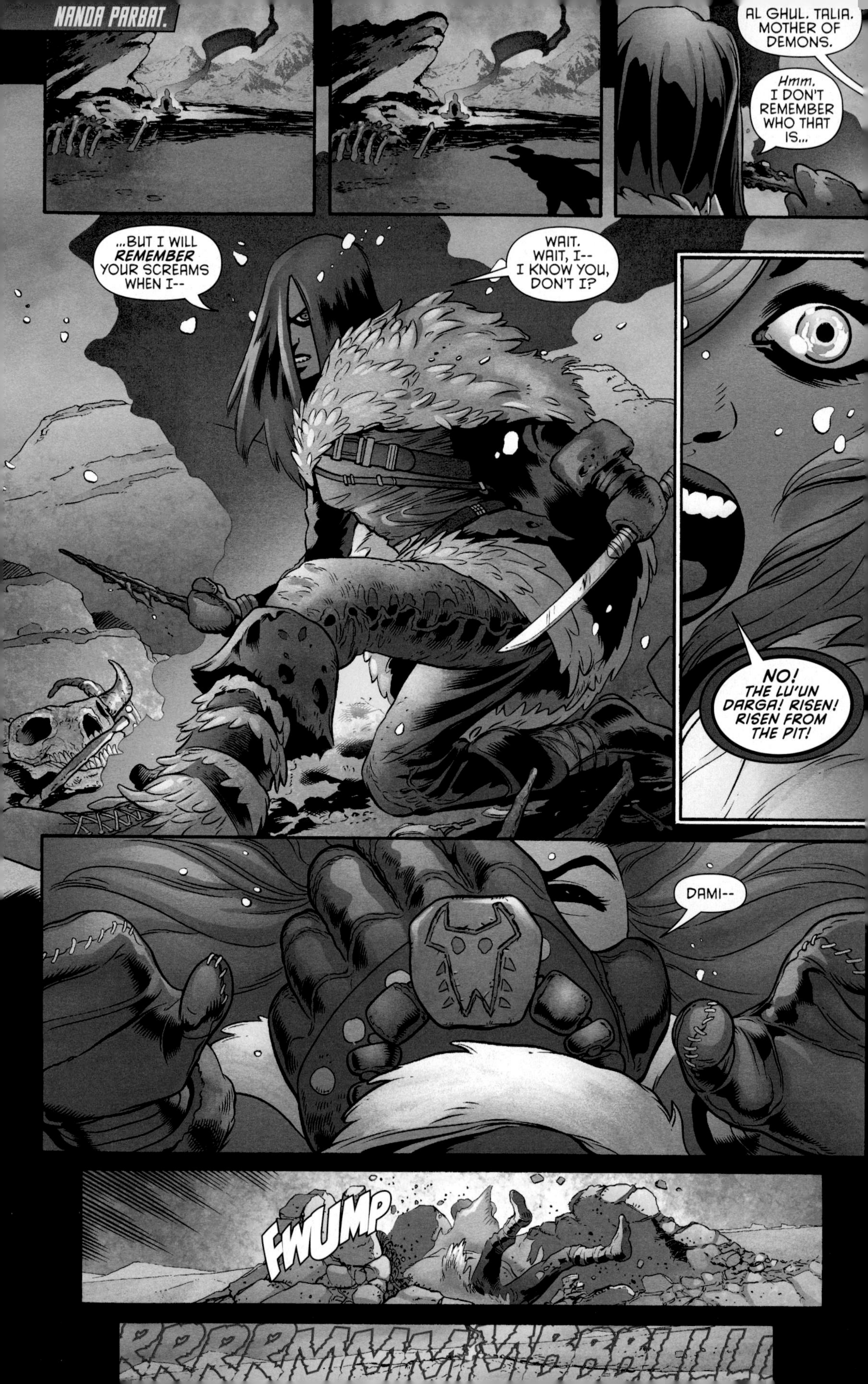
NANDA PARBAT.
AL GHUL. TALIA. MOTHER OF DEMONS.
Hmm. I DON'T REMEMBER WHO THAT IS...
...BUT I WILL REMEMBER YOUR SCREAMS WHEN I--
WAIT. WAIT, I-- I KNOW YOU, DON'T I?
NO! THE LU'UN DARGA! RISEN! RISEN FROM THE PIT!
DAMI--
FWUMP

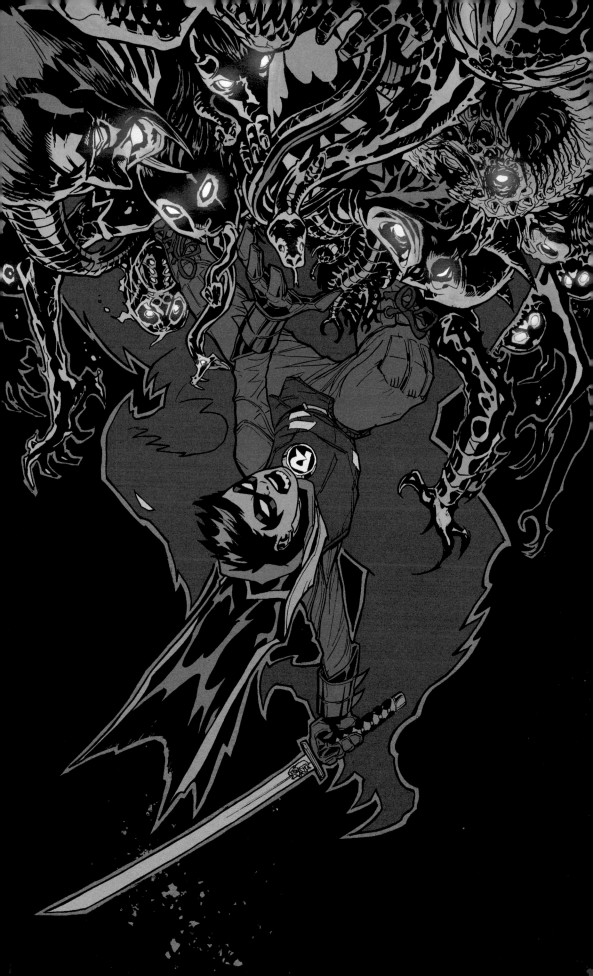

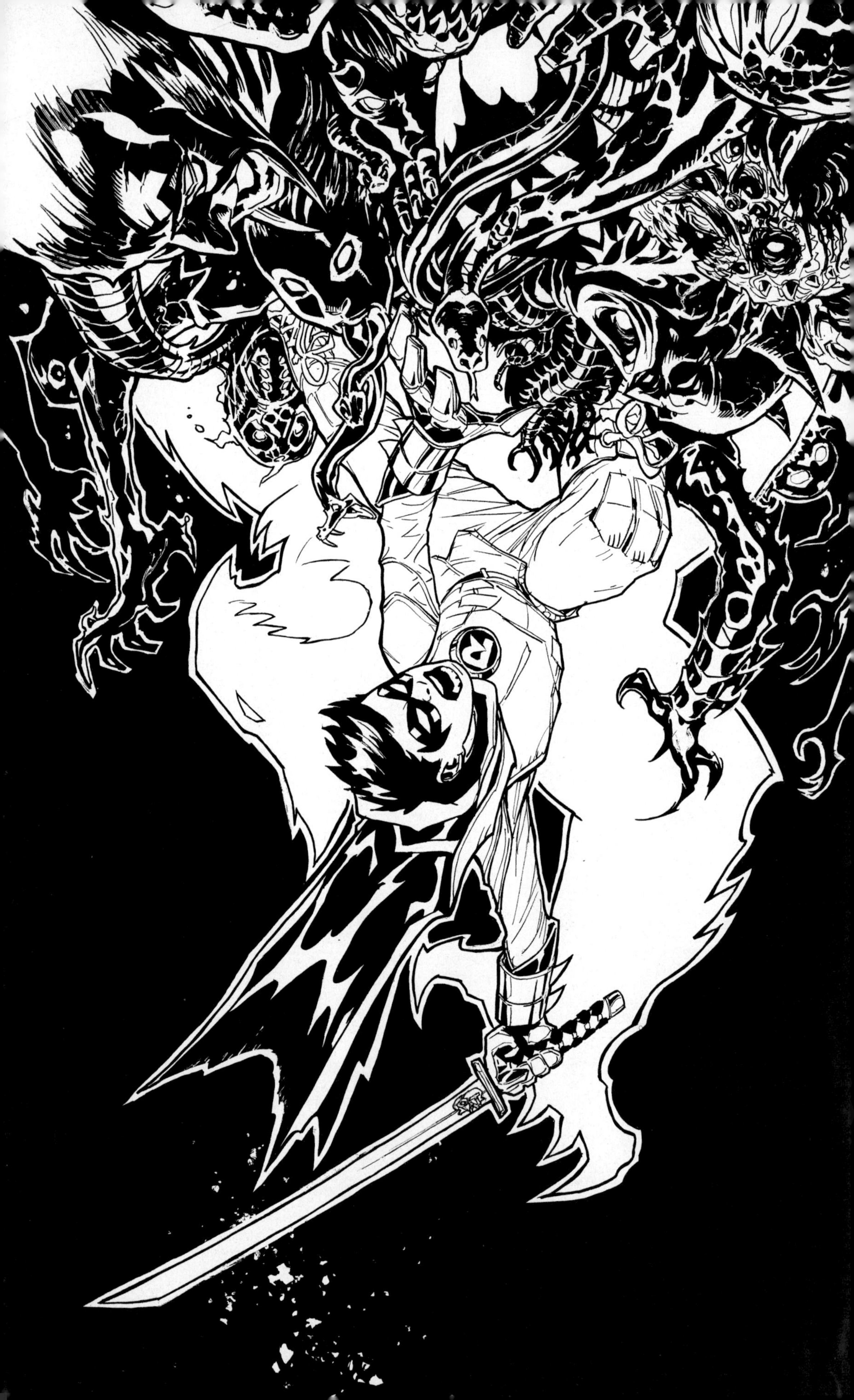

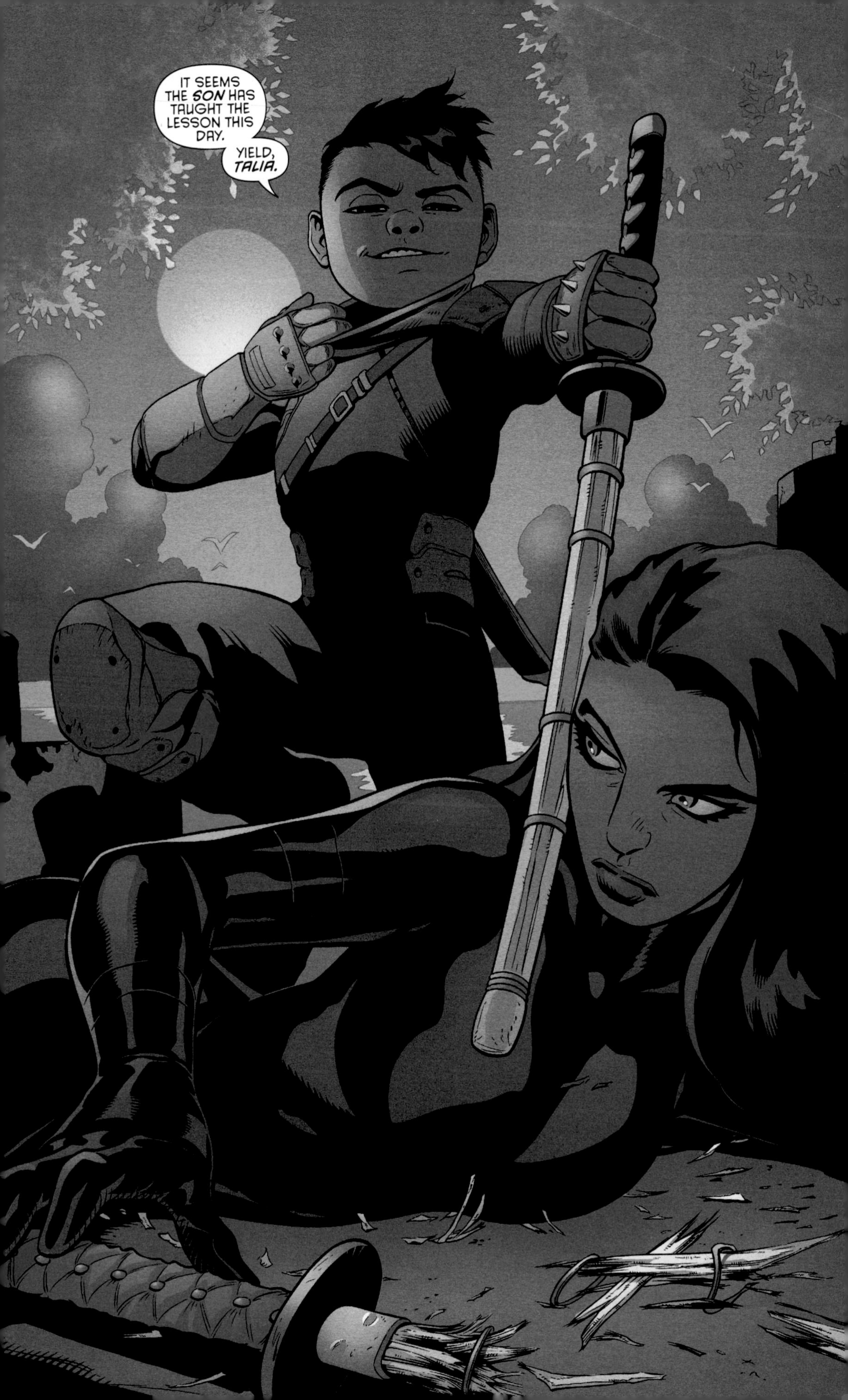
IT SEEMS THE SON HAS TAUGHT THE LESSON THIS DAY.
YIELD, TALIA.

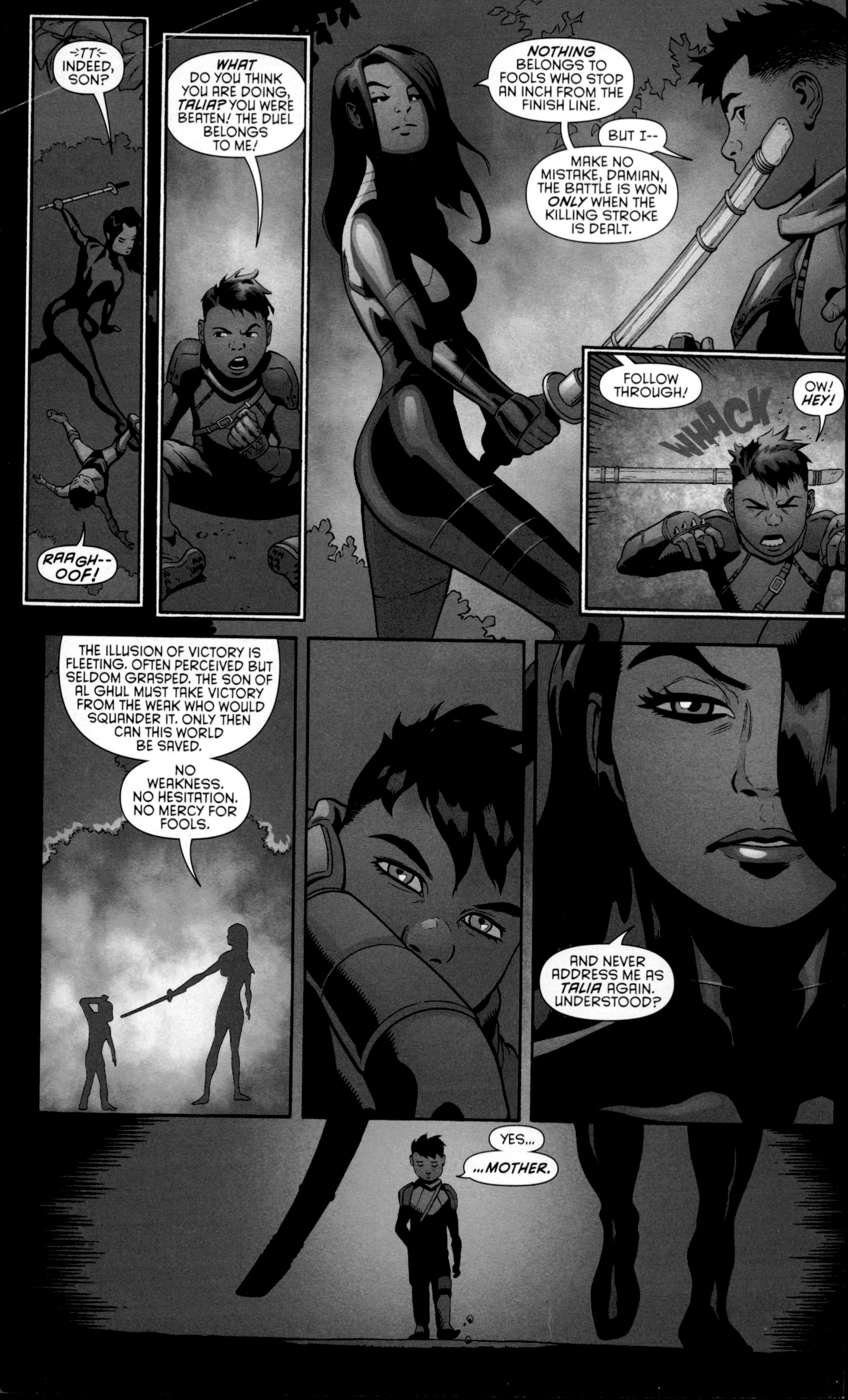

-TT- INDEED, SON?
RAAGH-- OOF!
WHAT DO YOU THINK YOU ARE DOING, TALIA? YOU WERE BEATEN! THE DUEL BELONGS TO ME!
NOTHING BELONGS TO FOOLS WHO STOP AN INCH FROM THE FINISH LINE.
BUT I--
MAKE NO MISTAKE, DAMIAN, THE BATTLE IS WON ONLY WHEN THE KILLING STROKE IS DEALT.
FOLLOW THROUGH!
WHACK
OW! HEY!
THE ILLUSION OF VICTORY IS FLEETING. OFTEN PERCEIVED BUT SELDOM GRASPED. THE SON OF AL GHUL MUST TAKE VICTORY FROM THE WEAK WHO WOULD SQUANDER IT. ONLY THEN CAN THIS WORLD BE SAVED.
NO WEAKNESS. NO HESITATION. NO MERCY FOR FOOLS.
AND NEVER ADDRESS ME AS TALIA AGAIN. UNDERSTOOD?
YES...
...MOTHER.

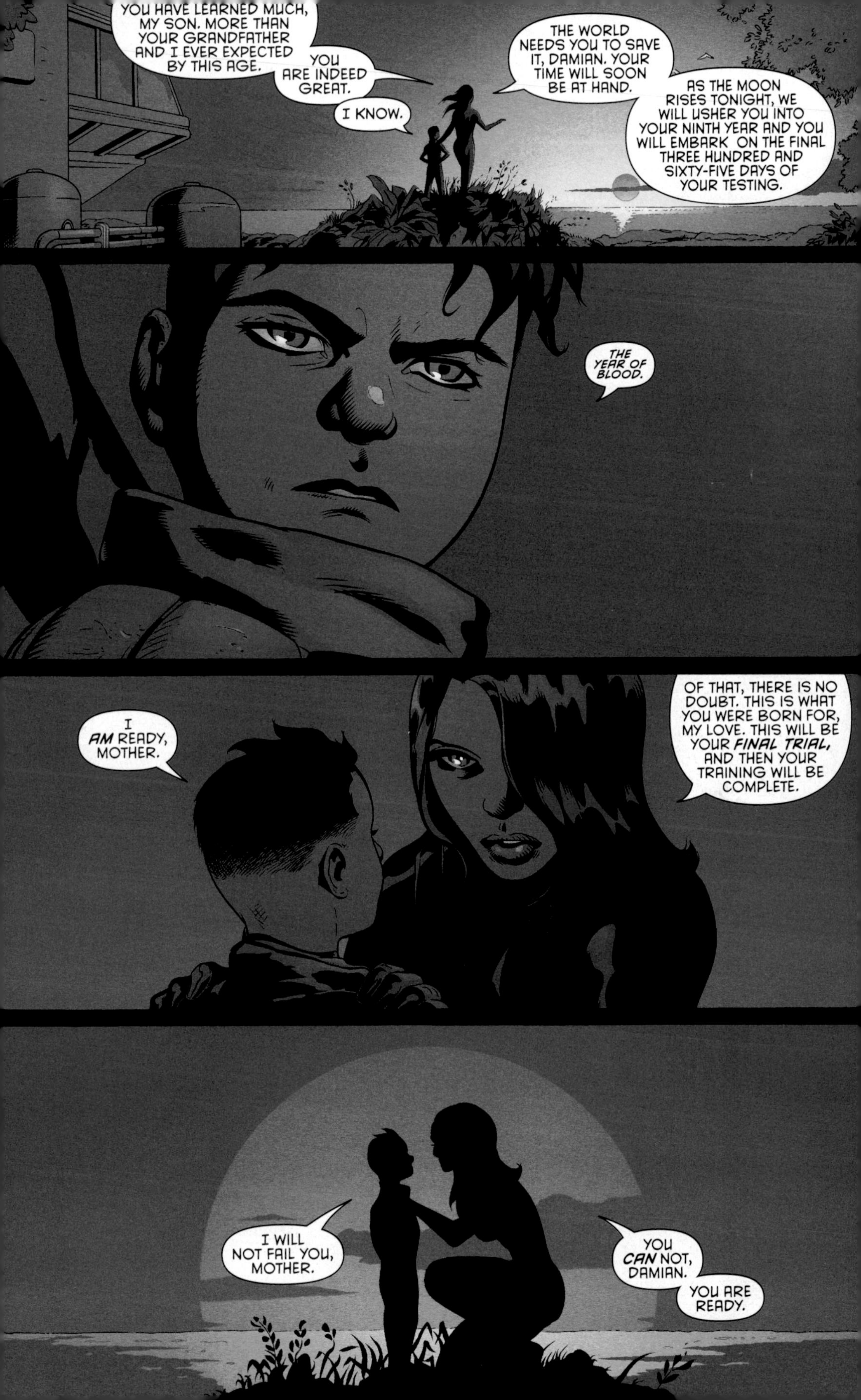
YOU HAVE LEARNED MUCH, MY SON. MORE THAN YOUR GRANDFATHER AND I EVER EXPECTED BY THIS AGE.
YOU ARE INDEED GREAT.
I KNOW.
THE WORLD NEEDS YOU TO SAVE IT, DAMIAN. YOUR TIME WILL SOON BE AT HAND.
AS THE MOON RISES TONIGHT, WE WILL USHER YOU INTO YOUR NINTH YEAR AND YOU WILL EMBARK ON THE FINAL THREE HUNDRED AND SIXTY-FIVE DAYS OF YOUR TESTING.
THE YEAR OF BLOOD.
I AM READY, MOTHER.
OF THAT, THERE IS NO DOUBT. THIS IS WHAT YOU WERE BORN FOR, MY LOVE. THIS WILL BE YOUR FINAL TRIAL, AND THEN YOUR TRAINING WILL BE COMPLETE.
I WILL NOT FAIL YOU, MOTHER.
YOU CAN NOT, DAMIAN.
YOU ARE READY.

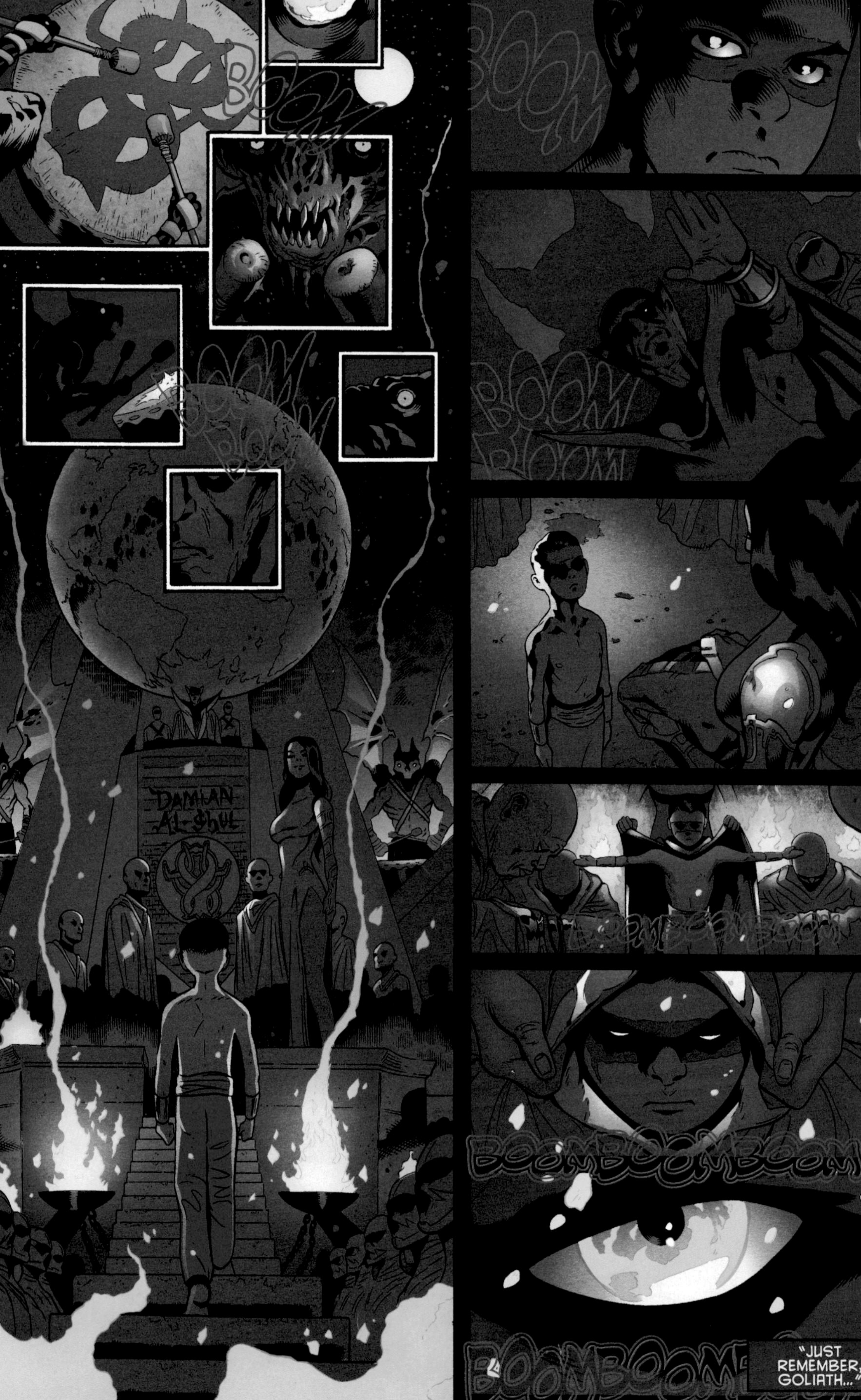
BOOM
BOOM
BOOM
DAMIAN AL-GHUL
BOOM
BOOM
BOOM
BOOMBOOMBOOM
BOOMBOOMBOOM
"JUST REMEMBER, GOLIATH..."

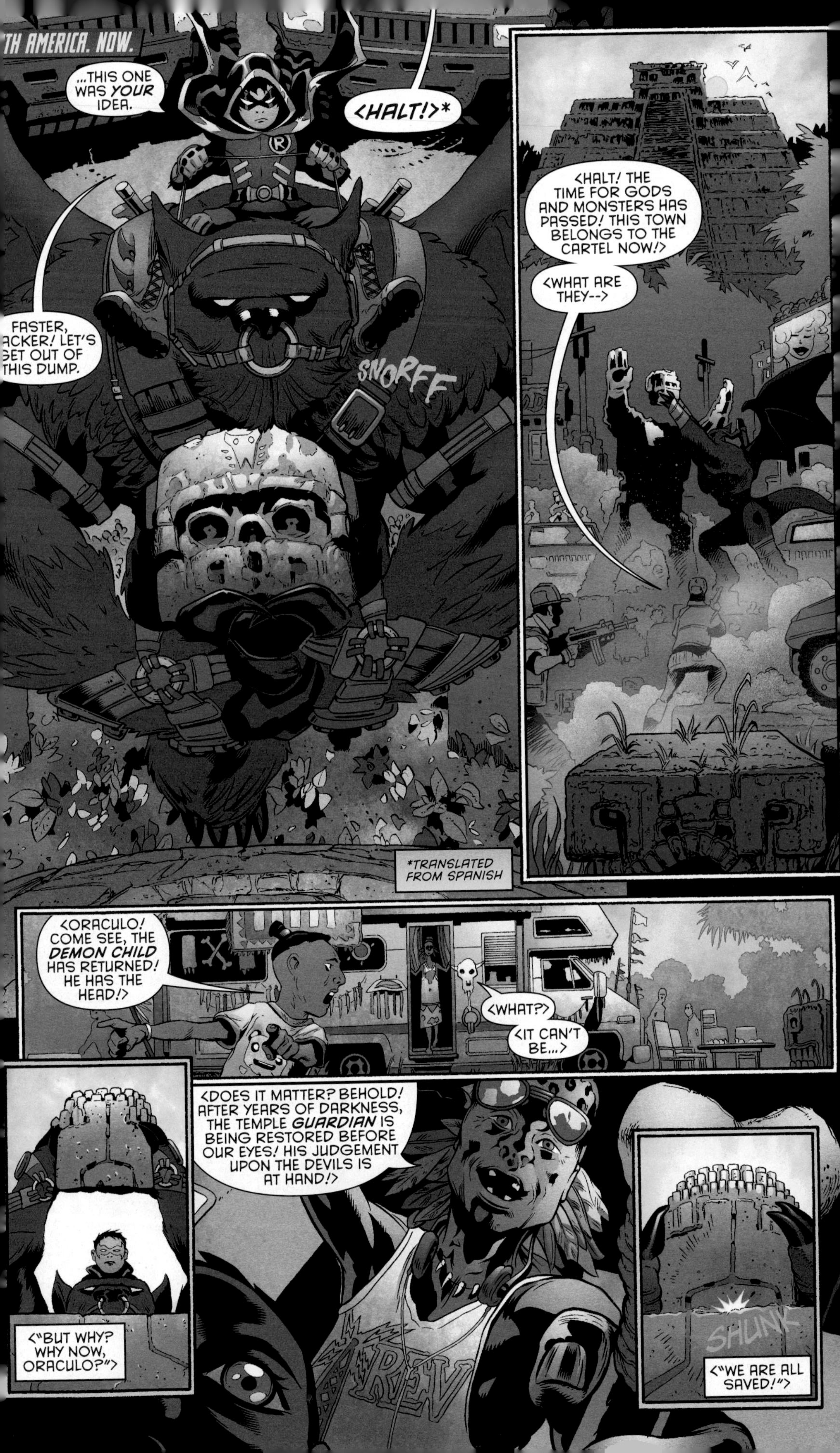
TH AMERICA. NOW.
...THIS ONE WAS *YOUR* IDEA.
<HALT!>*
FASTER, ACKER! LET'S GET OUT OF THIS DUMP.
SNORFF
<HALT! THE TIME FOR GODS AND MONSTERS HAS PASSED! THIS TOWN BELONGS TO THE CARTEL NOW!>
<WHAT ARE THEY-->
*TRANSLATED FROM SPANISH
<ORACULO! COME SEE, THE *DEMON CHILD* HAS RETURNED! HE HAS THE HEAD!>
<WHAT?>
<IT CAN'T BE...>
<DOES IT MATTER? BEHOLD! AFTER YEARS OF DARKNESS, THE TEMPLE *GUARDIAN* IS BEING RESTORED BEFORE OUR EYES! HIS JUDGEMENT UPON THE DEVILS IS AT HAND!>
<"BUT WHY? WHY NOW, ORACULO?">
SHUNK
<"WE ARE ALL SAVED!">

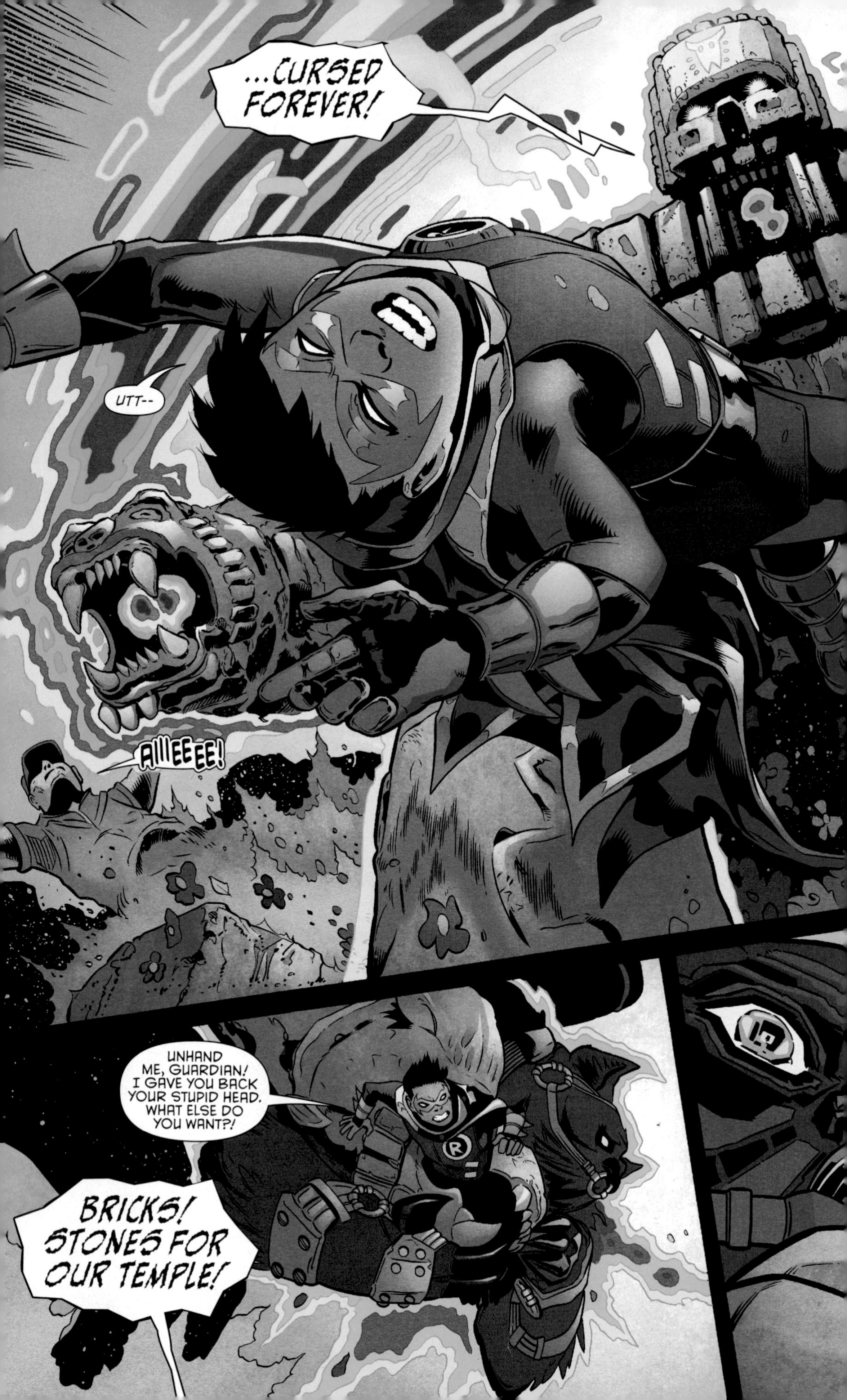
...CURSED FOREVER!
UTT--
AIIIEEEE!
UNHAND ME, GUARDIAN! I GAVE YOU BACK YOUR STUPID HEAD. WHAT ELSE DO YOU WANT?!
BRICKS! STONES FOR OUR TEMPLE!

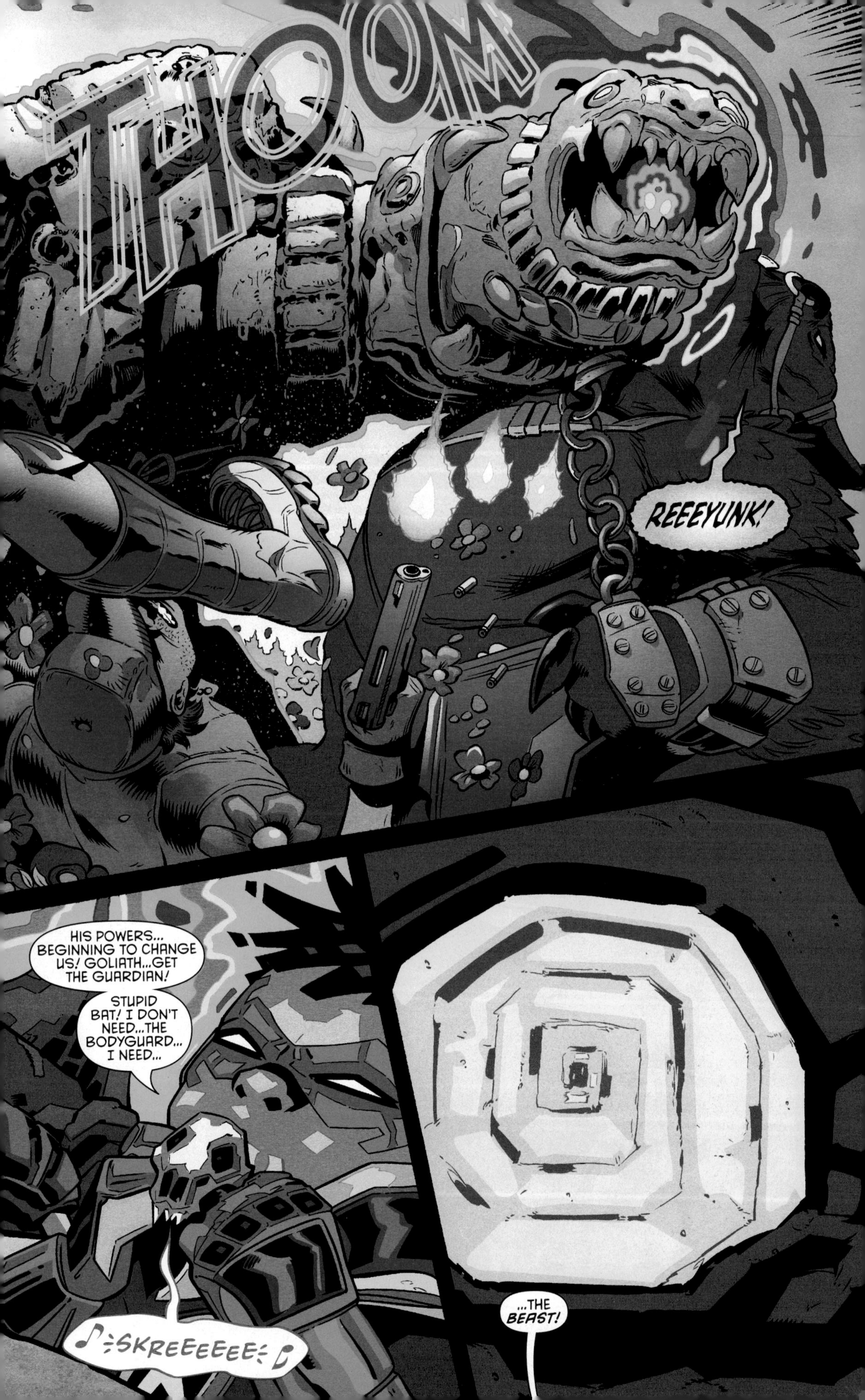
THOOM
REEEYUNK!
HIS POWERS... BEGINNING TO CHANGE US! GOLIATH...GET THE GUARDIAN!
STUPID BAT! I DON'T NEED...THE BODYGUARD... I NEED...
...THE BEAST!
SKREEEEEEE

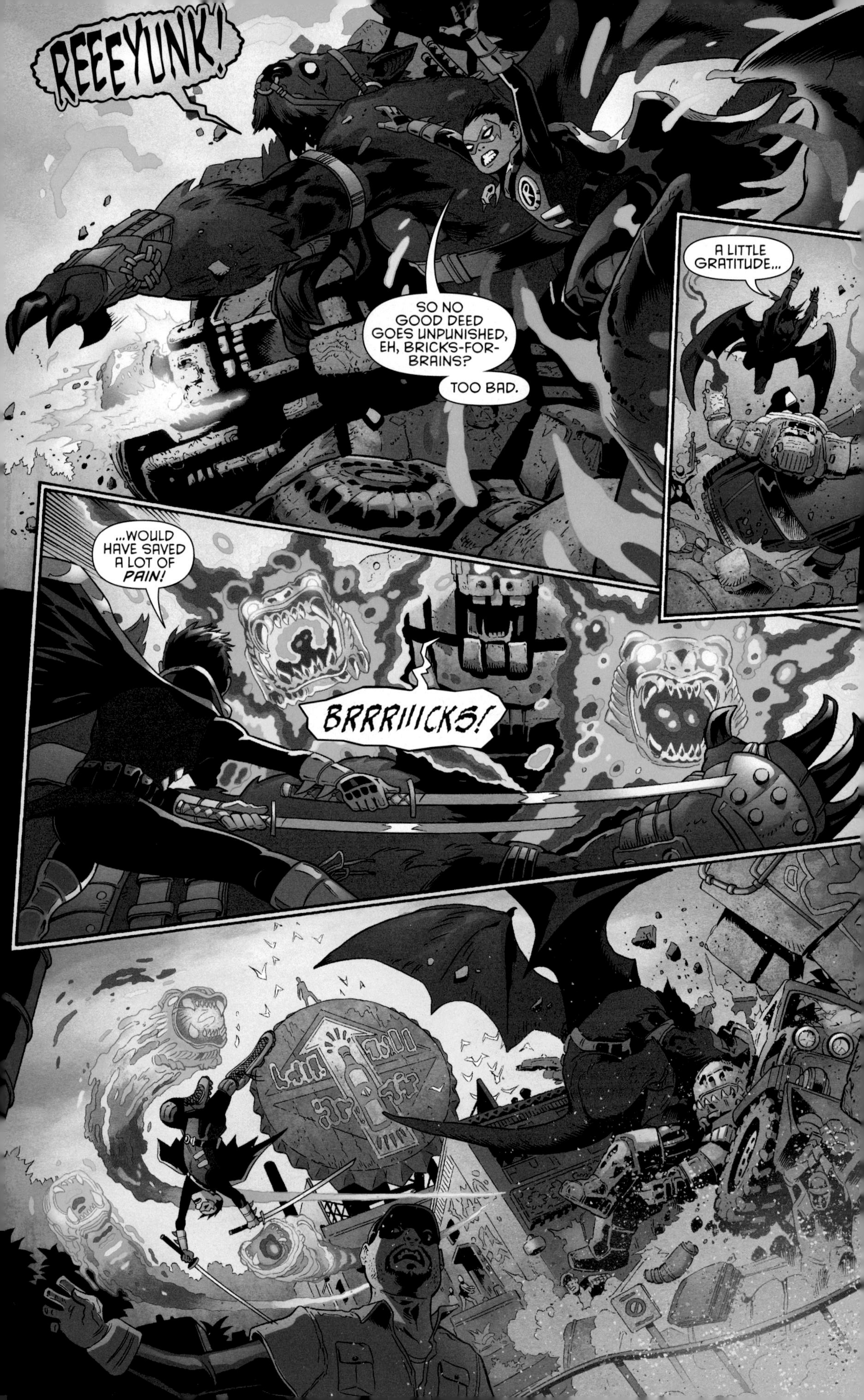
REEEYUNK!
SO NO GOOD DEED GOES UNPUNISHED, EH, BRICKS-FOR-BRAINS?
TOO BAD.
A LITTLE GRATITUDE...
...WOULD HAVE SAVED A LOT OF PAIN!
BRRRIIICKS!

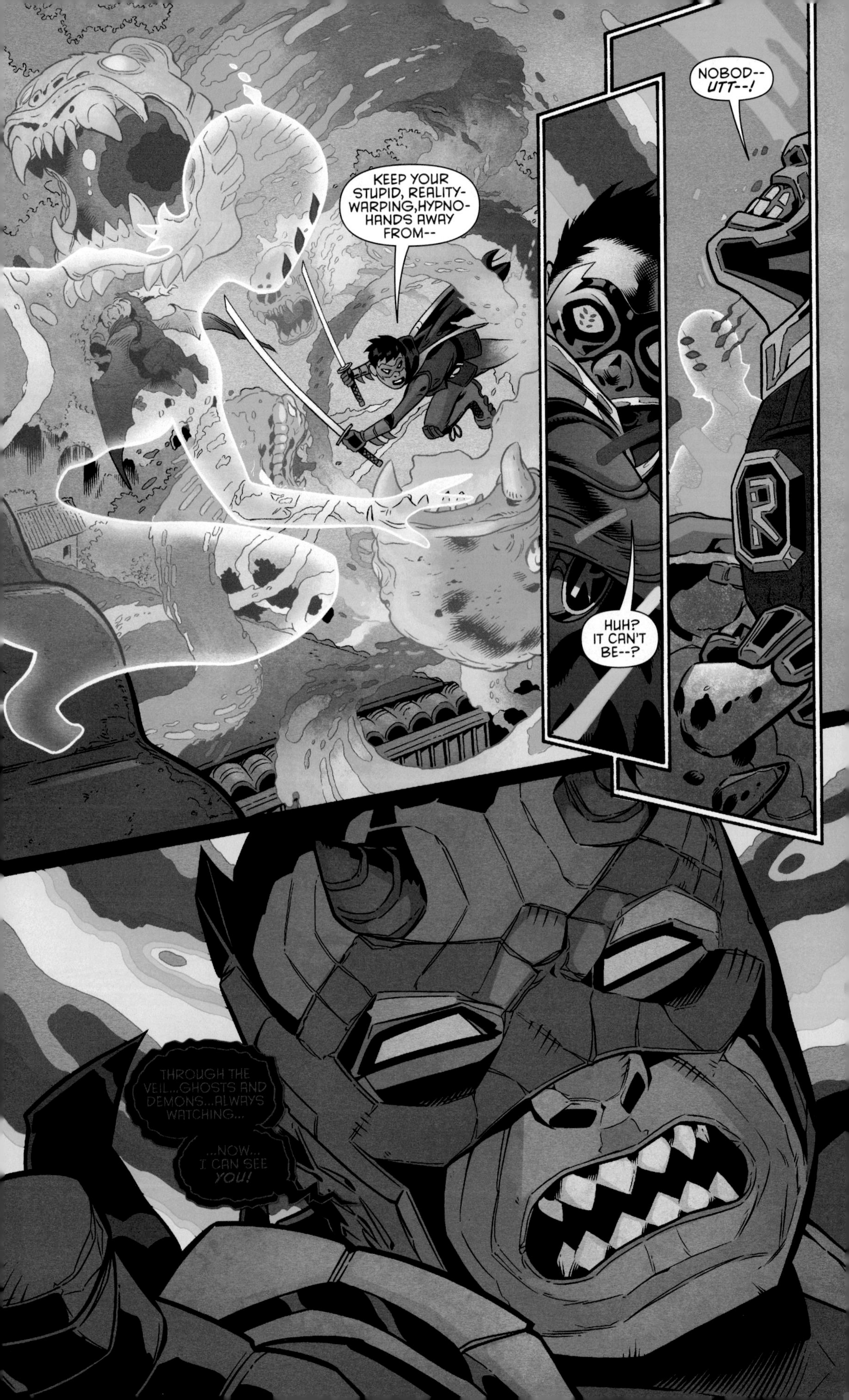
KEEP YOUR STUPID, REALITY-WARPING, HYPNO-HANDS AWAY FROM--
HUH? IT CAN'T BE--?
NOBOD-- UTT--!
THROUGH THE VEIL...GHOSTS AND DEMONS...ALWAYS WATCHING...
...NOW... I CAN SEE YOU!

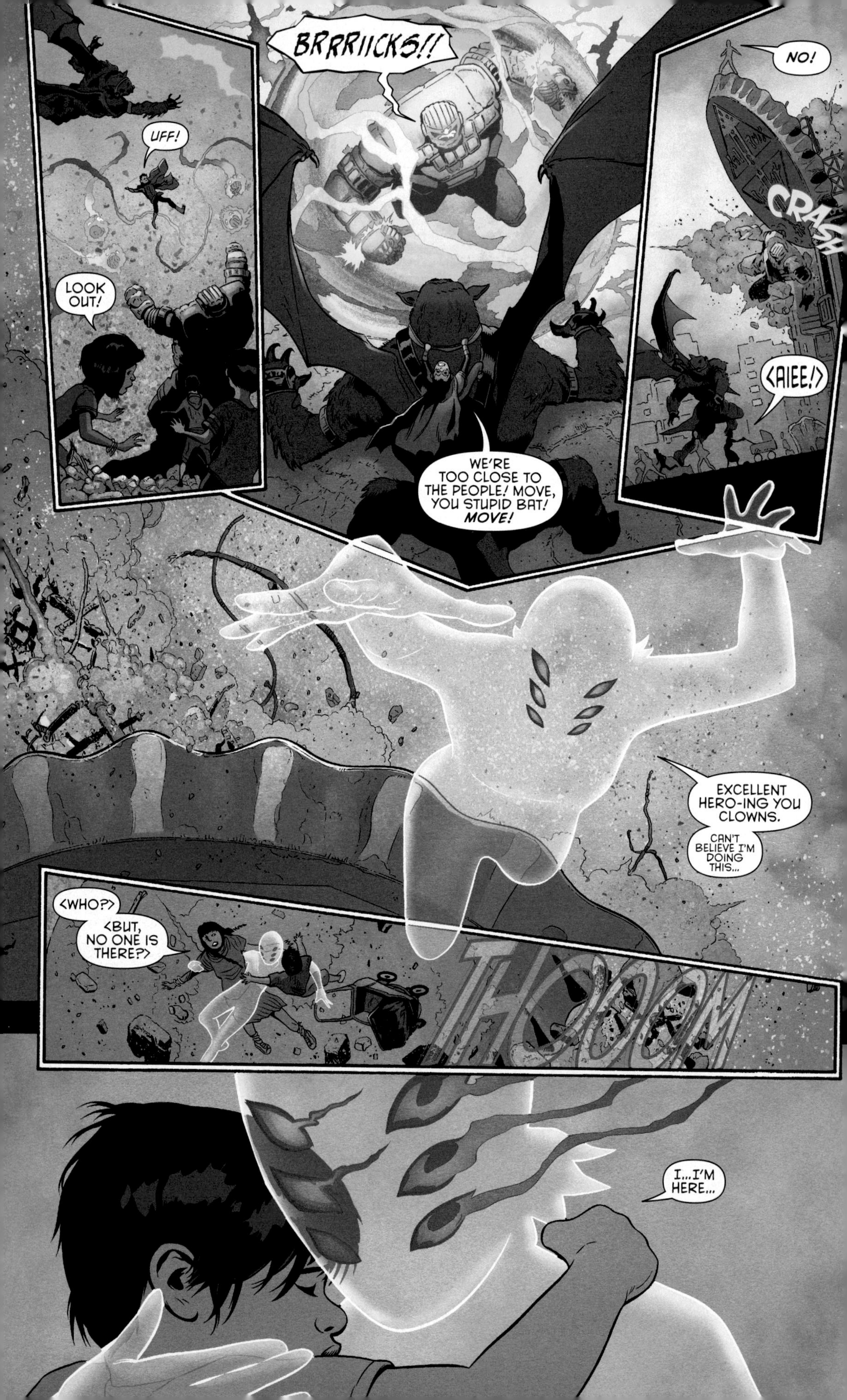

UFF!
LOOK OUT!
BRRRIICKS!!
WE'RE TOO CLOSE TO THE PEOPLE! MOVE, YOU STUPID BAT! MOVE!
NO!
CRASH
<AIEE!>
EXCELLENT HERO-ING YOU CLOWNS.
CAN'T BELIEVE I'M DOING THIS...
<WHO?>
<BUT, NO ONE IS THERE?>
THOOOM
I...I'M HERE...

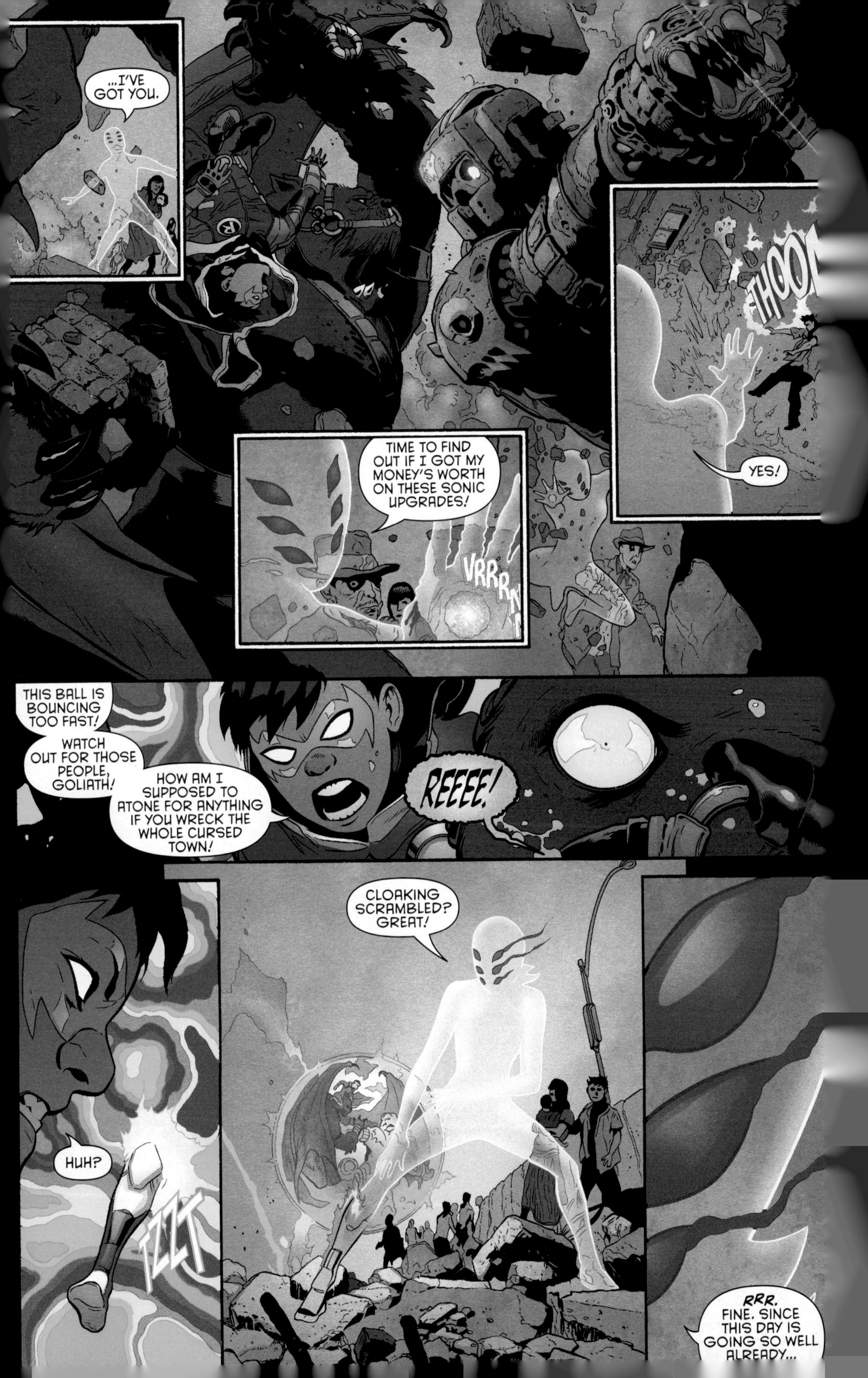
...I'VE GOT YOU.
THOOM
YES!
TIME TO FIND OUT IF I GOT MY MONEY'S WORTH ON THESE SONIC UPGRADES!
VRRRN
THIS BALL IS BOUNCING TOO FAST!
WATCH OUT FOR THOSE PEOPLE, GOLIATH!
HOW AM I SUPPOSED TO ATONE FOR ANYTHING IF YOU WRECK THE WHOLE CURSED TOWN!
REEEE!
HUH?
TZZT
CLOAKING SCRAMBLED? GREAT!
RRR. FINE. SINCE THIS DAY IS GOING SO WELL ALREADY...

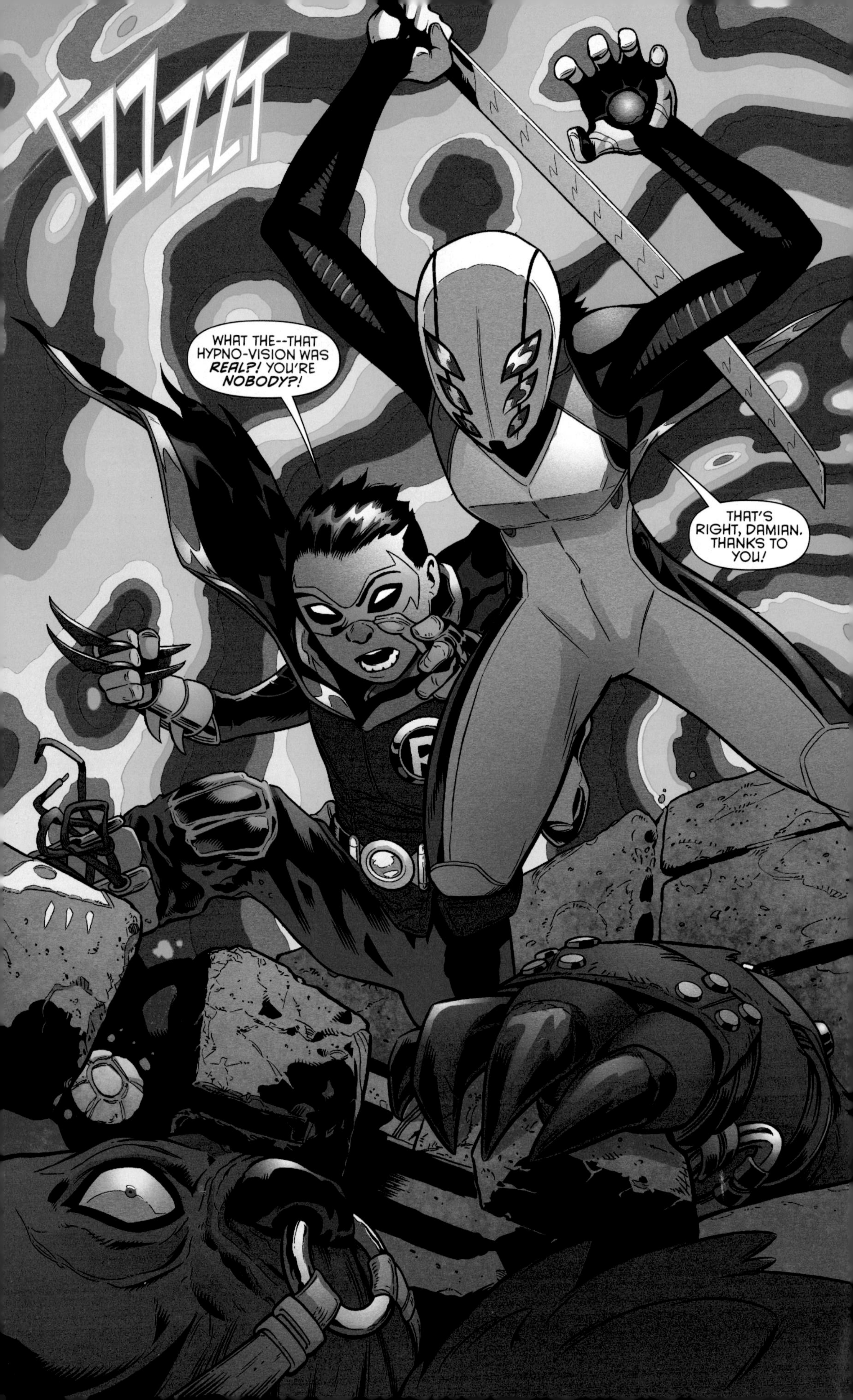
TZZZZZT
WHAT THE--THAT HYPNO-VISION WAS *REAL?!* YOU'RE *NOBODY?!*
THAT'S RIGHT, DAMIAN. THANKS TO YOU!

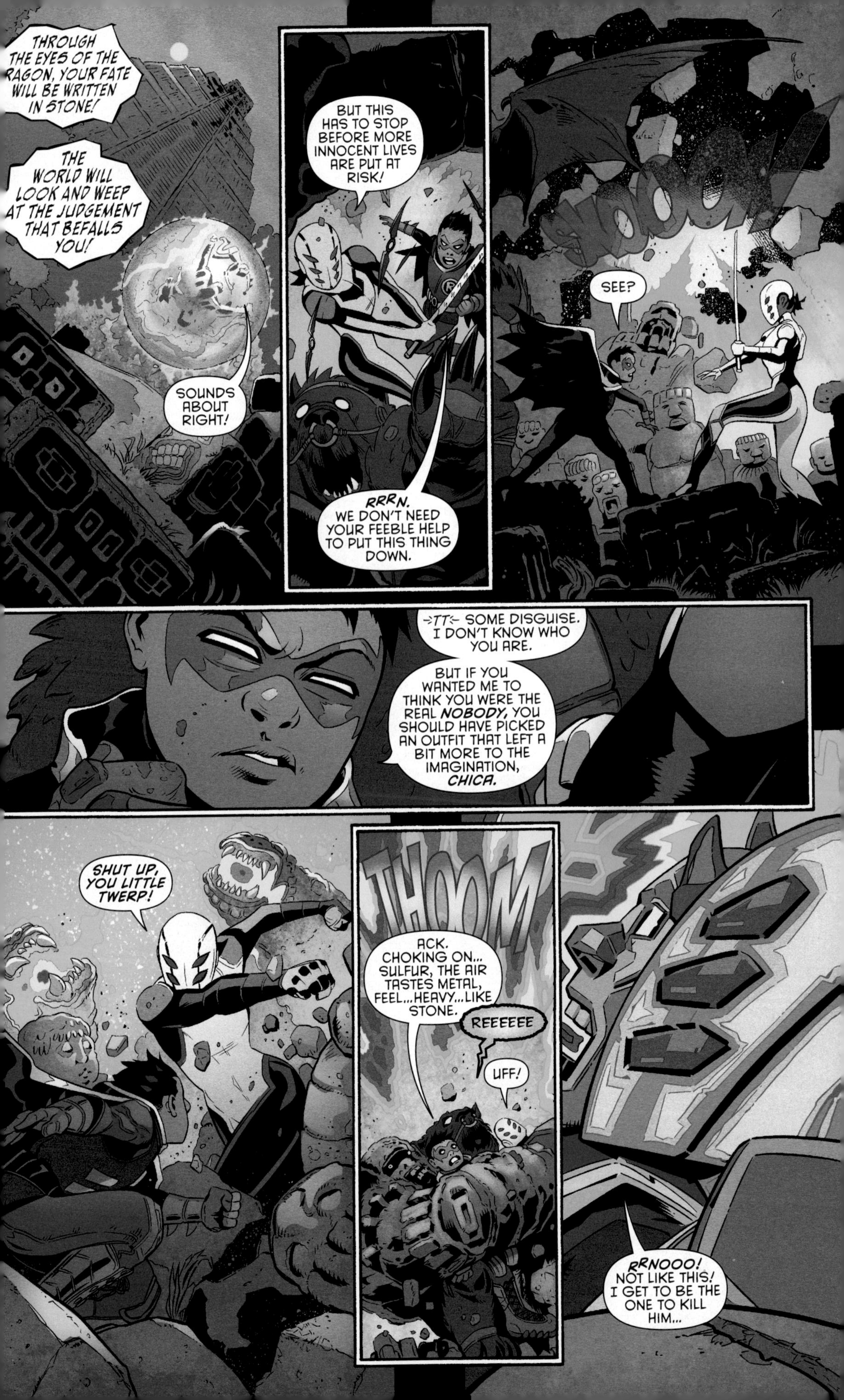
THROUGH THE EYES OF THE RAGON, YOUR FATE WILL BE WRITTEN IN STONE!
THE WORLD WILL LOOK AND WEEP AT THE JUDGEMENT THAT BEFALLS YOU!
SOUNDS ABOUT RIGHT!
BUT THIS HAS TO STOP BEFORE MORE INNOCENT LIVES ARE PUT AT RISK!
RRRN. WE DON'T NEED YOUR FEEBLE HELP TO PUT THIS THING DOWN.
SEE?
-TT- SOME DISGUISE. I DON'T KNOW WHO YOU ARE.
BUT IF YOU WANTED ME TO THINK YOU WERE THE REAL NOBODY, YOU SHOULD HAVE PICKED AN OUTFIT THAT LEFT A BIT MORE TO THE IMAGINATION, CHICA.
SHUT UP, YOU LITTLE TWERP!
THOOM
ACK. CHOKING ON... SULFUR, THE AIR TASTES METAL, FEEL...HEAVY...LIKE STONE.
REEEEEE
UFF!
RRNOOO! NOT LIKE THIS! I GET TO BE THE ONE TO KILL HIM...

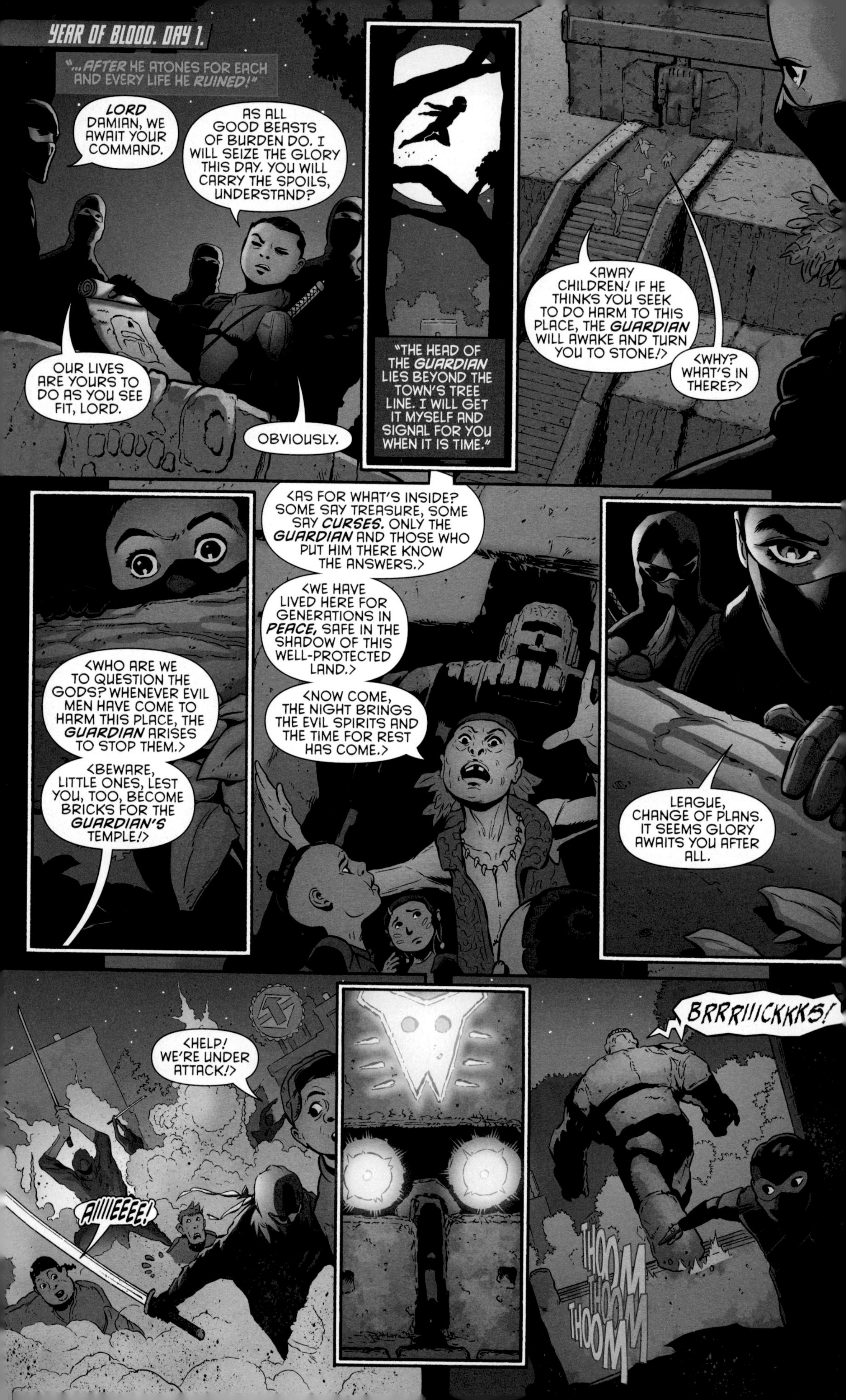

YEAR OF BLOOD. DAY 1.
"...AFTER HE ATONES FOR EACH AND EVERY LIFE HE RUINED!"
LORD DAMIAN, WE AWAIT YOUR COMMAND.
AS ALL GOOD BEASTS OF BURDEN DO. I WILL SEIZE THE GLORY THIS DAY. YOU WILL CARRY THE SPOILS, UNDERSTAND?
OUR LIVES ARE YOURS TO DO AS YOU SEE FIT, LORD.
OBVIOUSLY.
"THE HEAD OF THE GUARDIAN LIES BEYOND THE TOWN'S TREE LINE. I WILL GET IT MYSELF AND SIGNAL FOR YOU WHEN IT IS TIME."
<AWAY CHILDREN! IF HE THINKS YOU SEEK TO DO HARM TO THIS PLACE, THE GUARDIAN WILL AWAKE AND TURN YOU TO STONE!>
<WHY? WHAT'S IN THERE?>
<AS FOR WHAT'S INSIDE? SOME SAY TREASURE, SOME SAY CURSES. ONLY THE GUARDIAN AND THOSE WHO PUT HIM THERE KNOW THE ANSWERS.>
<WE HAVE LIVED HERE FOR GENERATIONS IN PEACE, SAFE IN THE SHADOW OF THIS WELL-PROTECTED LAND.>
<NOW COME, THE NIGHT BRINGS THE EVIL SPIRITS AND THE TIME FOR REST HAS COME.>
<WHO ARE WE TO QUESTION THE GODS? WHENEVER EVIL MEN HAVE COME TO HARM THIS PLACE, THE GUARDIAN ARISES TO STOP THEM.>
<BEWARE, LITTLE ONES, LEST YOU, TOO, BECOME BRICKS FOR THE GUARDIAN'S TEMPLE!>
LEAGUE, CHANGE OF PLANS. IT SEEMS GLORY AWAITS YOU AFTER ALL.
<HELP! WE'RE UNDER ATTACK!>
AIIIEEEE!
BRRRIIICKKKS!
THOOM THOOM THOOM

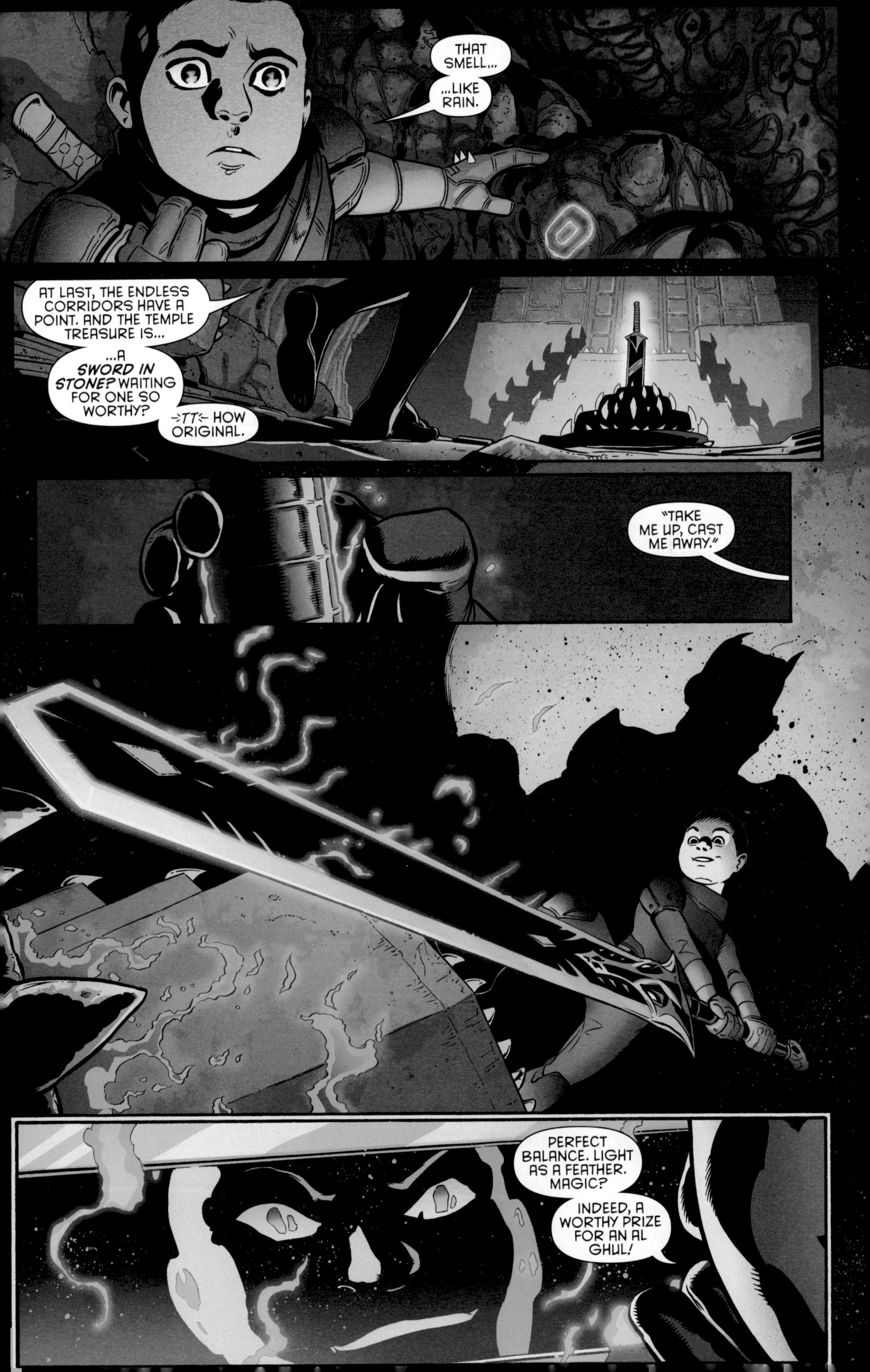
THAT SMELL...
...LIKE RAIN.
AT LAST, THE ENDLESS CORRIDORS HAVE A POINT. AND THE TEMPLE TREASURE IS...
...A SWORD IN STONE? WAITING FOR ONE SO WORTHY?
-TT- HOW ORIGINAL.
"TAKE ME UP, CAST ME AWAY."
PERFECT BALANCE. LIGHT AS A FEATHER. MAGIC?
INDEED, A WORTHY PRIZE FOR AN AL GHUL!

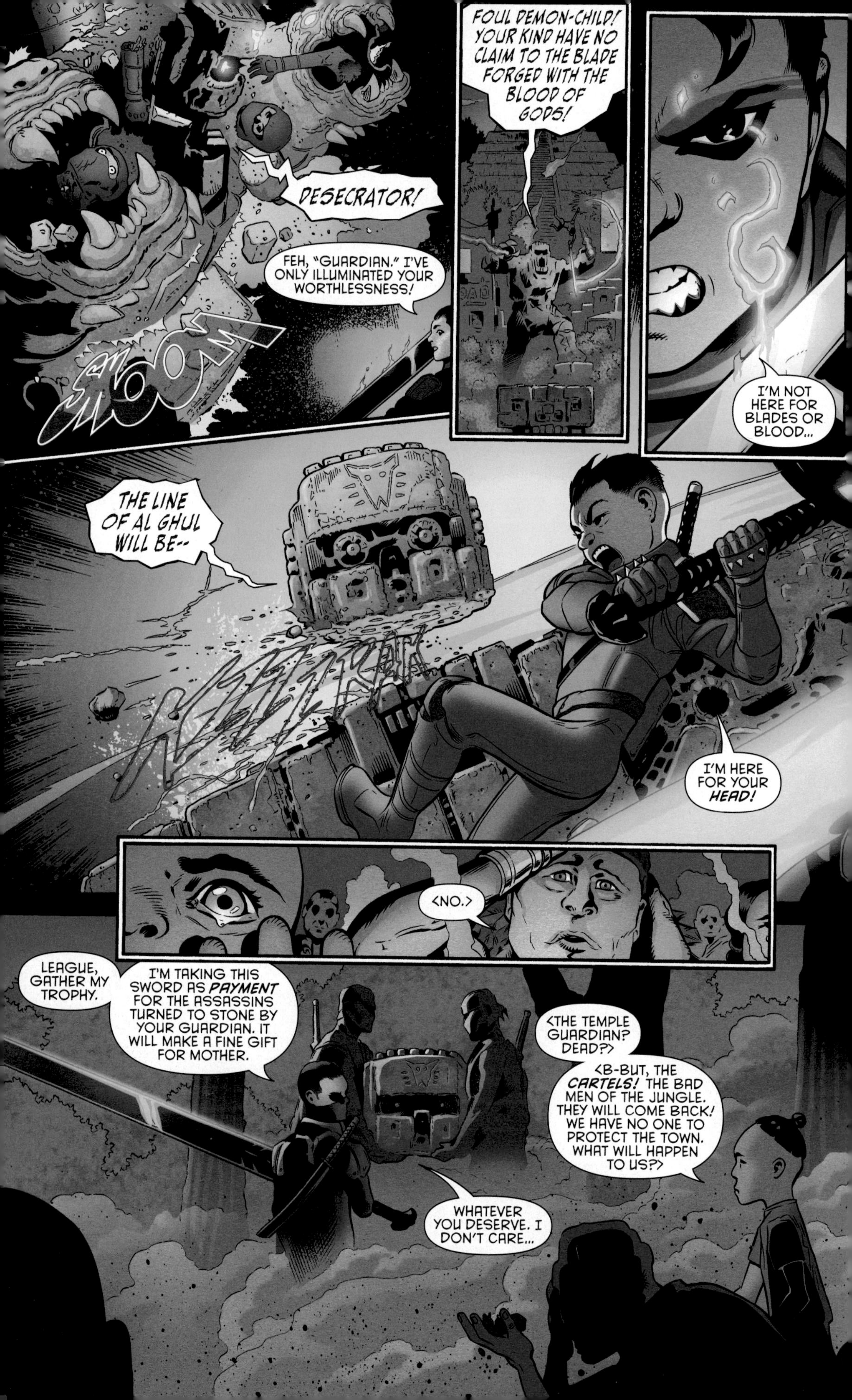
DESECRATOR!
FEH, "GUARDIAN." I'VE ONLY ILLUMINATED YOUR WORTHLESSNESS!
FOUL DEMON-CHILD! YOUR KIND HAVE NO CLAIM TO THE BLADE FORGED WITH THE BLOOD OF GODS!
I'M NOT HERE FOR BLADES OR BLOOD...
THE LINE OF AL GHUL WILL BE--
I'M HERE FOR YOUR HEAD!
<NO.>
LEAGUE, GATHER MY TROPHY.
I'M TAKING THIS SWORD AS PAYMENT FOR THE ASSASSINS TURNED TO STONE BY YOUR GUARDIAN. IT WILL MAKE A FINE GIFT FOR MOTHER.
<THE TEMPLE GUARDIAN? DEAD?>
<B-BUT, THE CARTELS! THE BAD MEN OF THE JUNGLE. THEY WILL COME BACK! WE HAVE NO ONE TO PROTECT THE TOWN. WHAT WILL HAPPEN TO US?>
WHATEVER YOU DESERVE. I DON'T CARE...

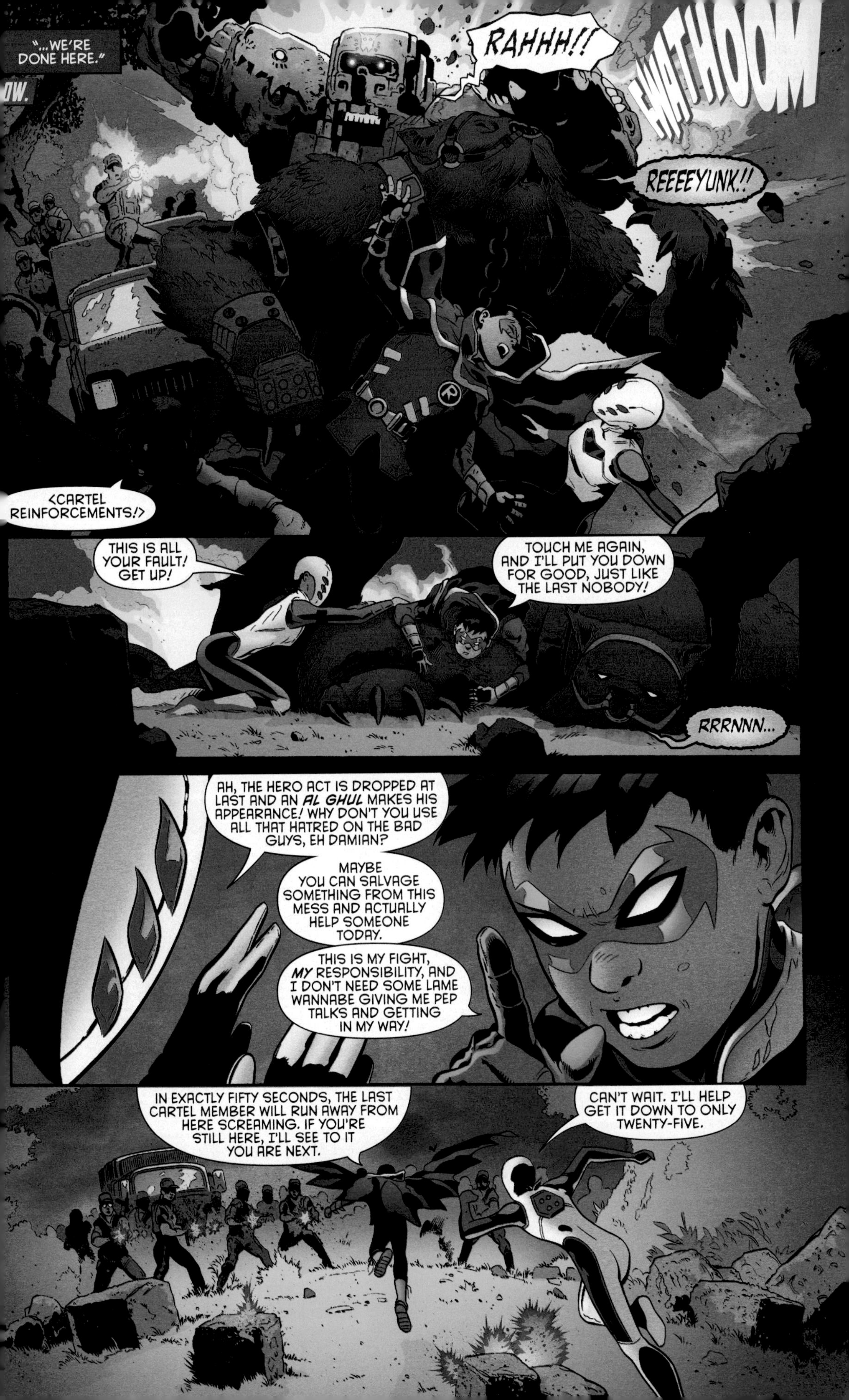
"...WE'RE DONE HERE."
RAHHH!!
SWATHOOM
REEEEYUNK!!
<CARTEL REINFORCEMENTS!>
THIS IS ALL YOUR FAULT! GET UP!
TOUCH ME AGAIN, AND I'LL PUT YOU DOWN FOR GOOD, JUST LIKE THE LAST NOBODY!
RRRNNN...
AH, THE HERO ACT IS DROPPED AT LAST AND AN AL GHUL MAKES HIS APPEARANCE! WHY DON'T YOU USE ALL THAT HATRED ON THE BAD GUYS, EH DAMIAN?
MAYBE YOU CAN SALVAGE SOMETHING FROM THIS MESS AND ACTUALLY HELP SOMEONE TODAY.
THIS IS MY FIGHT, MY RESPONSIBILITY, AND I DON'T NEED SOME LAME WANNABE GIVING ME PEP TALKS AND GETTING IN MY WAY!
IN EXACTLY FIFTY SECONDS, THE LAST CARTEL MEMBER WILL RUN AWAY FROM HERE SCREAMING. IF YOU'RE STILL HERE, I'LL SEE TO IT YOU ARE NEXT.
CAN'T WAIT. I'LL HELP GET IT DOWN TO ONLY TWENTY-FIVE.

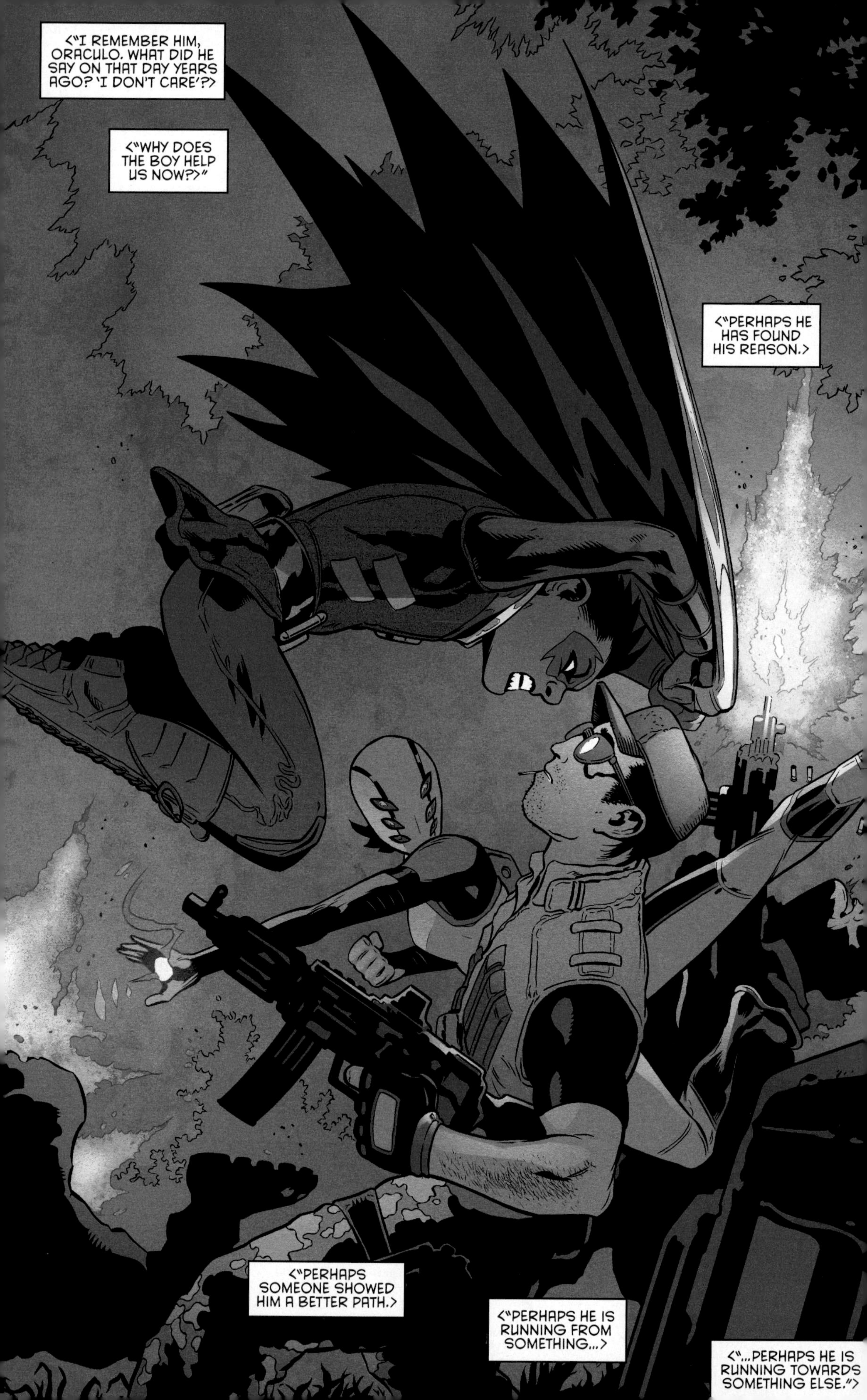
<"I REMEMBER HIM, ORACULO. WHAT DID HE SAY ON THAT DAY YEARS AGO? 'I DON'T CARE'?>
<"WHY DOES THE BOY HELP US NOW?>"
<"PERHAPS HE HAS FOUND HIS REASON.>
<"PERHAPS SOMEONE SHOWED HIM A BETTER PATH.>
<"PERHAPS HE IS RUNNING FROM SOMETHING...>
<"...PERHAPS HE IS RUNNING TOWARDS SOMETHING ELSE.">

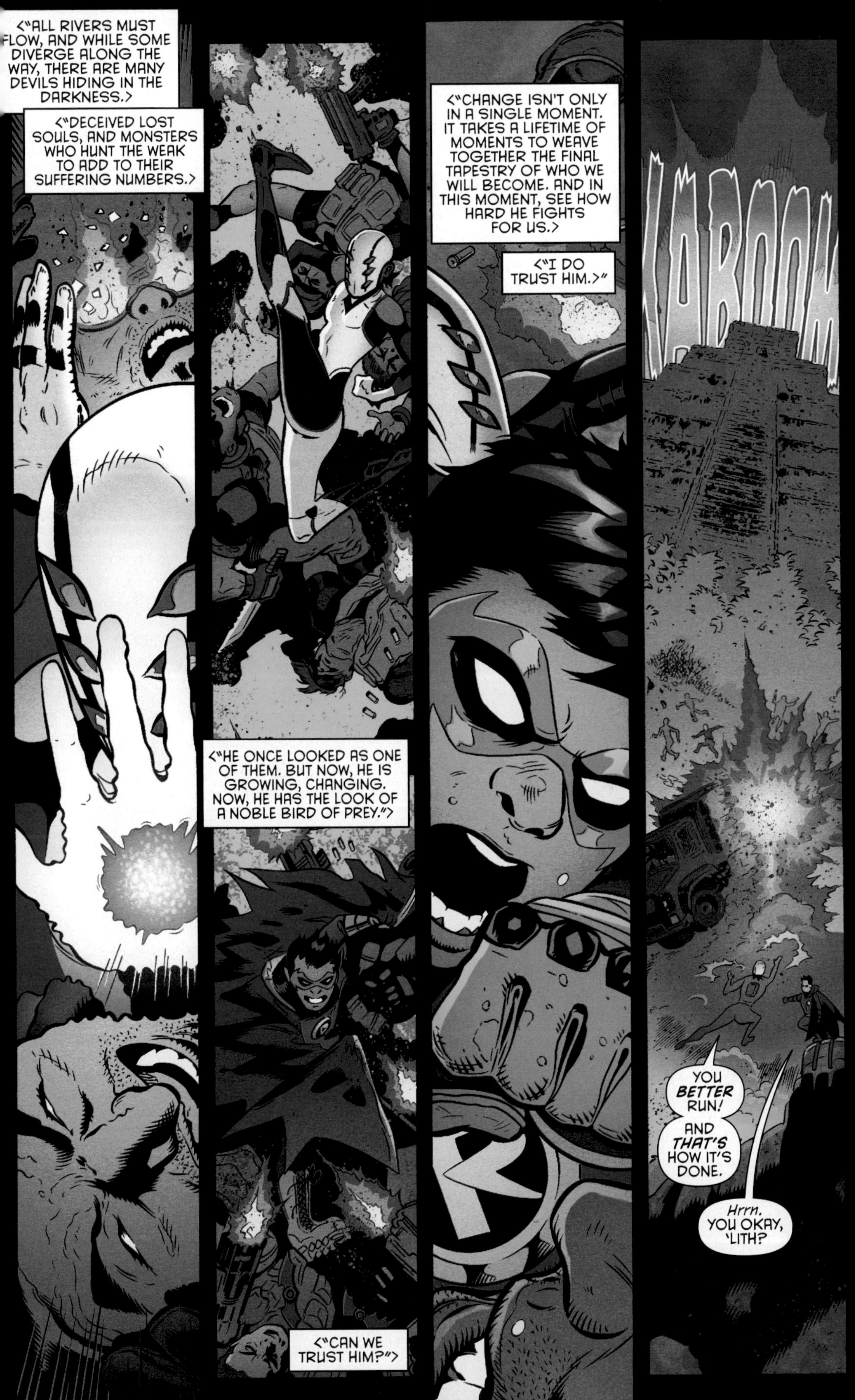
<"ALL RIVERS MUST FLOW, AND WHILE SOME DIVERGE ALONG THE WAY, THERE ARE MANY DEVILS HIDING IN THE DARKNESS.>
<"DECEIVED LOST SOULS, AND MONSTERS WHO HUNT THE WEAK TO ADD TO THEIR SUFFERING NUMBERS.>
<"HE ONCE LOOKED AS ONE OF THEM. BUT NOW, HE IS GROWING, CHANGING. NOW, HE HAS THE LOOK OF A NOBLE BIRD OF PREY.">
<"CAN WE TRUST HIM?">
<"CHANGE ISN'T ONLY IN A SINGLE MOMENT. IT TAKES A LIFETIME OF MOMENTS TO WEAVE TOGETHER THE FINAL TAPESTRY OF WHO WE WILL BECOME. AND IN THIS MOMENT, SEE HOW HARD HE FIGHTS FOR US.>
<"I DO TRUST HIM.>"
YOU *BETTER* RUN!
AND *THAT'S* HOW IT'S DONE.
Hrrn. YOU OKAY, 'LITH?

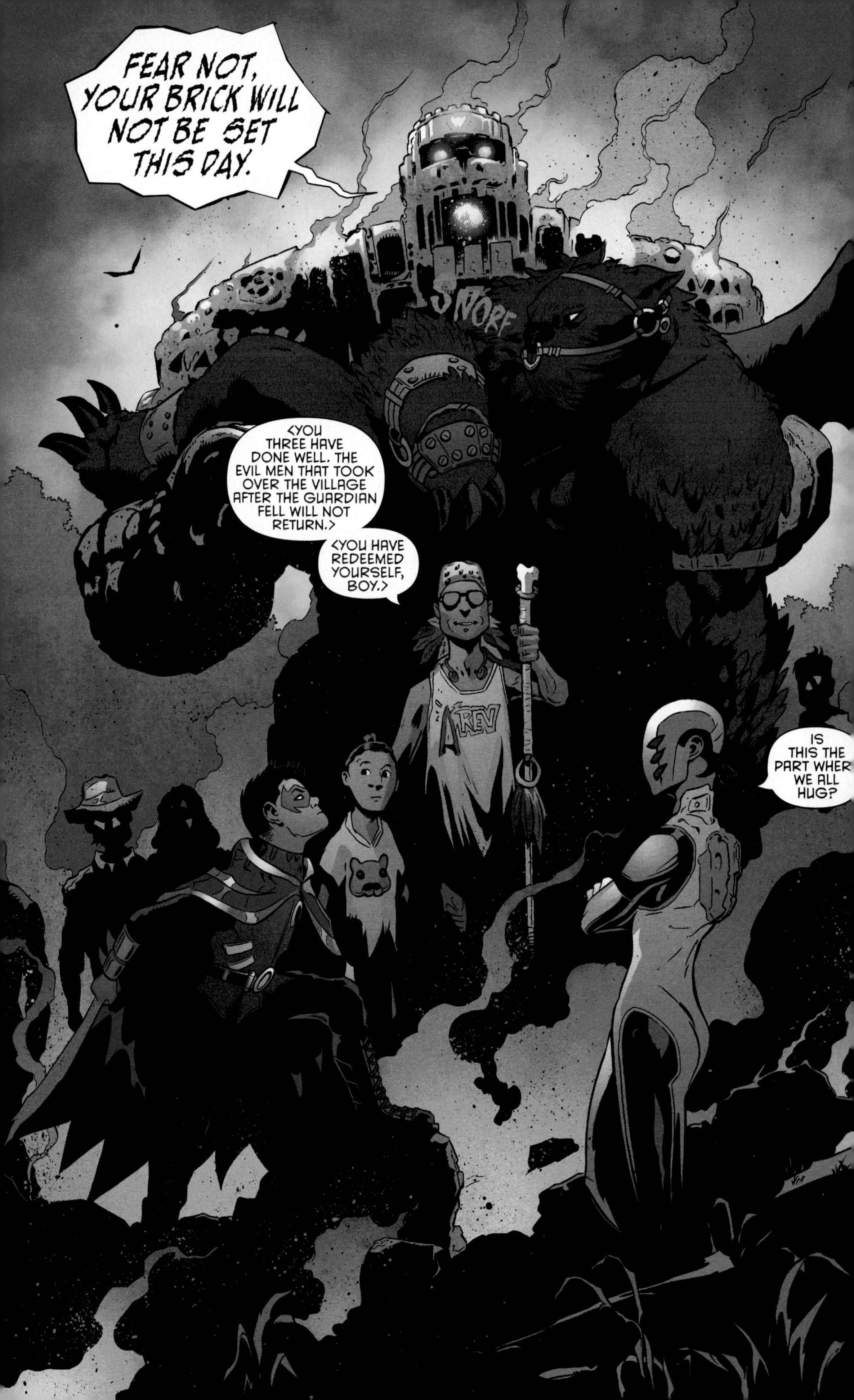
FEAR NOT, YOUR BRICK WILL NOT BE SET THIS DAY.
<YOU THREE HAVE DONE WELL. THE EVIL MEN THAT TOOK OVER THE VILLAGE AFTER THE GUARDIAN FELL WILL NOT RETURN.>
<YOU HAVE REDEEMED YOURSELF, BOY.>
IS THIS THE PART WHER WE ALL HUG?

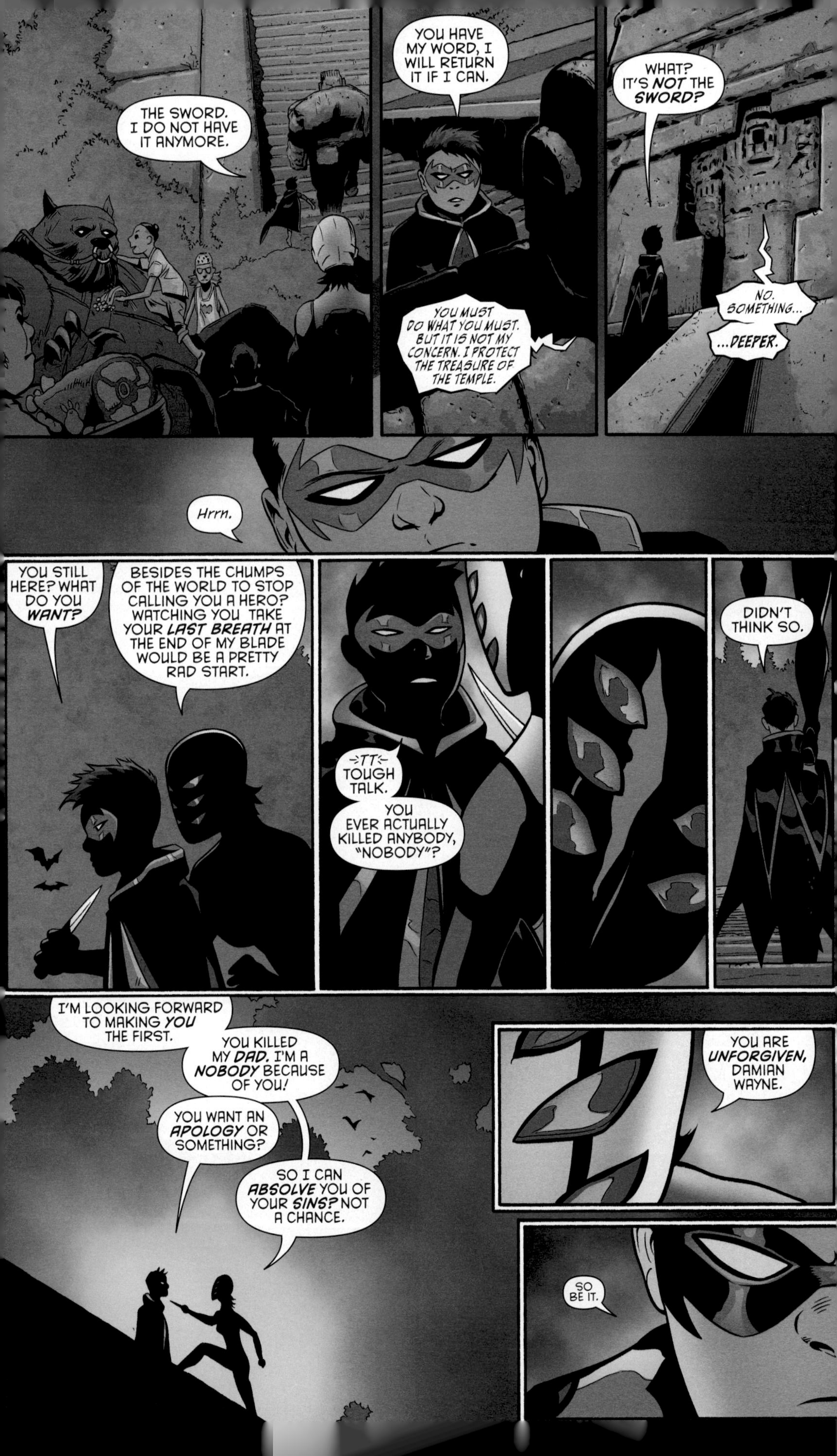
THE SWORD. I DO NOT HAVE IT ANYMORE.
YOU HAVE MY WORD, I WILL RETURN IT IF I CAN.
YOU MUST DO WHAT YOU MUST. BUT IT IS NOT MY CONCERN. I PROTECT THE TREASURE OF THE TEMPLE.
WHAT? IT'S NOT THE SWORD?
NO. SOMETHING...
...DEEPER.
Hrrn.
YOU STILL HERE? WHAT DO YOU WANT?
BESIDES THE CHUMPS OF THE WORLD TO STOP CALLING YOU A HERO? WATCHING YOU TAKE YOUR LAST BREATH AT THE END OF MY BLADE WOULD BE A PRETTY RAD START.
-TT- TOUGH TALK.
YOU EVER ACTUALLY KILLED ANYBODY, "NOBODY"?
DIDN'T THINK SO.
I'M LOOKING FORWARD TO MAKING YOU THE FIRST.
YOU KILLED MY DAD. I'M A NOBODY BECAUSE OF YOU!
YOU WANT AN APOLOGY OR SOMETHING?
SO I CAN ABSOLVE YOU OF YOUR SINS? NOT A CHANCE.
YOU ARE UNFORGIVEN, DAMIAN WAYNE.
SO BE IT.

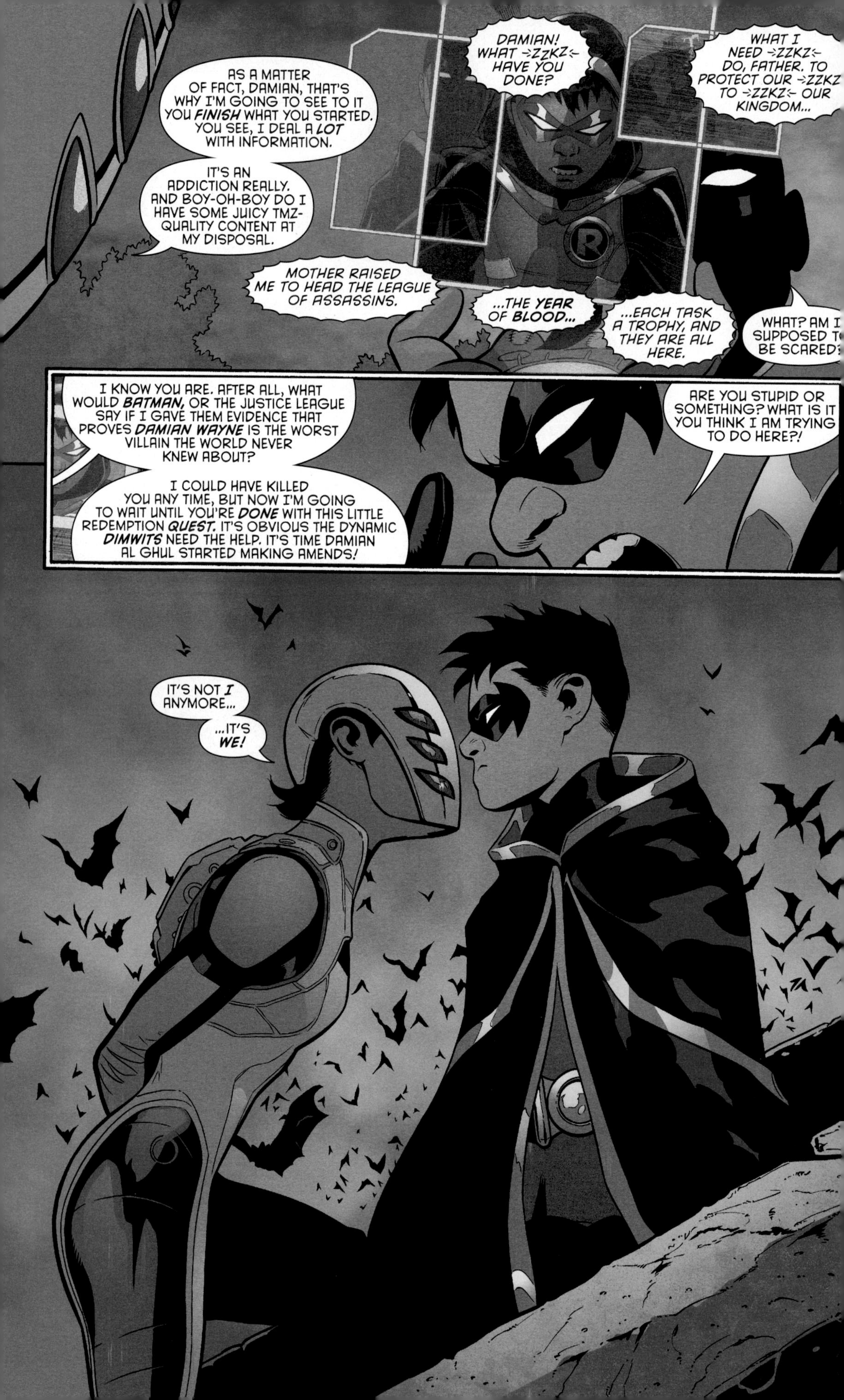
AS A MATTER OF FACT, DAMIAN, THAT'S WHY I'M GOING TO SEE TO IT YOU FINISH WHAT YOU STARTED. YOU SEE, I DEAL A LOT WITH INFORMATION.
IT'S AN ADDICTION REALLY. AND BOY-OH-BOY DO I HAVE SOME JUICY TMZ-QUALITY CONTENT AT MY DISPOSAL.
DAMIAN! WHAT ⇒ZZKZ⇐ HAVE YOU DONE?
WHAT I NEED ⇒ZZKZ⇐ DO, FATHER. TO PROTECT OUR ⇒ZZKZ TO ⇒ZZKZ⇐ OUR KINGDOM...
MOTHER RAISED ME TO HEAD THE LEAGUE OF ASSASSINS.
...THE YEAR OF BLOOD...
...EACH TASK A TROPHY, AND THEY ARE ALL HERE.
WHAT? AM I SUPPOSED TO BE SCARED?
I KNOW YOU ARE. AFTER ALL, WHAT WOULD BATMAN, OR THE JUSTICE LEAGUE SAY IF I GAVE THEM EVIDENCE THAT PROVES DAMIAN WAYNE IS THE WORST VILLAIN THE WORLD NEVER KNEW ABOUT?
I COULD HAVE KILLED YOU ANY TIME, BUT NOW I'M GOING TO WAIT UNTIL YOU'RE DONE WITH THIS LITTLE REDEMPTION QUEST. IT'S OBVIOUS THE DYNAMIC DIMWITS NEED THE HELP. IT'S TIME DAMIAN AL GHUL STARTED MAKING AMENDS!
ARE YOU STUPID OR SOMETHING? WHAT IS IT YOU THINK I AM TRYING TO DO HERE?!
IT'S NOT I ANYMORE...
...IT'S WE!

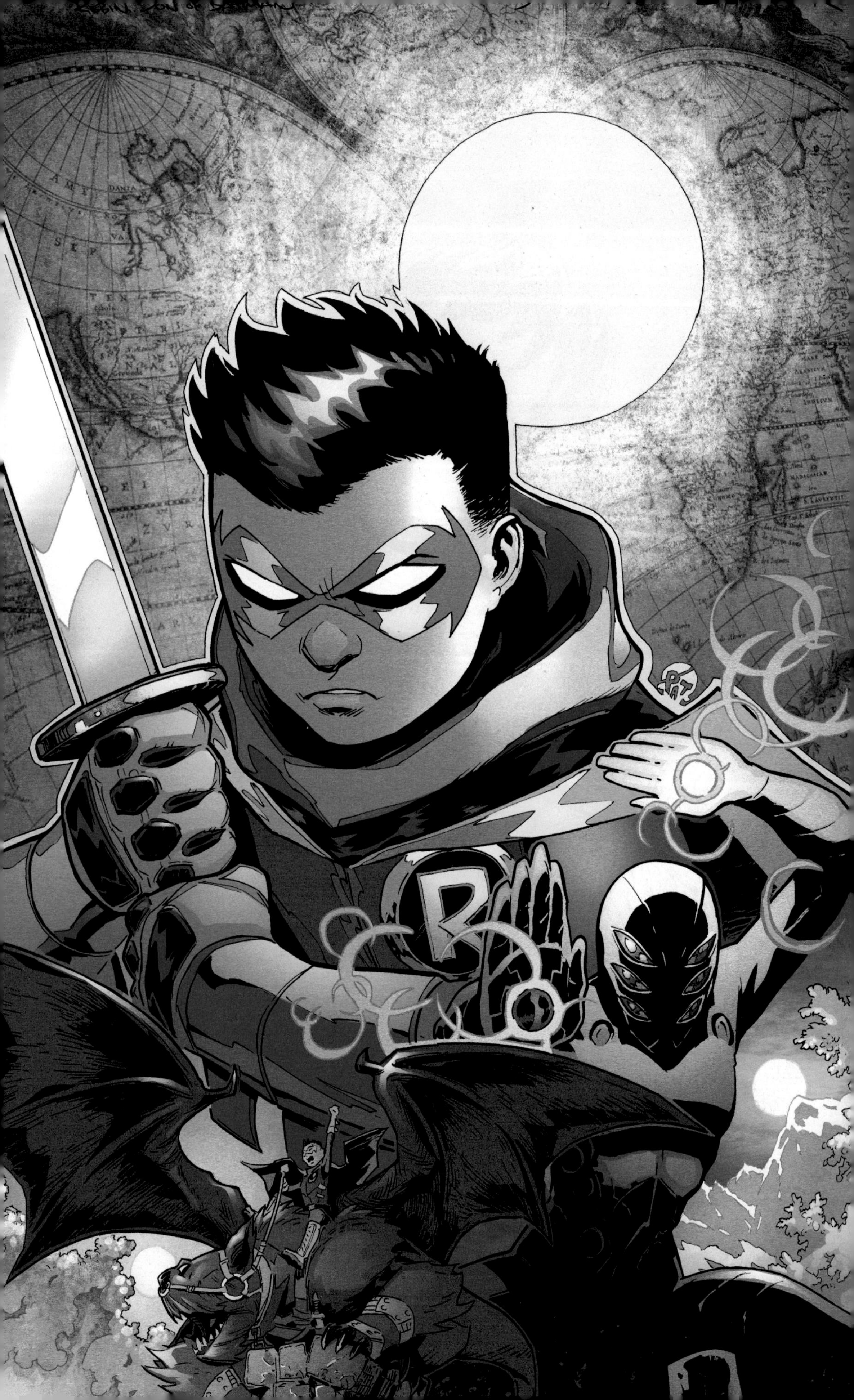

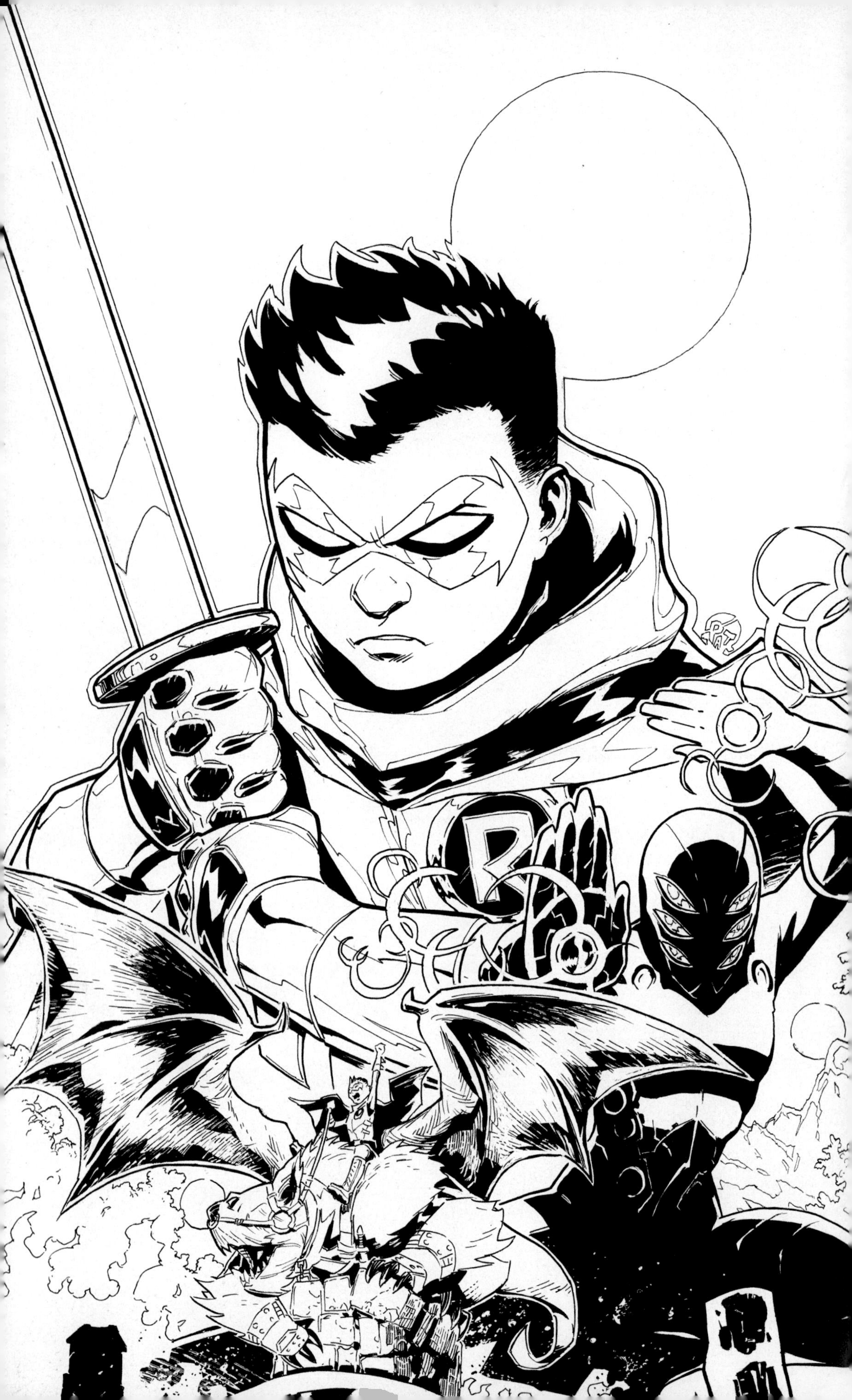

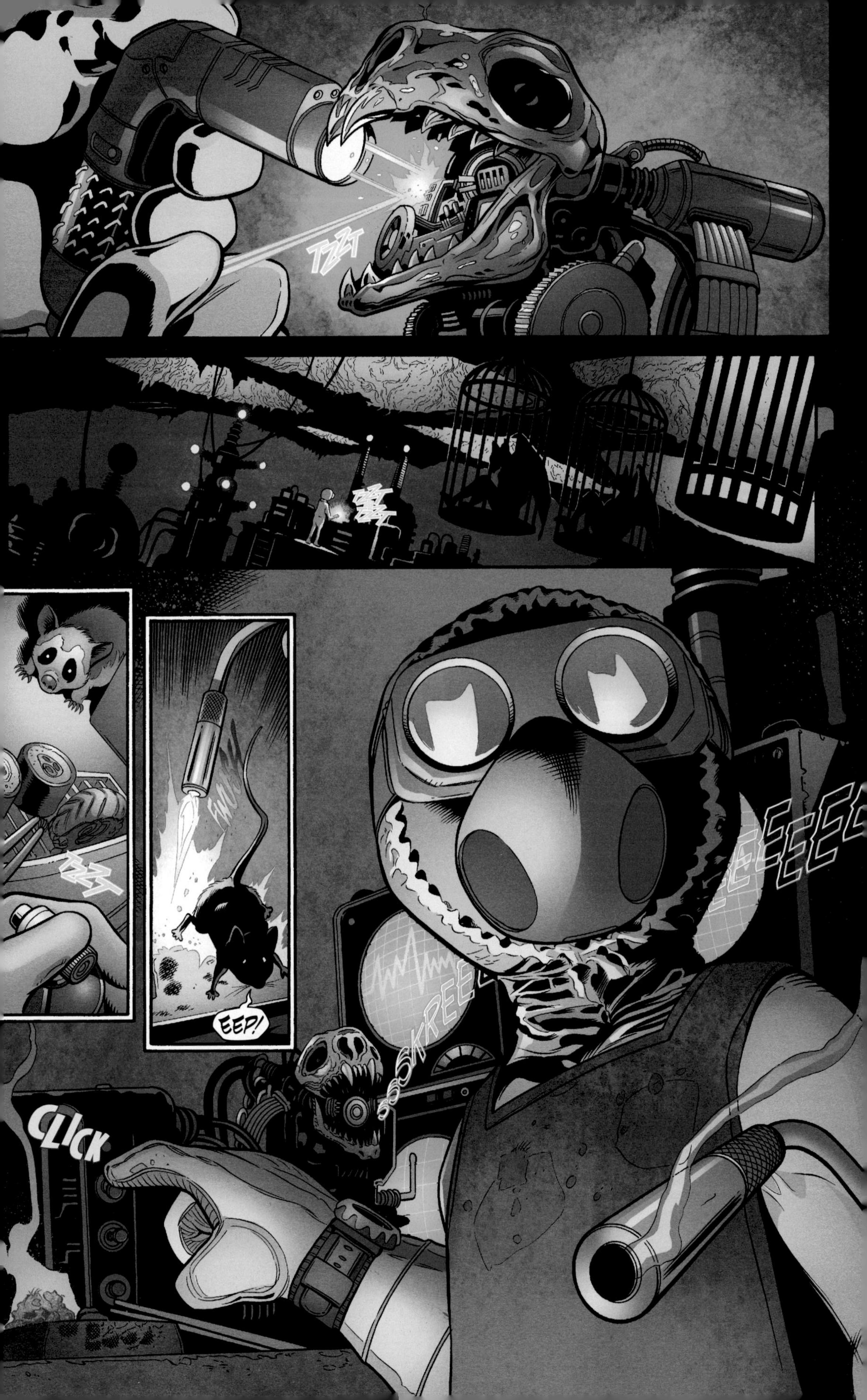
TZZT
TZZT
EEP!
SSSKREE
EEEEEE
CLICK

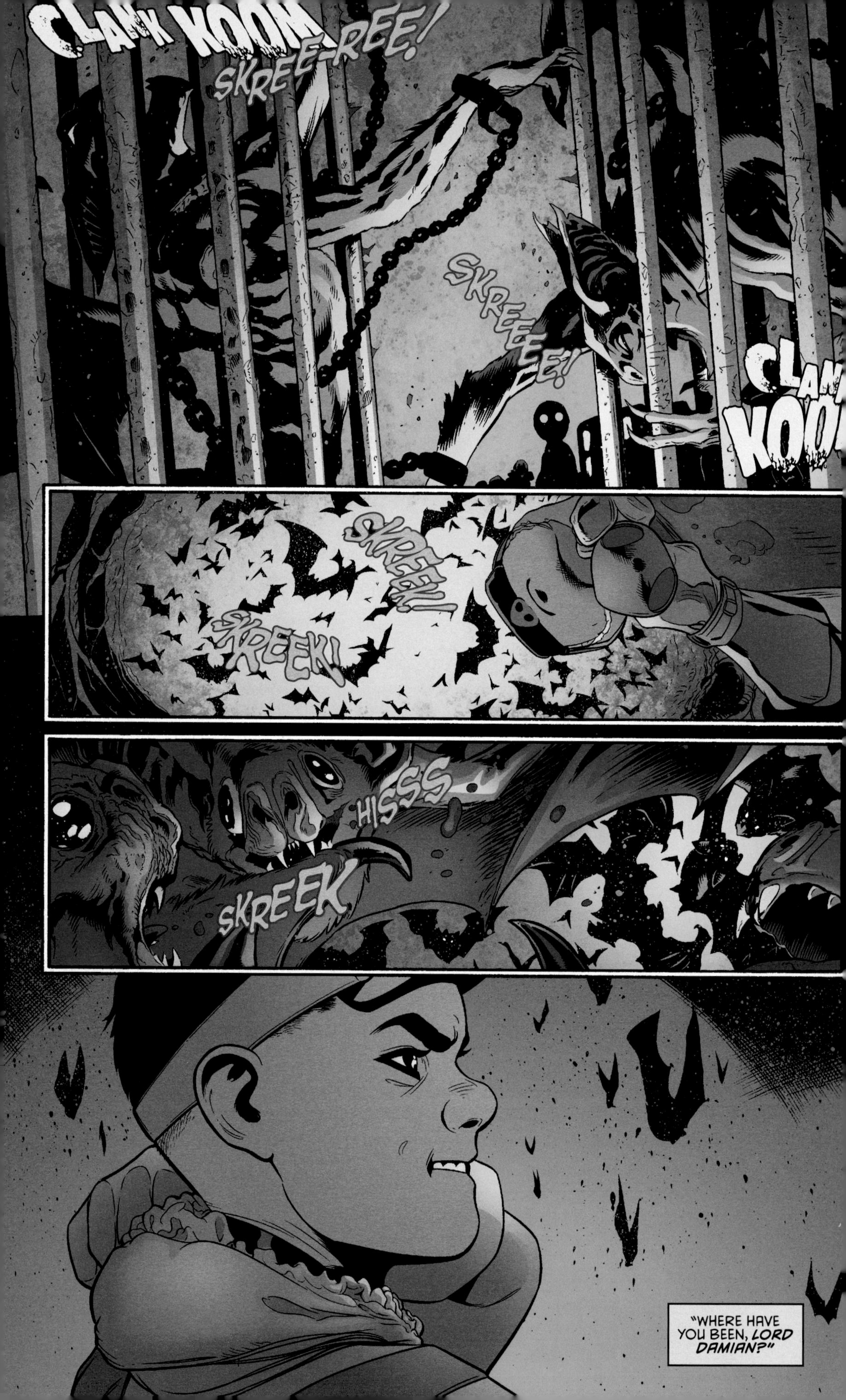
CLANK KOOM
SKREE-REE!
SKREEEEE!
CLANK KOOM
SKREEK!
SKREEK!
HISSSS
SKREEK
"WHERE HAVE YOU BEEN, LORD DAMIAN?"

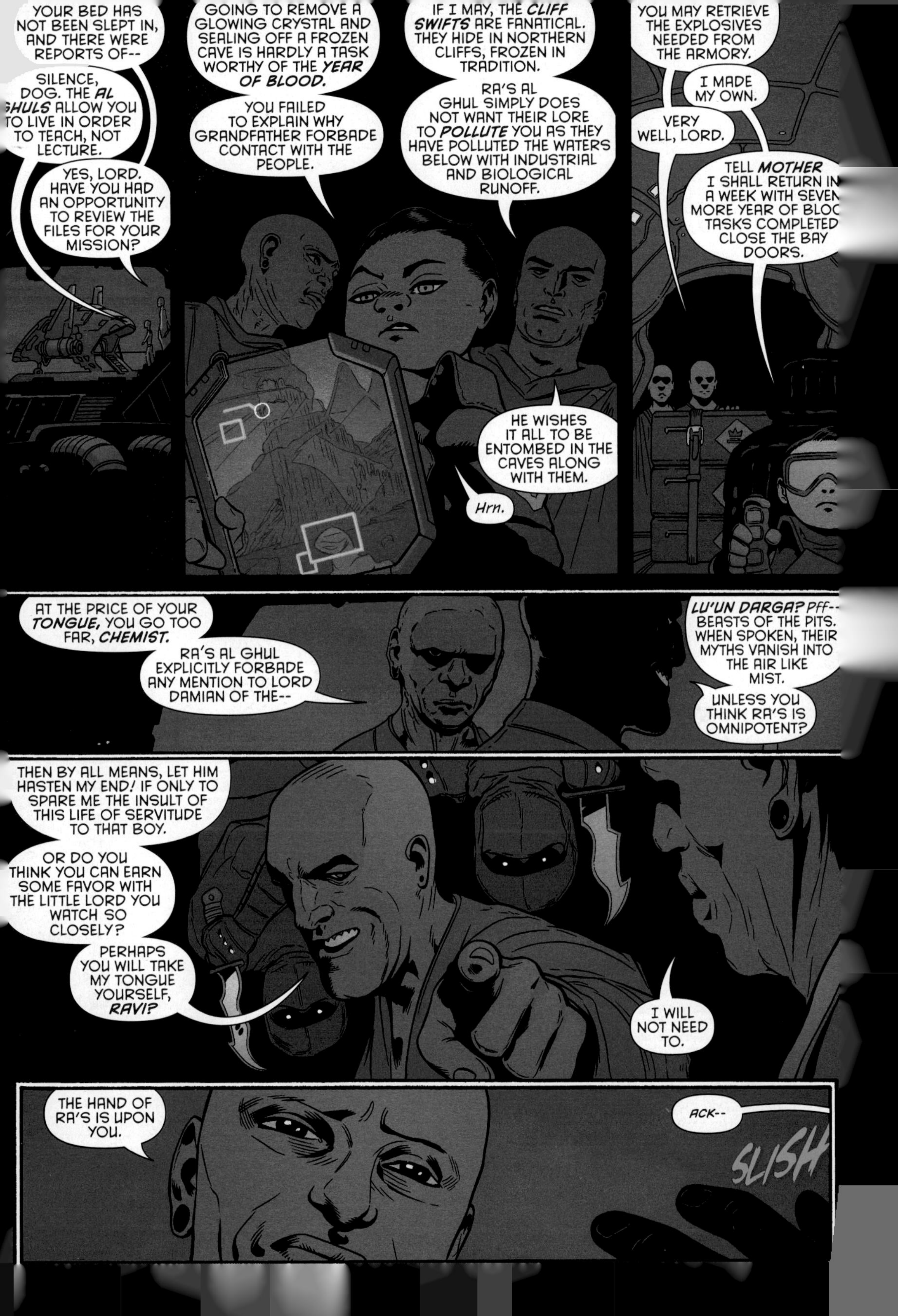
YOUR BED HAS NOT BEEN SLEPT IN, AND THERE WERE REPORTS OF--
SILENCE, DOG. THE AL GHULS ALLOW YOU TO LIVE IN ORDER TO TEACH, NOT LECTURE.
YES, LORD. HAVE YOU HAD AN OPPORTUNITY TO REVIEW THE FILES FOR YOUR MISSION?
GOING TO REMOVE A GLOWING CRYSTAL AND SEALING OFF A FROZEN CAVE IS HARDLY A TASK WORTHY OF THE YEAR OF BLOOD.
YOU FAILED TO EXPLAIN WHY GRANDFATHER FORBADE CONTACT WITH THE PEOPLE.
IF I MAY, THE CLIFF SWIFTS ARE FANATICAL. THEY HIDE IN NORTHERN CLIFFS, FROZEN IN TRADITION.
RA'S AL GHUL SIMPLY DOES NOT WANT THEIR LORE TO POLLUTE YOU AS THEY HAVE POLLUTED THE WATERS BELOW WITH INDUSTRIAL AND BIOLOGICAL RUNOFF.
HE WISHES IT ALL TO BE ENTOMBED IN THE CAVES ALONG WITH THEM.
Hrn.
YOU MAY RETRIEVE THE EXPLOSIVES NEEDED FROM THE ARMORY.
I MADE MY OWN.
VERY WELL, LORD.
TELL MOTHER I SHALL RETURN IN A WEEK WITH SEVEN MORE YEAR OF BLOO TASKS COMPLETED. CLOSE THE BAY DOORS.
AT THE PRICE OF YOUR TONGUE, YOU GO TOO FAR, CHEMIST.
RA'S AL GHUL EXPLICITLY FORBADE ANY MENTION TO LORD DAMIAN OF THE--
LU'UN DARGA? Pff-- BEASTS OF THE PITS. WHEN SPOKEN, THEIR MYTHS VANISH INTO THE AIR LIKE MIST.
UNLESS YOU THINK RA'S IS OMNIPOTENT?
THEN BY ALL MEANS, LET HIM HASTEN MY END! IF ONLY TO SPARE ME THE INSULT OF THIS LIFE OF SERVITUDE TO THAT BOY.
OR DO YOU THINK YOU CAN EARN SOME FAVOR WITH THE LITTLE LORD YOU WATCH SO CLOSELY?
PERHAPS YOU WILL TAKE MY TONGUE YOURSELF, RAVI?
I WILL NOT NEED TO.
THE HAND OF RA'S IS UPON YOU.
ACK--
SLISH

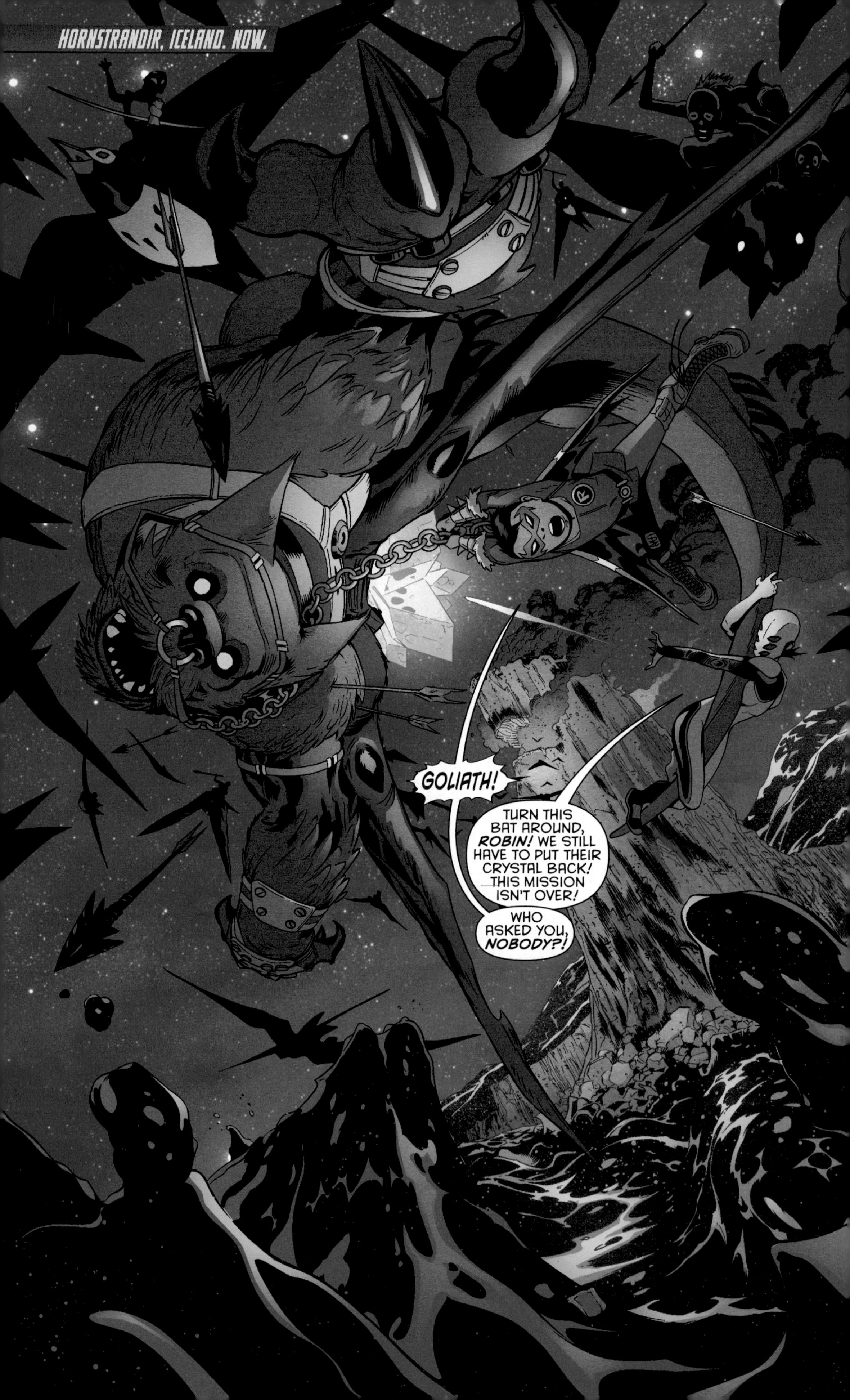
HORNSTRANDIR, ICELAND. NOW.
GOLIATH!
TURN THIS BAT AROUND, ROBIN! WE STILL HAVE TO PUT THEIR CRYSTAL BACK! THIS MISSION ISN'T OVER!
WHO ASKED YOU, NOBODY?!

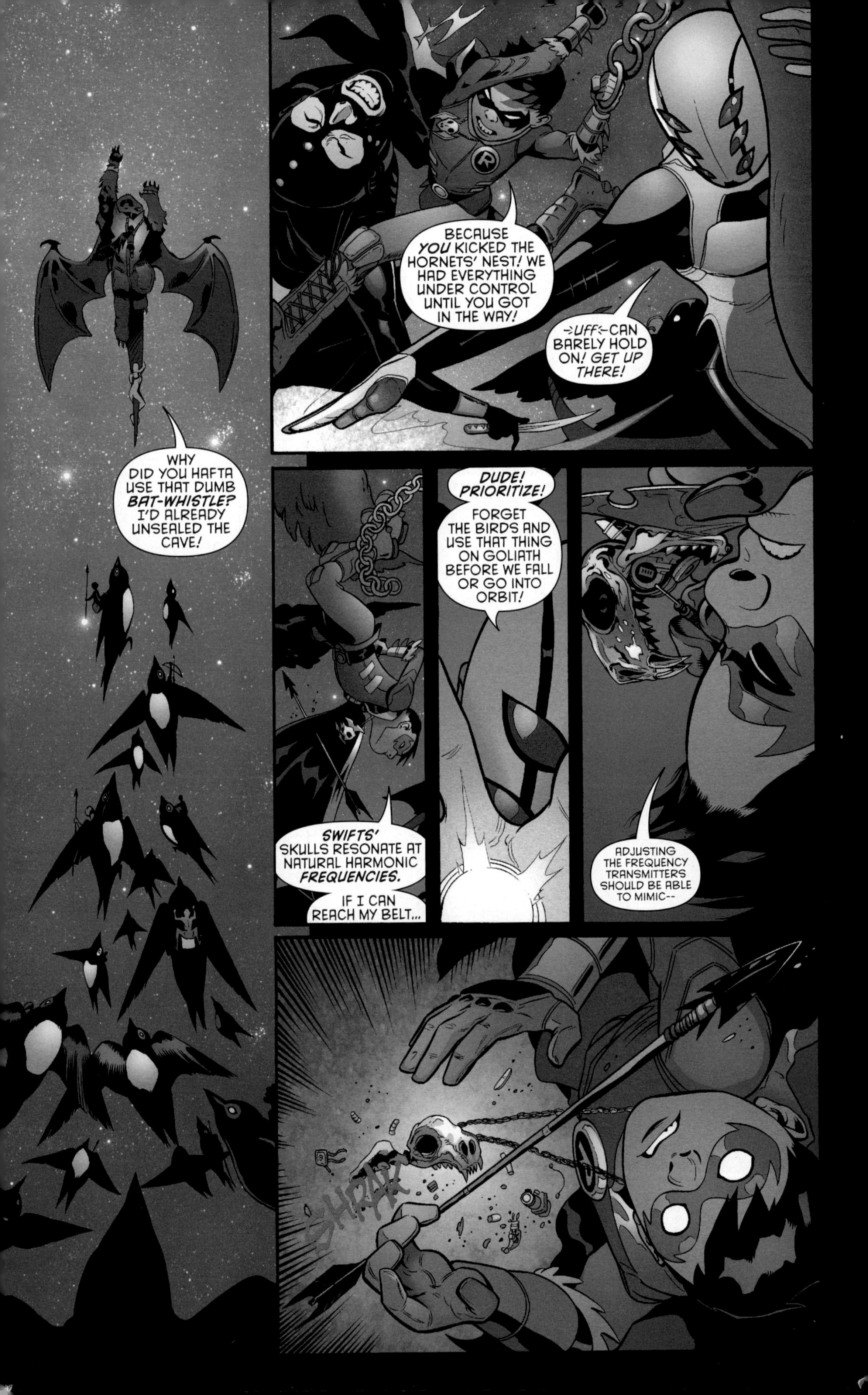

WHY DID YOU HAFTA USE THAT DUMB BAT-WHISTLE? I'D ALREADY UNSEALED THE CAVE!
BECAUSE YOU KICKED THE HORNETS' NEST! WE HAD EVERYTHING UNDER CONTROL UNTIL YOU GOT IN THE WAY!
-UFF- CAN BARELY HOLD ON! GET UP THERE!
SWIFTS' SKULLS RESONATE AT NATURAL HARMONIC FREQUENCIES.
IF I CAN REACH MY BELT...
DUDE! PRIORITIZE!
FORGET THE BIRDS AND USE THAT THING ON GOLIATH BEFORE WE FALL OR GO INTO ORBIT!
ADJUSTING THE FREQUENCY TRANSMITTERS SHOULD BE ABLE TO MIMIC--
SHRAK

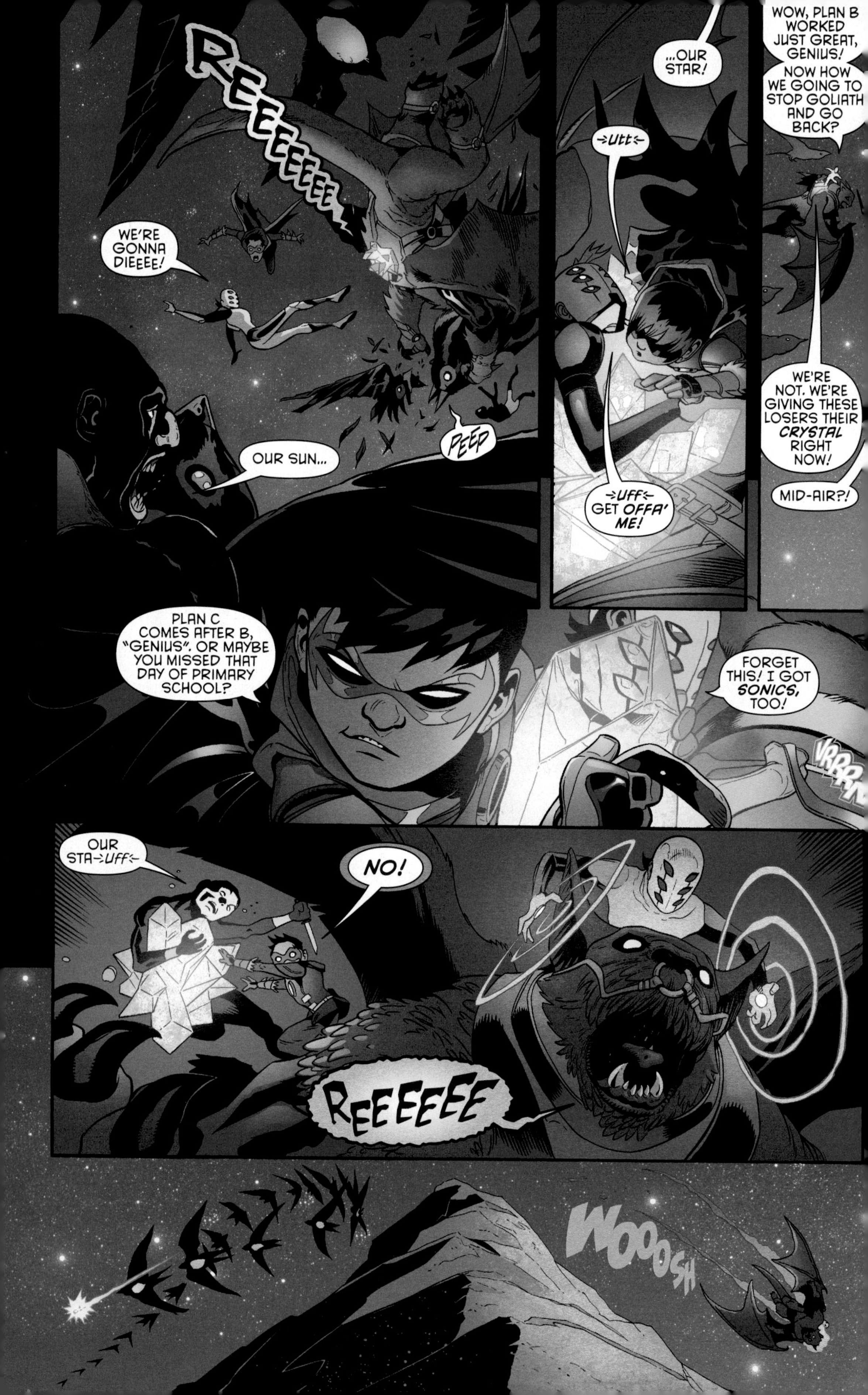
REEEEEEEE
WE'RE GONNA DIEEEE!
OUR SUN...
PEEP
...OUR STAR!
UFF
UFF GET OFFA' ME!
WOW, PLAN B WORKED JUST GREAT, GENIUS!
NOW HOW WE GOING TO STOP GOLIATH AND GO BACK?
WE'RE NOT. WE'RE GIVING THESE LOSERS THEIR CRYSTAL RIGHT NOW!
MID-AIR?!
PLAN C COMES AFTER B, "GENIUS". OR MAYBE YOU MISSED THAT DAY OF PRIMARY SCHOOL?
FORGET THIS! I GOT SONICS, TOO!
VRBRR
OUR STA-UFF
NO!
REEEEEE
WOOOSH

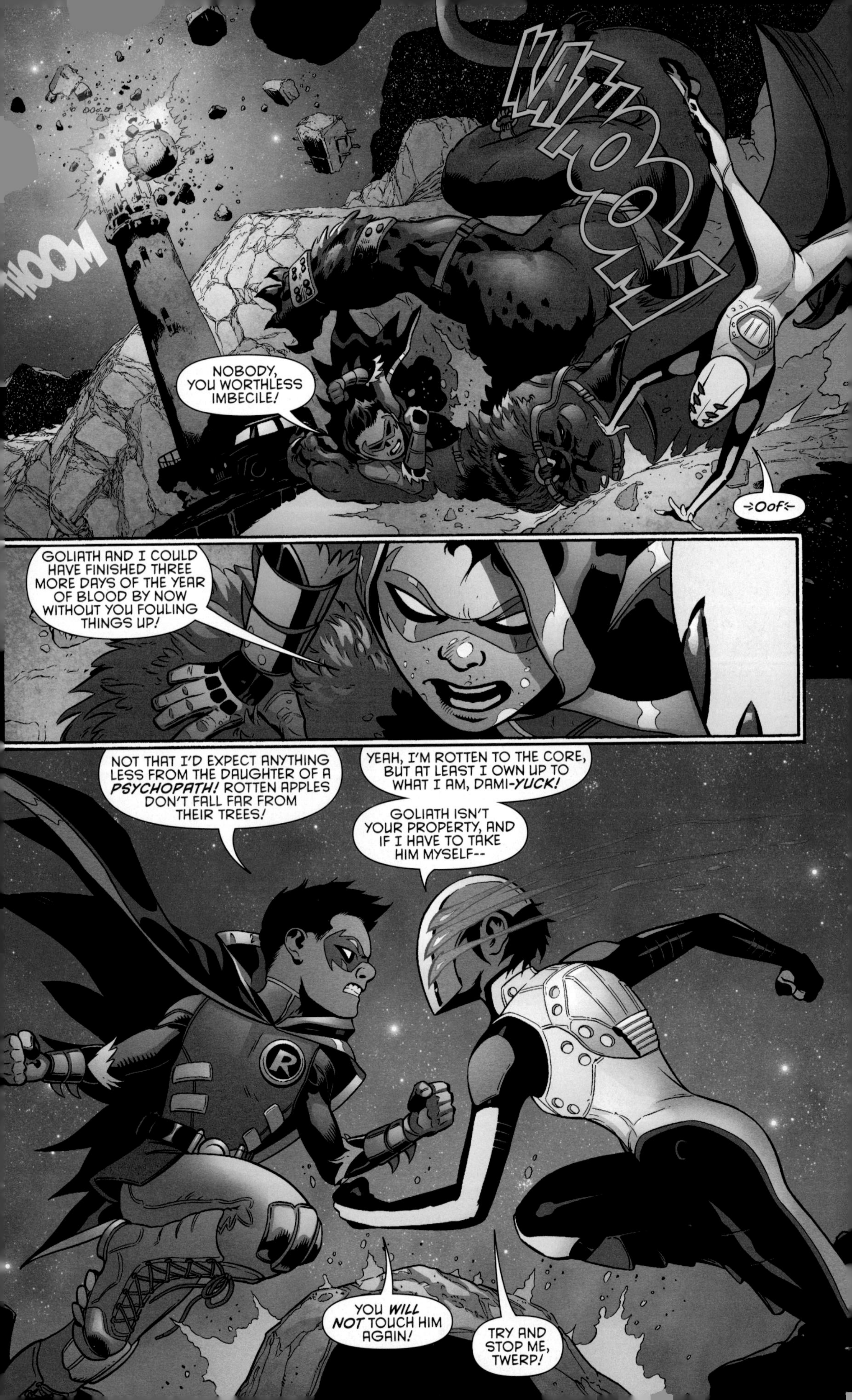
THOOM
WHOOOOM
NOBODY, YOU WORTHLESS IMBECILE!
Oof
GOLIATH AND I COULD HAVE FINISHED THREE MORE DAYS OF THE YEAR OF BLOOD BY NOW WITHOUT YOU FOULING THINGS UP!
NOT THAT I'D EXPECT ANYTHING LESS FROM THE DAUGHTER OF A PSYCHOPATH! ROTTEN APPLES DON'T FALL FAR FROM THEIR TREES!
YEAH, I'M ROTTEN TO THE CORE, BUT AT LEAST I OWN UP TO WHAT I AM, DAMI-YUCK!
GOLIATH ISN'T YOUR PROPERTY, AND IF I HAVE TO TAKE HIM MYSELF--
YOU WILL NOT TOUCH HIM AGAIN!
TRY AND STOP ME, TWERP!

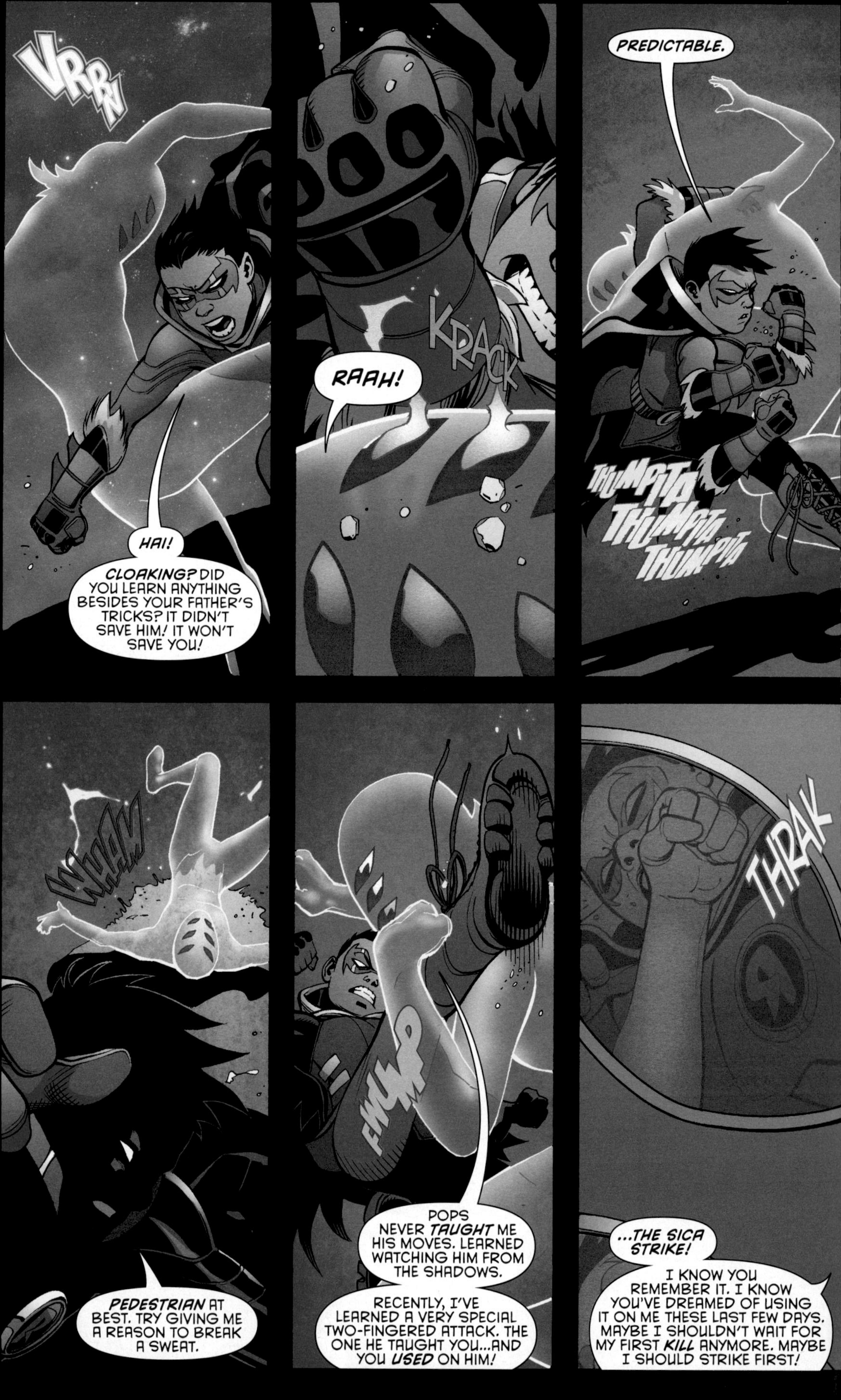
VRRN
HAI!
CLOAKING? DID YOU LEARN ANYTHING BESIDES YOUR FATHER'S TRICKS? IT DIDN'T SAVE HIM! IT WON'T SAVE YOU!
KRACK
RAAH!
PREDICTABLE.
THUMPITA THUMPITA THUMPIT
WHAM
PEDESTRIAN AT BEST. TRY GIVING ME A REASON TO BREAK A SWEAT.
FWUMP
POPS NEVER TAUGHT ME HIS MOVES. LEARNED WATCHING HIM FROM THE SHADOWS.
RECENTLY, I'VE LEARNED A VERY SPECIAL TWO-FINGERED ATTACK. THE ONE HE TAUGHT YOU...AND YOU USED ON HIM!
THRAK
...THE SICA STRIKE!
I KNOW YOU REMEMBER IT. I KNOW YOU'VE DREAMED OF USING IT ON ME THESE LAST FEW DAYS. MAYBE I SHOULDN'T WAIT FOR MY FIRST KILL ANYMORE. MAYBE I SHOULD STRIKE FIRST!

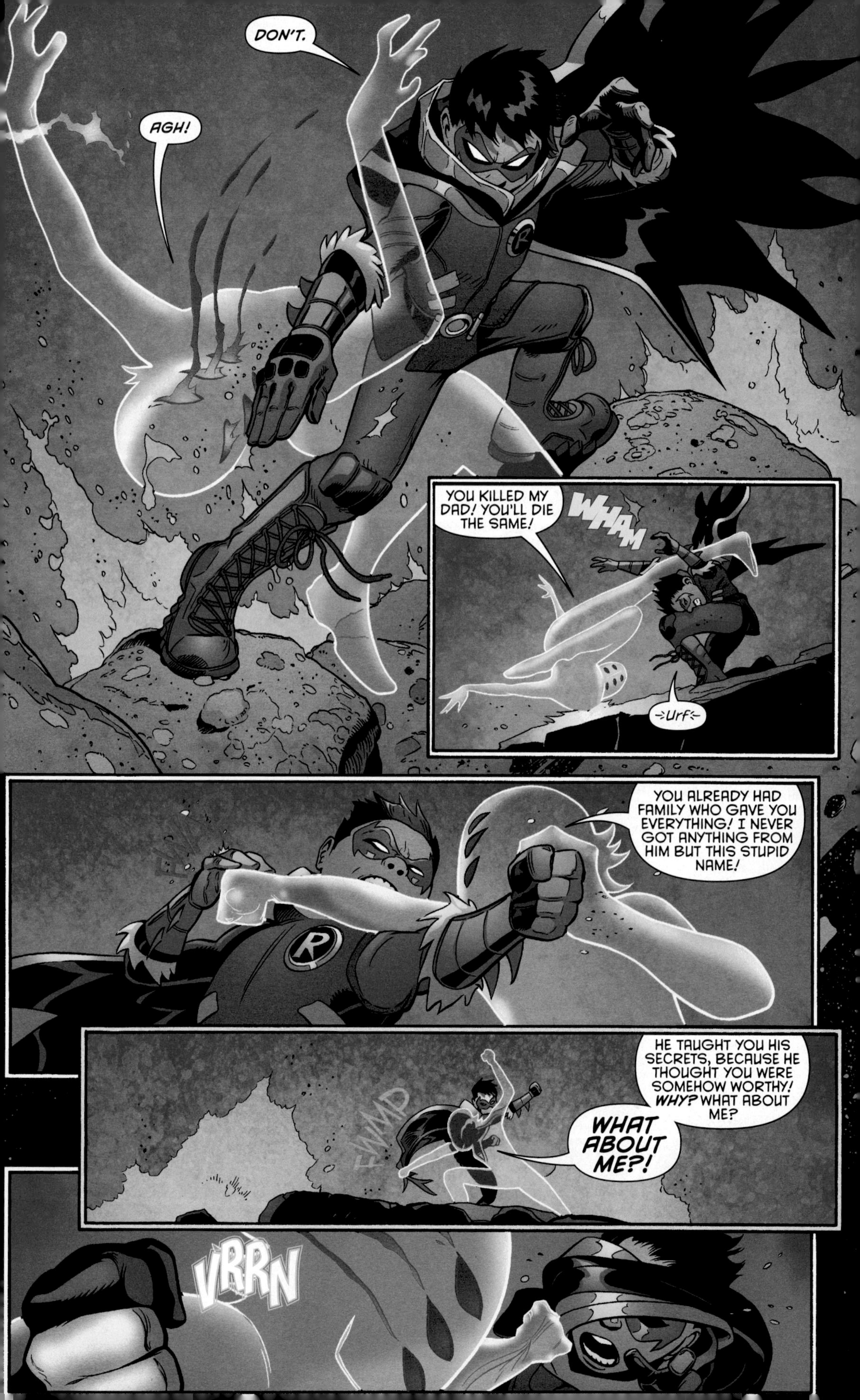
AGH!
DON'T.
YOU KILLED MY DAD! YOU'LL DIE THE SAME!
WHAM
-Urf-
YOU ALREADY HAD FAMILY WHO GAVE YOU EVERYTHING! I NEVER GOT ANYTHING FROM HIM BUT THIS STUPID NAME!
FWMP
HE TAUGHT YOU HIS SECRETS, BECAUSE HE THOUGHT YOU WERE SOMEHOW WORTHY! WHY? WHAT ABOUT ME?
WHAT ABOUT ME?!
VRRN

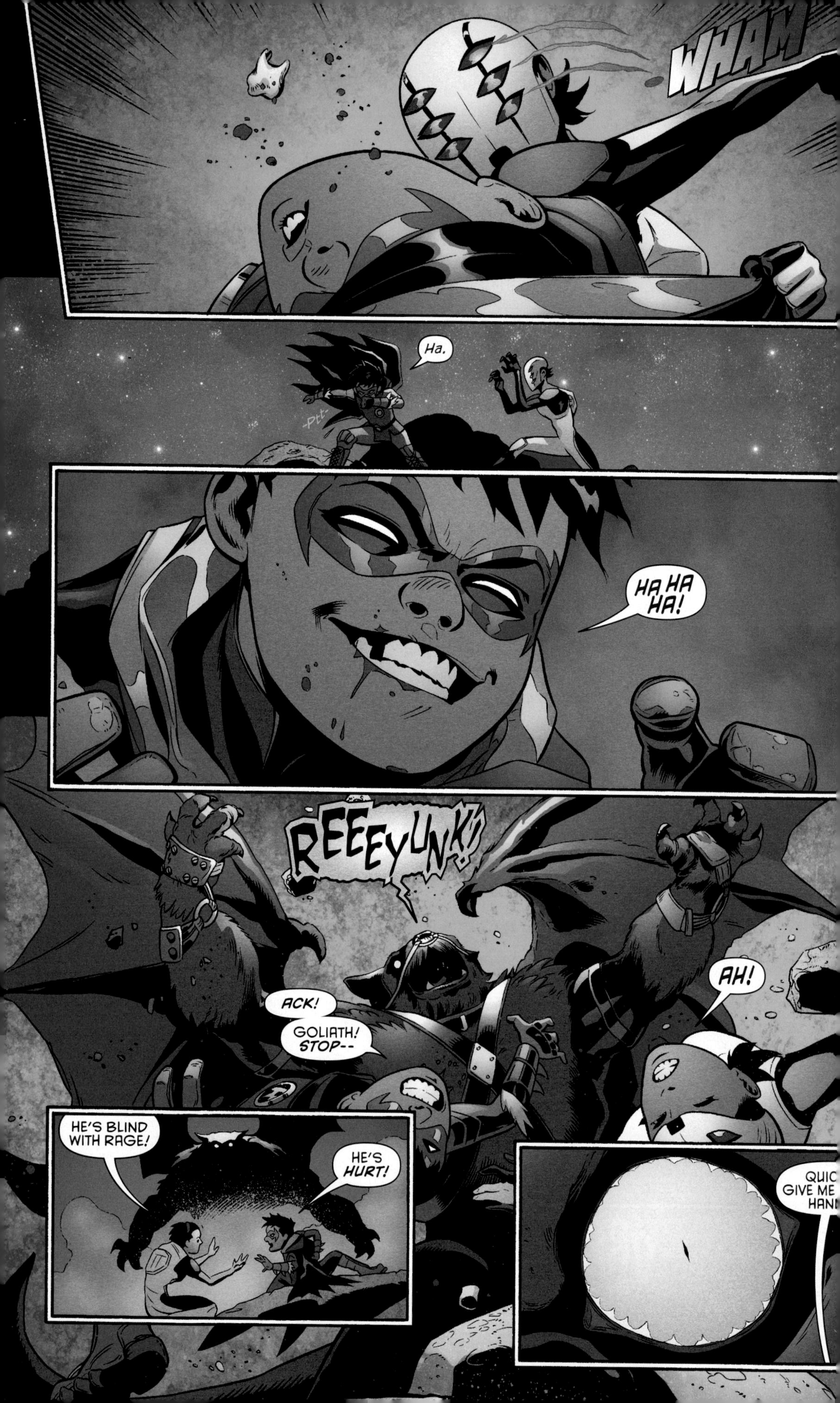
WHAM
Ha.
-Ptt-
HA HA
HA!
REEEYUNK!
ACK!
GOLIATH! STOP--
AH!
HE'S BLIND WITH RAGE!
HE'S HURT!
QUIC
GIVE ME
HAN

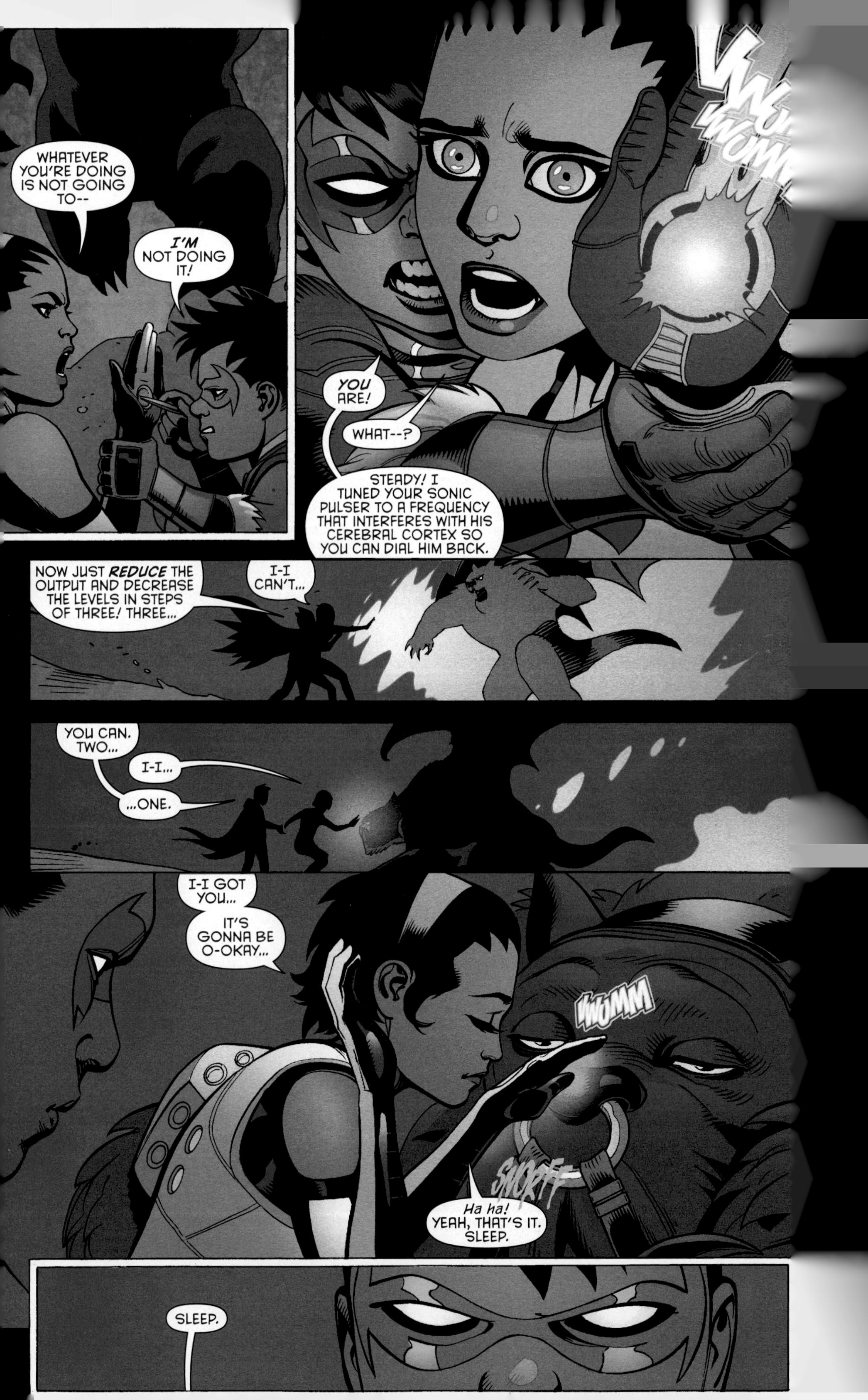
WHATEVER YOU'RE DOING IS NOT GOING TO--
I'M NOT DOING IT!
VWOMM VWOMM
YOU ARE!
WHAT--?
STEADY! I TUNED YOUR SONIC PULSER TO A FREQUENCY THAT INTERFERES WITH HIS CEREBRAL CORTEX SO YOU CAN DIAL HIM BACK.
NOW JUST REDUCE THE OUTPUT AND DECREASE THE LEVELS IN STEPS OF THREE! THREE...
I-I CAN'T...
YOU CAN. TWO...
I-I...
...ONE.
I-I GOT YOU...
IT'S GONNA BE O-OKAY...
VWOMM
SNORFF
Ha ha! YEAH, THAT'S IT. SLEEP.
SLEEP.

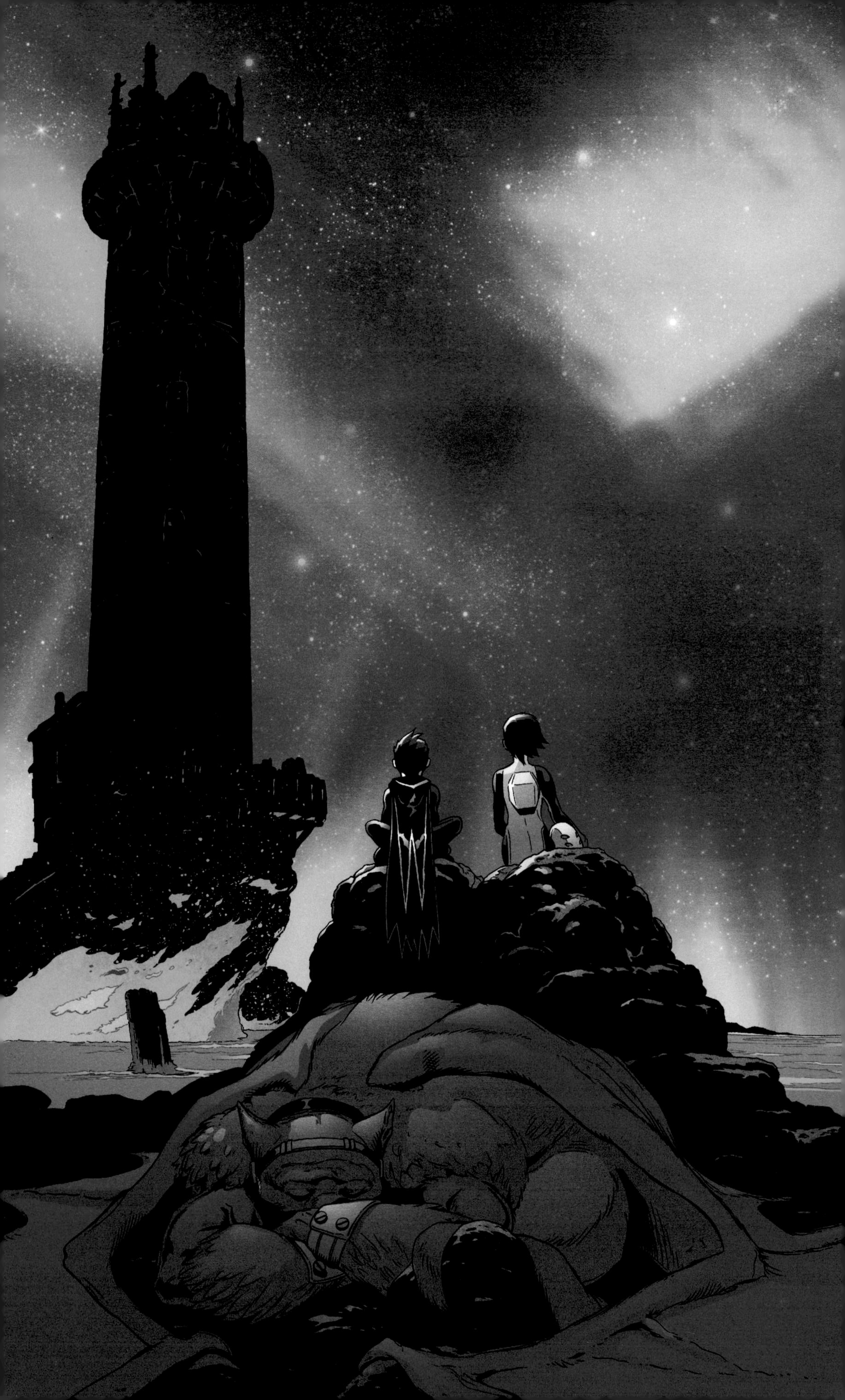

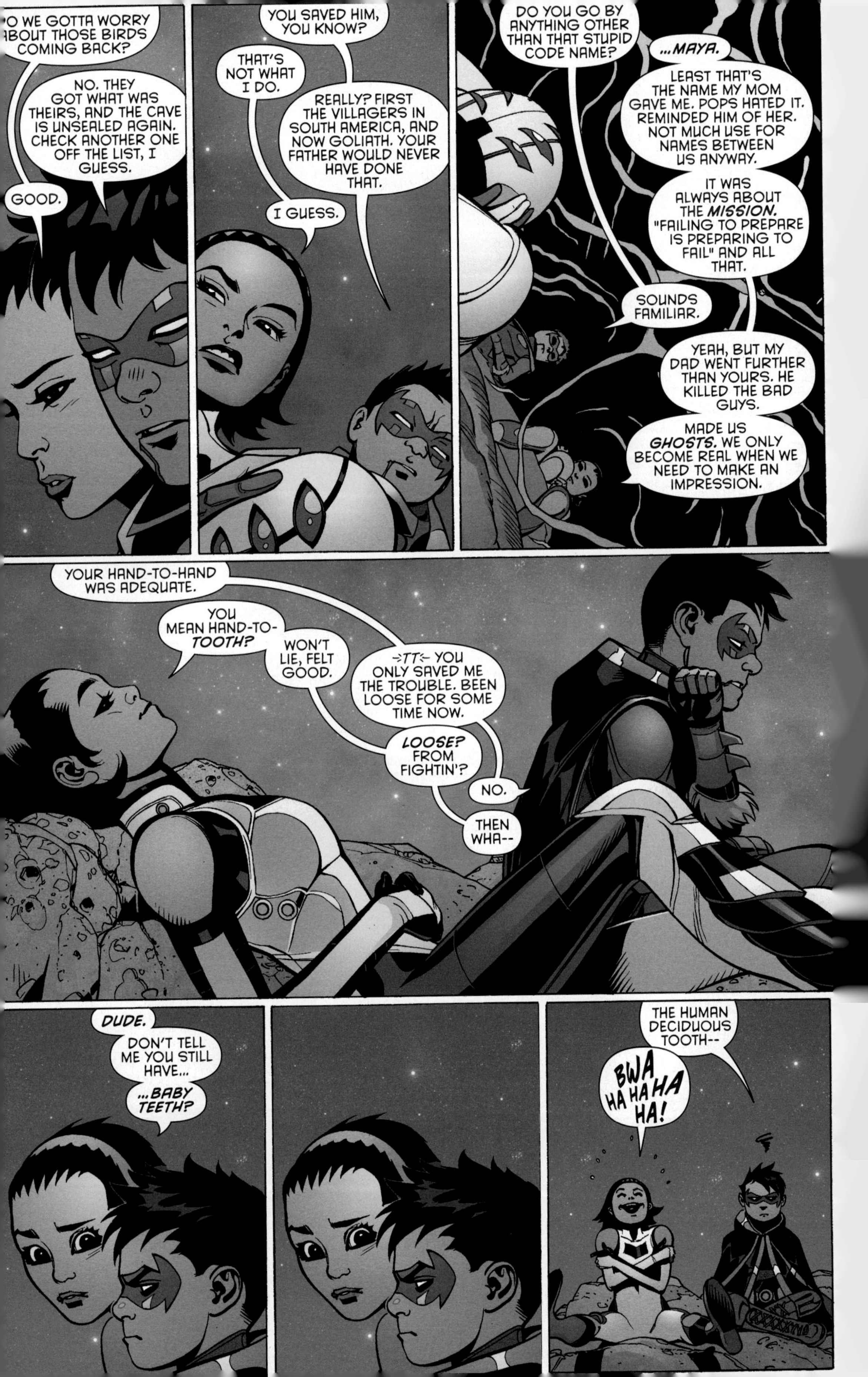
O WE GOTTA WORRY ABOUT THOSE BIRDS COMING BACK?
NO. THEY GOT WHAT WAS THEIRS, AND THE CAVE IS UNSEALED AGAIN. CHECK ANOTHER ONE OFF THE LIST, I GUESS.
GOOD.
YOU SAVED HIM, YOU KNOW?
THAT'S NOT WHAT I DO.
REALLY? FIRST THE VILLAGERS IN SOUTH AMERICA, AND NOW GOLIATH. YOUR FATHER WOULD NEVER HAVE DONE THAT.
I GUESS.
DO YOU GO BY ANYTHING OTHER THAN THAT STUPID CODE NAME?
...MAYA.
LEAST THAT'S THE NAME MY MOM GAVE ME. POPS HATED IT. REMINDED HIM OF HER. NOT MUCH USE FOR NAMES BETWEEN US ANYWAY.
IT WAS ALWAYS ABOUT THE MISSION. "FAILING TO PREPARE IS PREPARING TO FAIL" AND ALL THAT.
SOUNDS FAMILIAR.
YEAH, BUT MY DAD WENT FURTHER THAN YOURS. HE KILLED THE BAD GUYS.
MADE US GHOSTS. WE ONLY BECOME REAL WHEN WE NEED TO MAKE AN IMPRESSION.
YOUR HAND-TO-HAND WAS ADEQUATE.
YOU MEAN HAND-TO-TOOTH?
WON'T LIE, FELT GOOD.
TT YOU ONLY SAVED ME THE TROUBLE. BEEN LOOSE FOR SOME TIME NOW.
LOOSE? FROM FIGHTIN'?
NO.
THEN WHA--
DUDE.
DON'T TELL ME YOU STILL HAVE...
...BABY TEETH?
THE HUMAN DECIDUOUS TOOTH--
BWA HA HA HA HA!

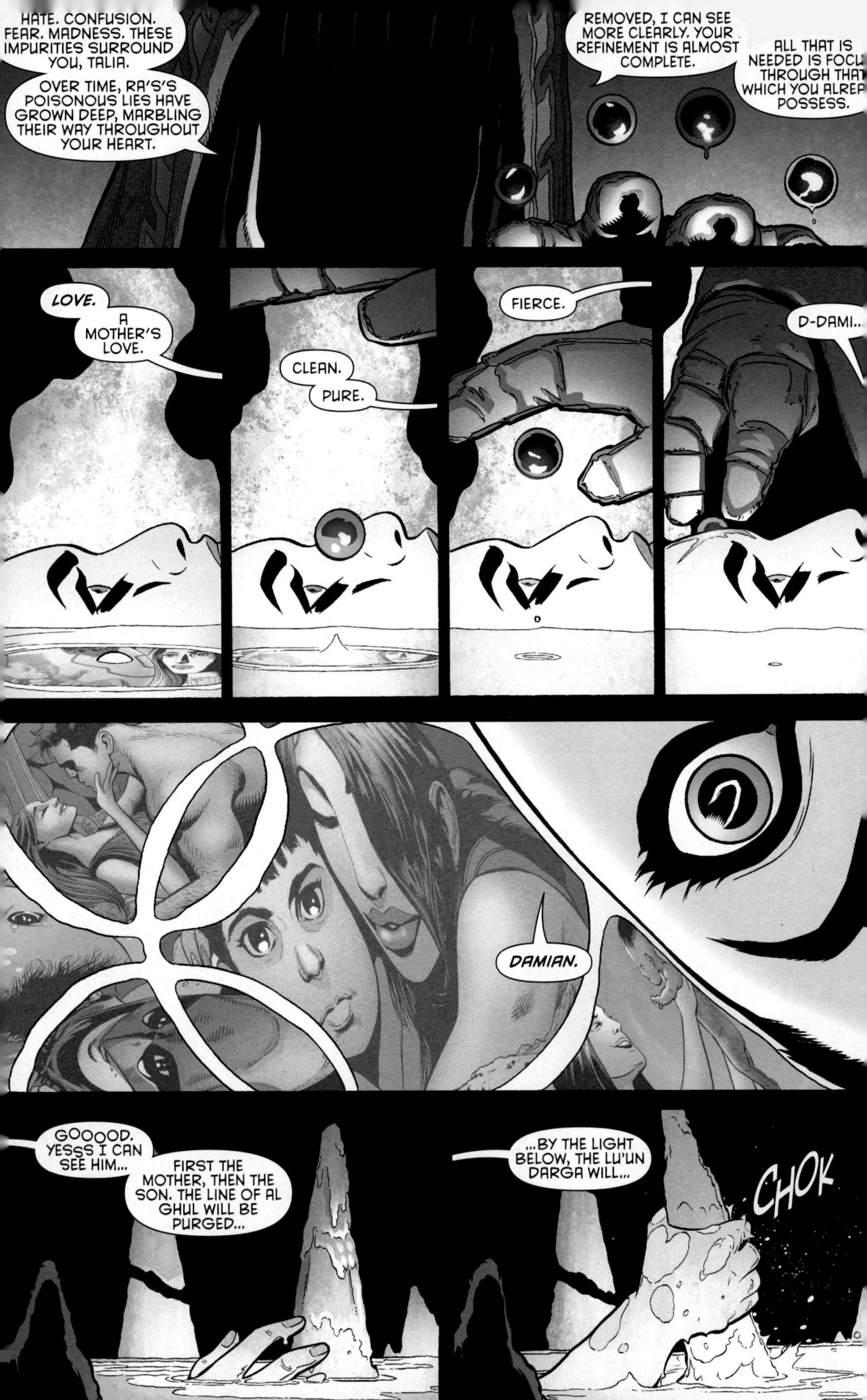
HATE. CONFUSION. FEAR. MADNESS. THESE IMPURITIES SURROUND YOU, TALIA.
OVER TIME, RA'S'S POISONOUS LIES HAVE GROWN DEEP, MARBLING THEIR WAY THROUGHOUT YOUR HEART.
REMOVED, I CAN SEE MORE CLEARLY. YOUR REFINEMENT IS ALMOST COMPLETE.
LOVE.
A MOTHER'S LOVE.
CLEAN.
PURE.
FIERCE.
D-DAMI...
DAMIAN.
GOOOOD. YESSS I CAN SEE HIM...
FIRST THE MOTHER, THEN THE SON. THE LINE OF AL GHUL WILL BE PURGED...
...BY THE LIGHT BELOW, THE LU'UN DARGA WILL...
CHOK

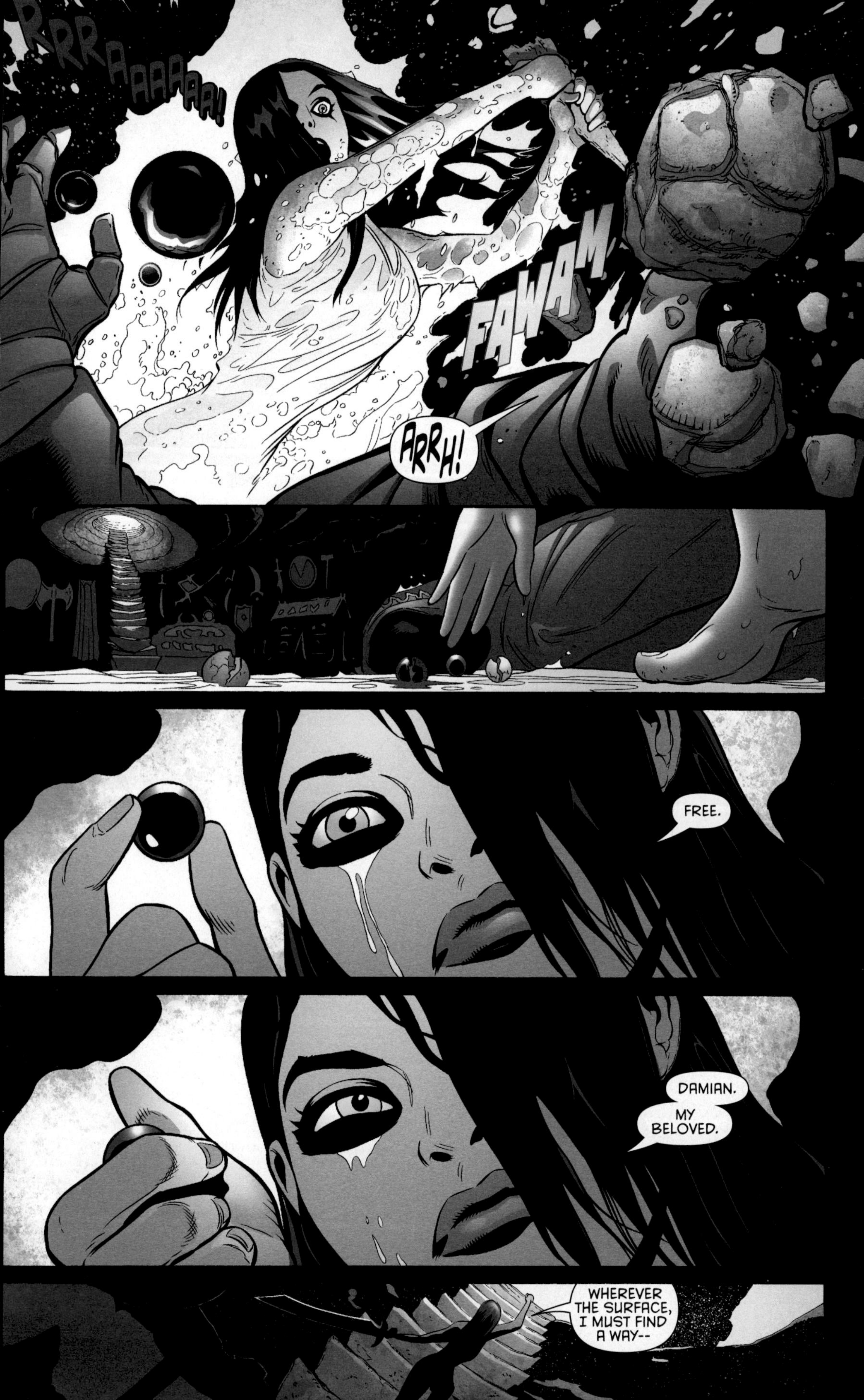
RRRAAAAAAA!
FAWAM
ARRH!
FREE.
DAMIAN.
MY BELOVED.
WHEREVER THE SURFACE, I MUST FIND A WAY--

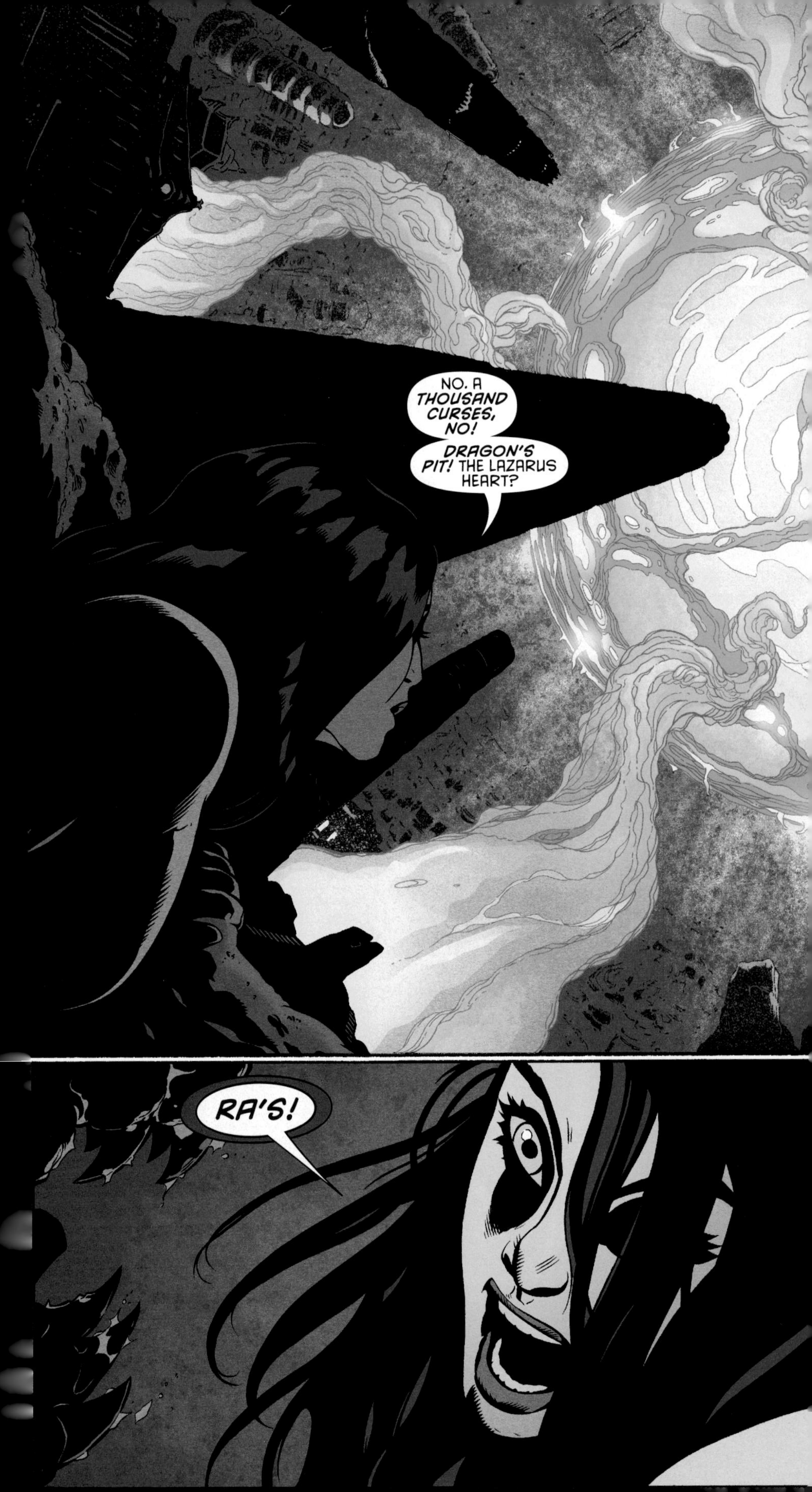
NO. A THOUSAND CURSES, NO!
DRAGON'S PIT! THE LAZARUS HEART?
RA'S!

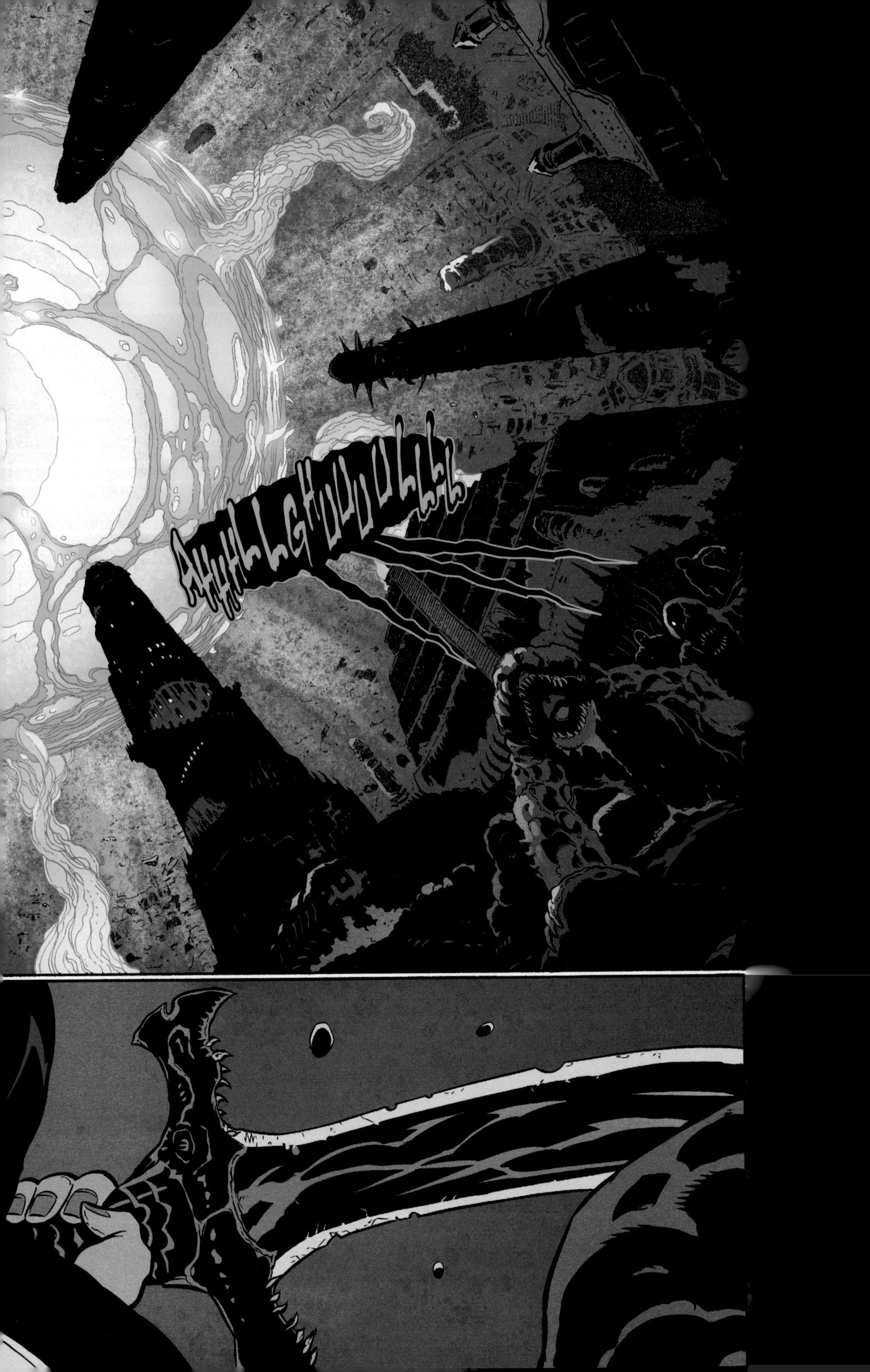
AHHLLGHUUUULLLL

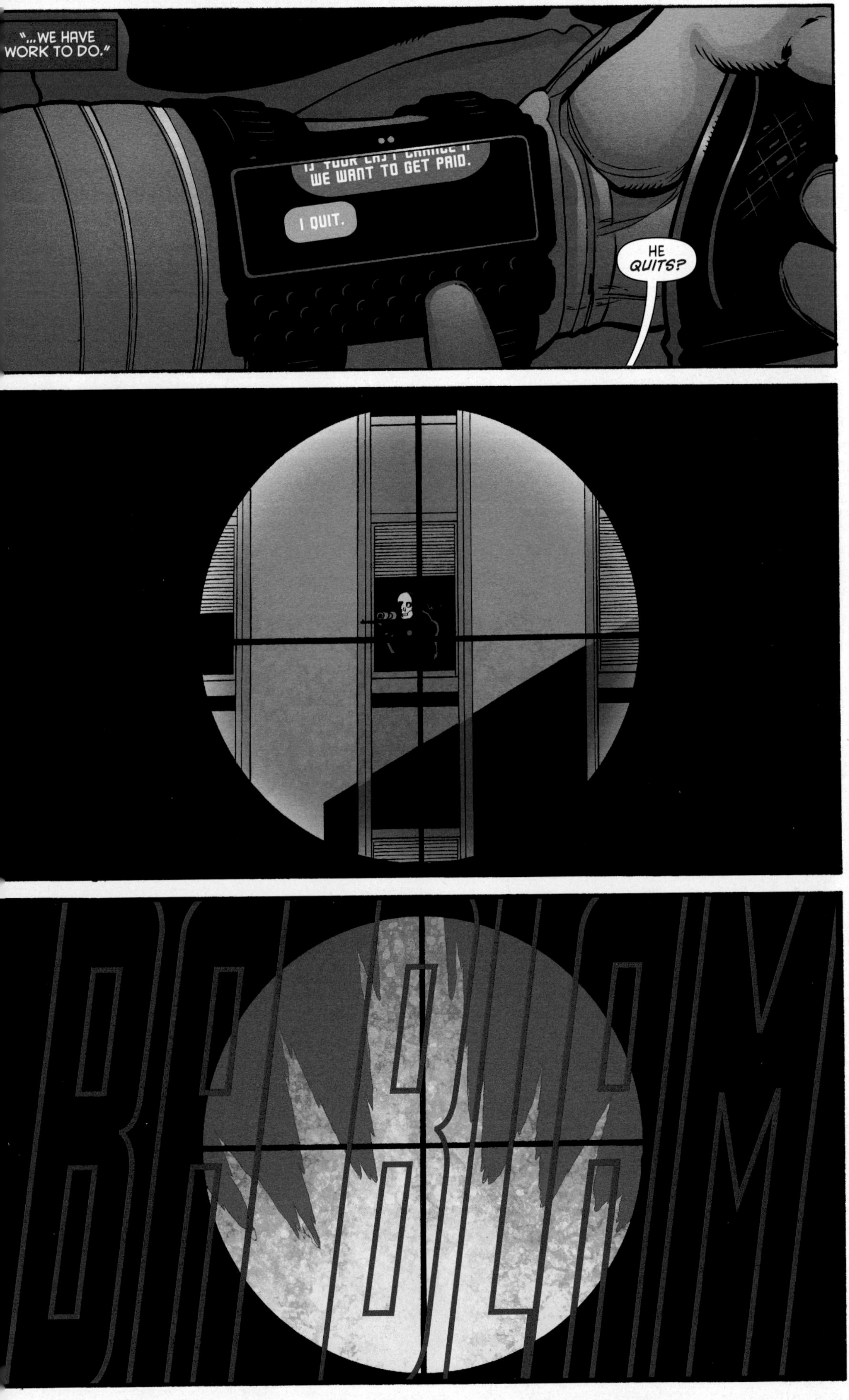
"...WE HAVE WORK TO DO."
WE WANT TO GET PAID.
I QUIT.
HE QUITS?

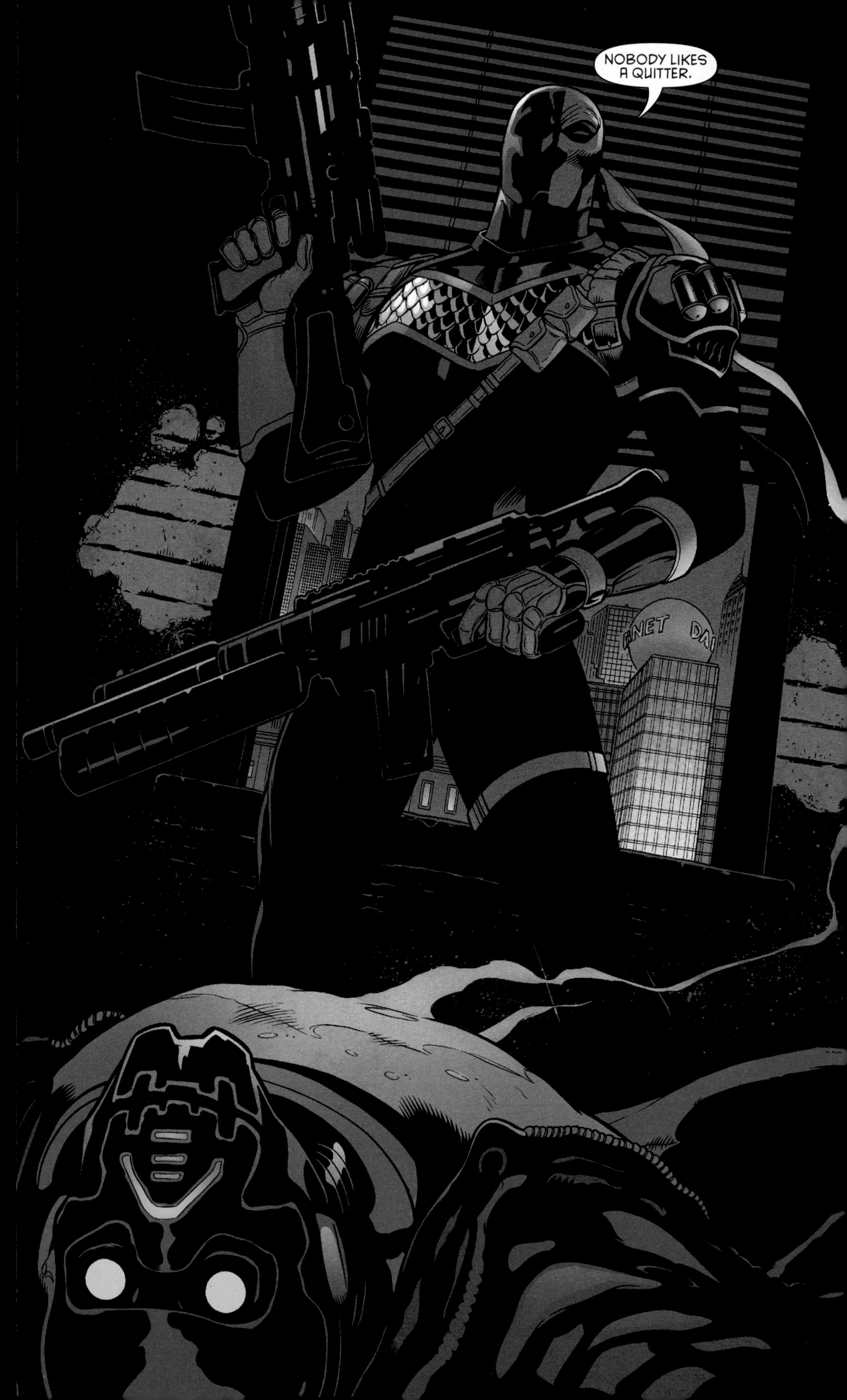
NOBODY LIKES A QUITTER.

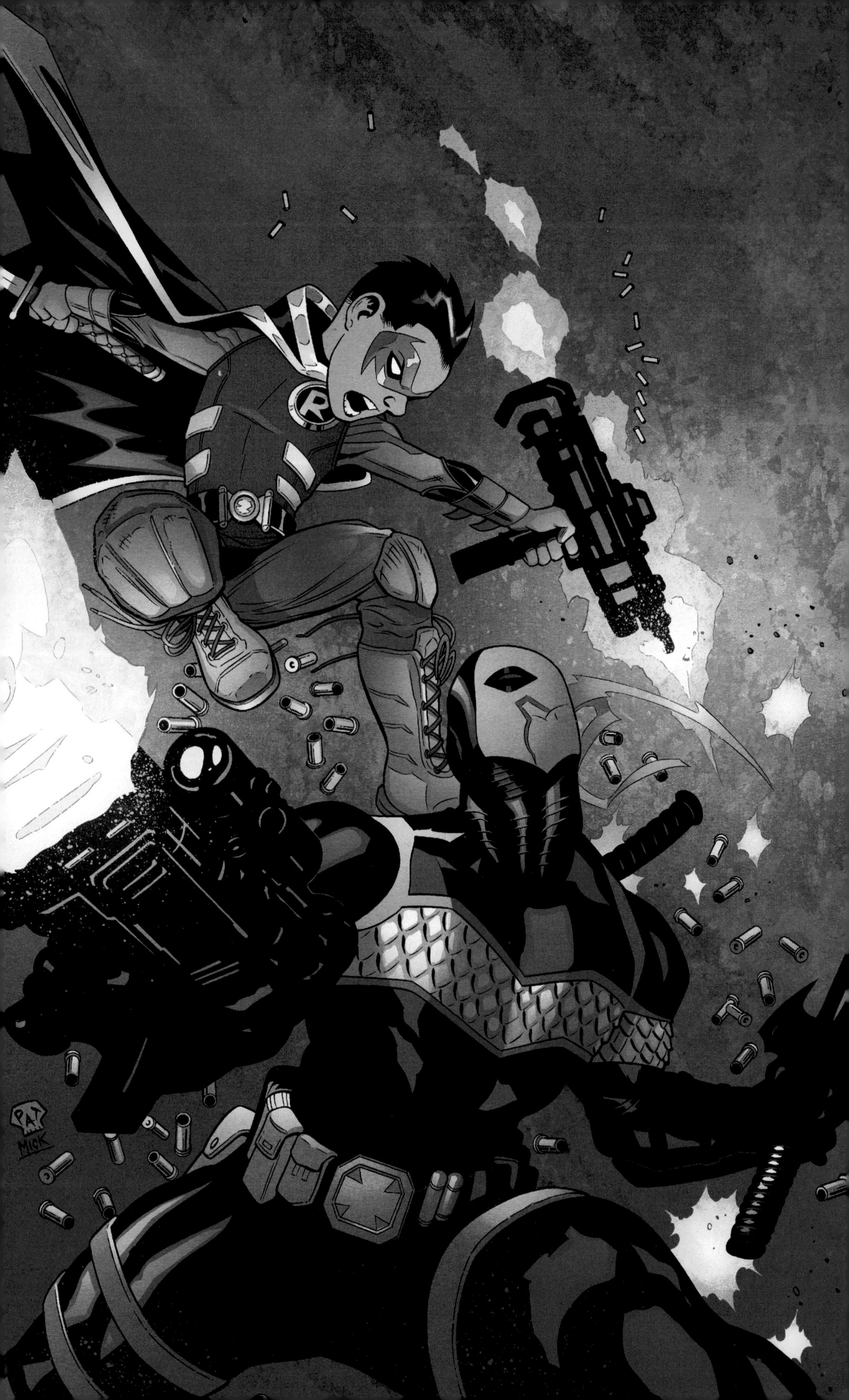

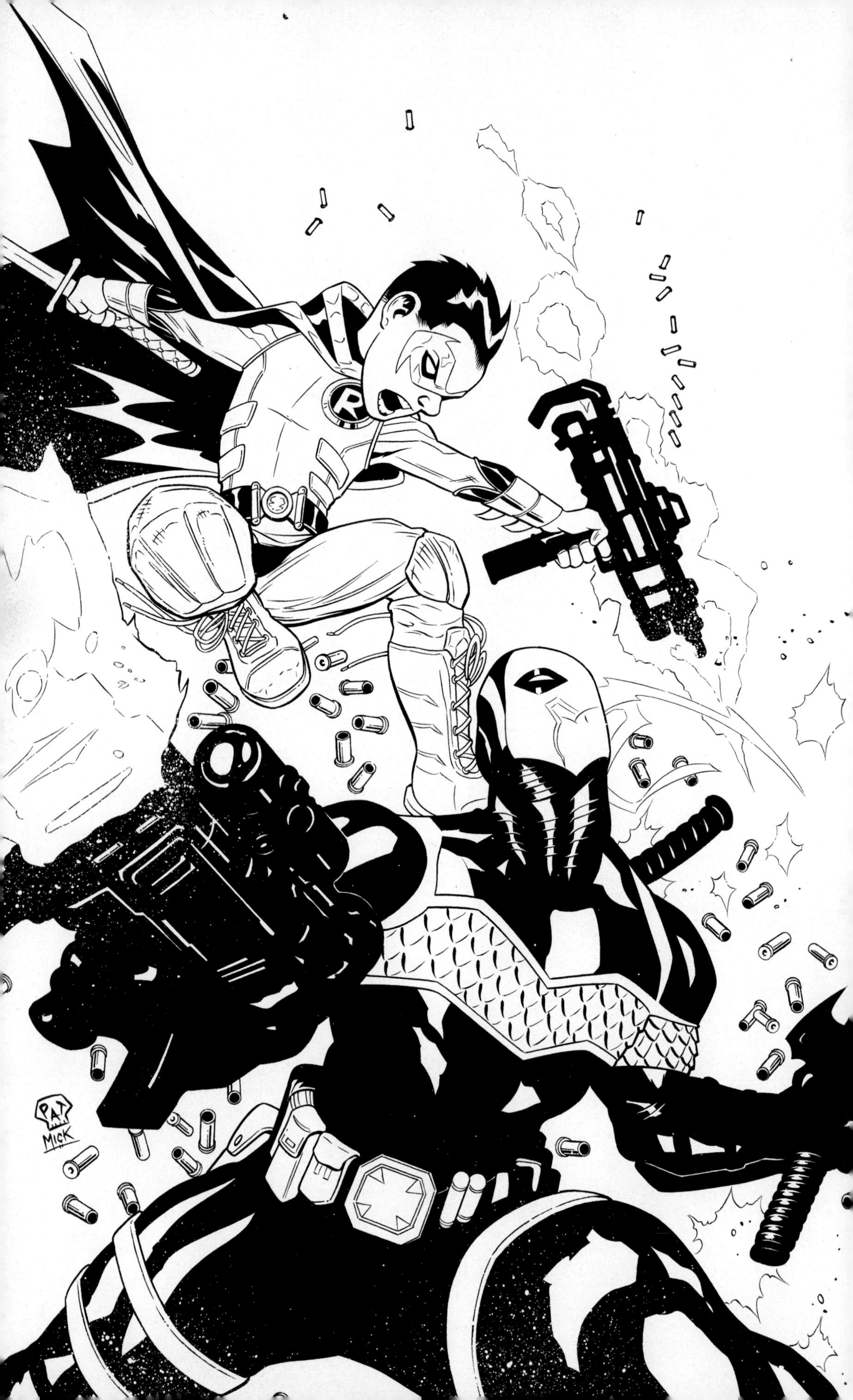
PAT
MICK

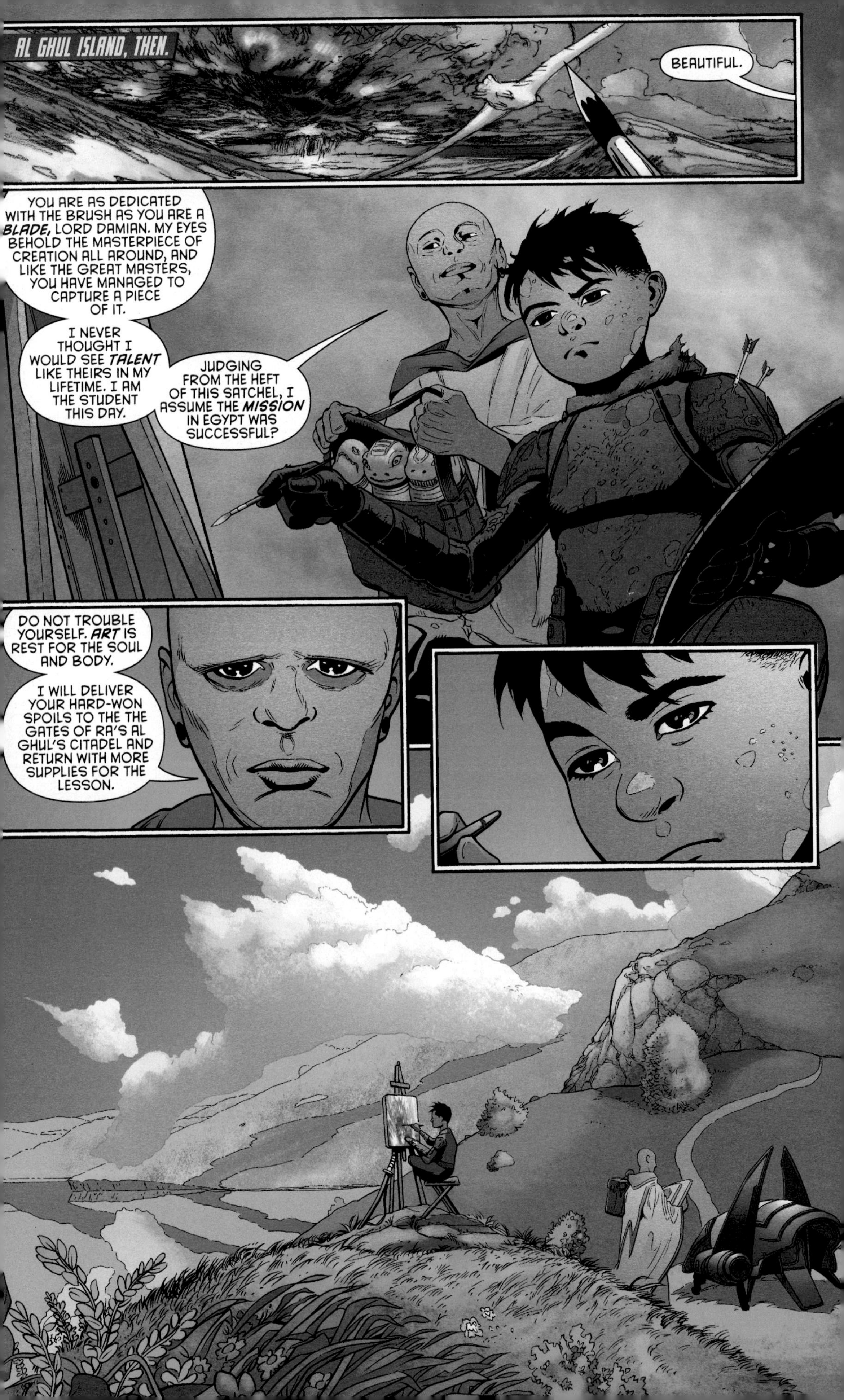
AL GHUL ISLAND, THEN.
BEAUTIFUL.
YOU ARE AS DEDICATED WITH THE BRUSH AS YOU ARE A BLADE, LORD DAMIAN. MY EYES BEHOLD THE MASTERPIECE OF CREATION ALL AROUND, AND LIKE THE GREAT MASTERS, YOU HAVE MANAGED TO CAPTURE A PIECE OF IT.
I NEVER THOUGHT I WOULD SEE TALENT LIKE THEIRS IN MY LIFETIME. I AM THE STUDENT THIS DAY.
JUDGING FROM THE HEFT OF THIS SATCHEL, I ASSUME THE MISSION IN EGYPT WAS SUCCESSFUL?
DO NOT TROUBLE YOURSELF. ART IS REST FOR THE SOUL AND BODY.
I WILL DELIVER YOUR HARD-WON SPOILS TO THE THE GATES OF RA'S AL GHUL'S CITADEL AND RETURN WITH MORE SUPPLIES FOR THE LESSON.

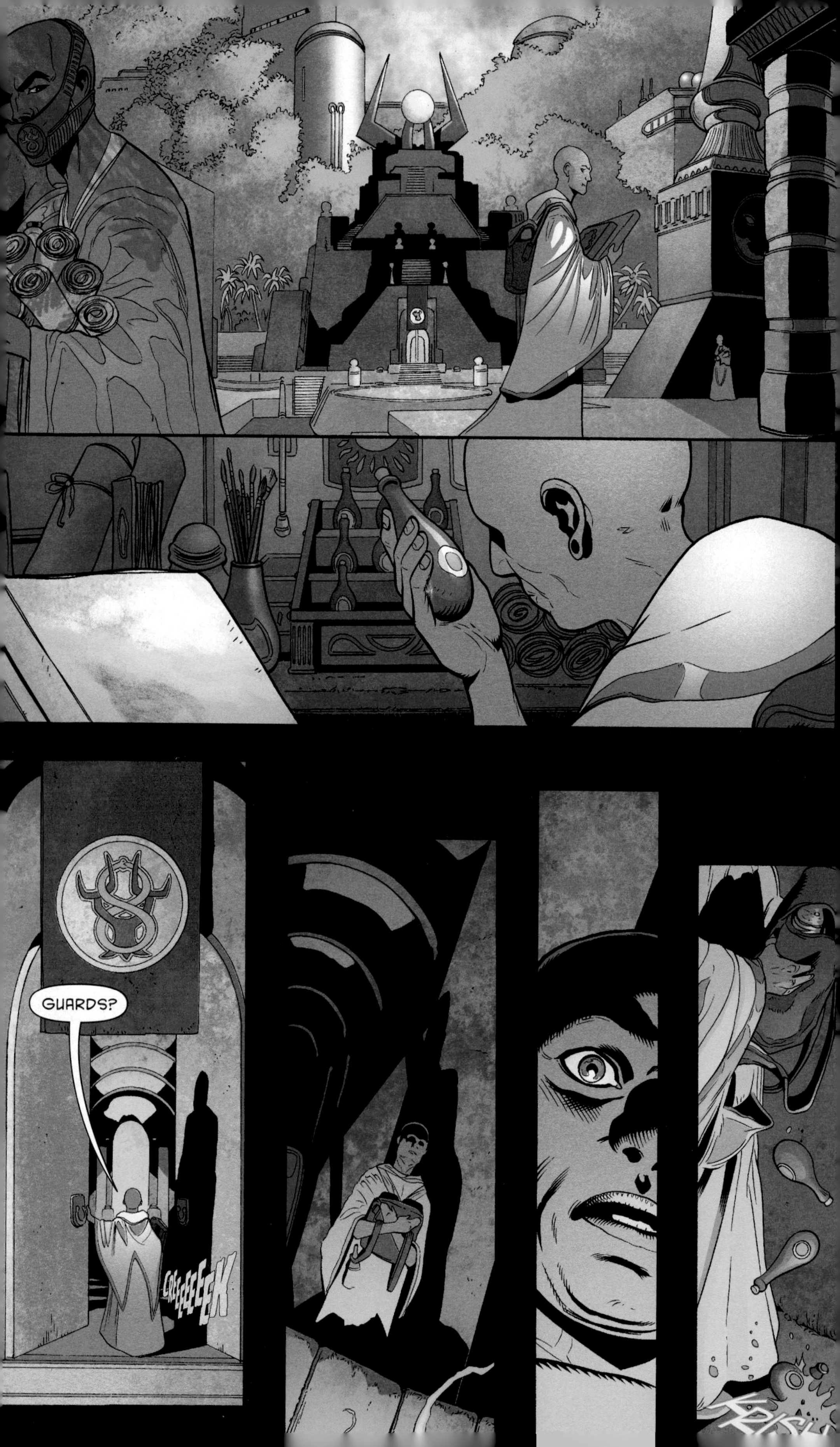

GUARDS?
CREEEEEEEK

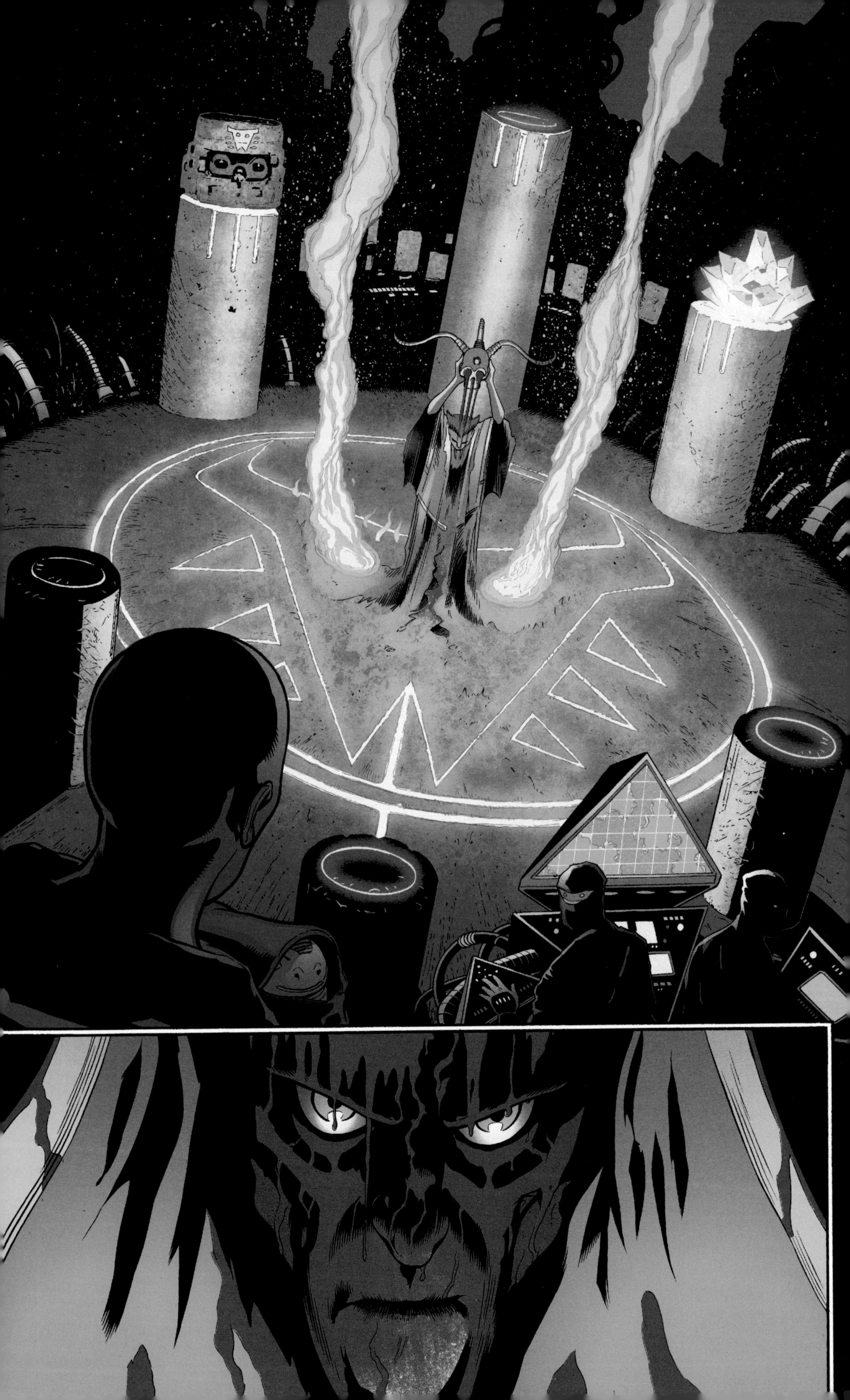

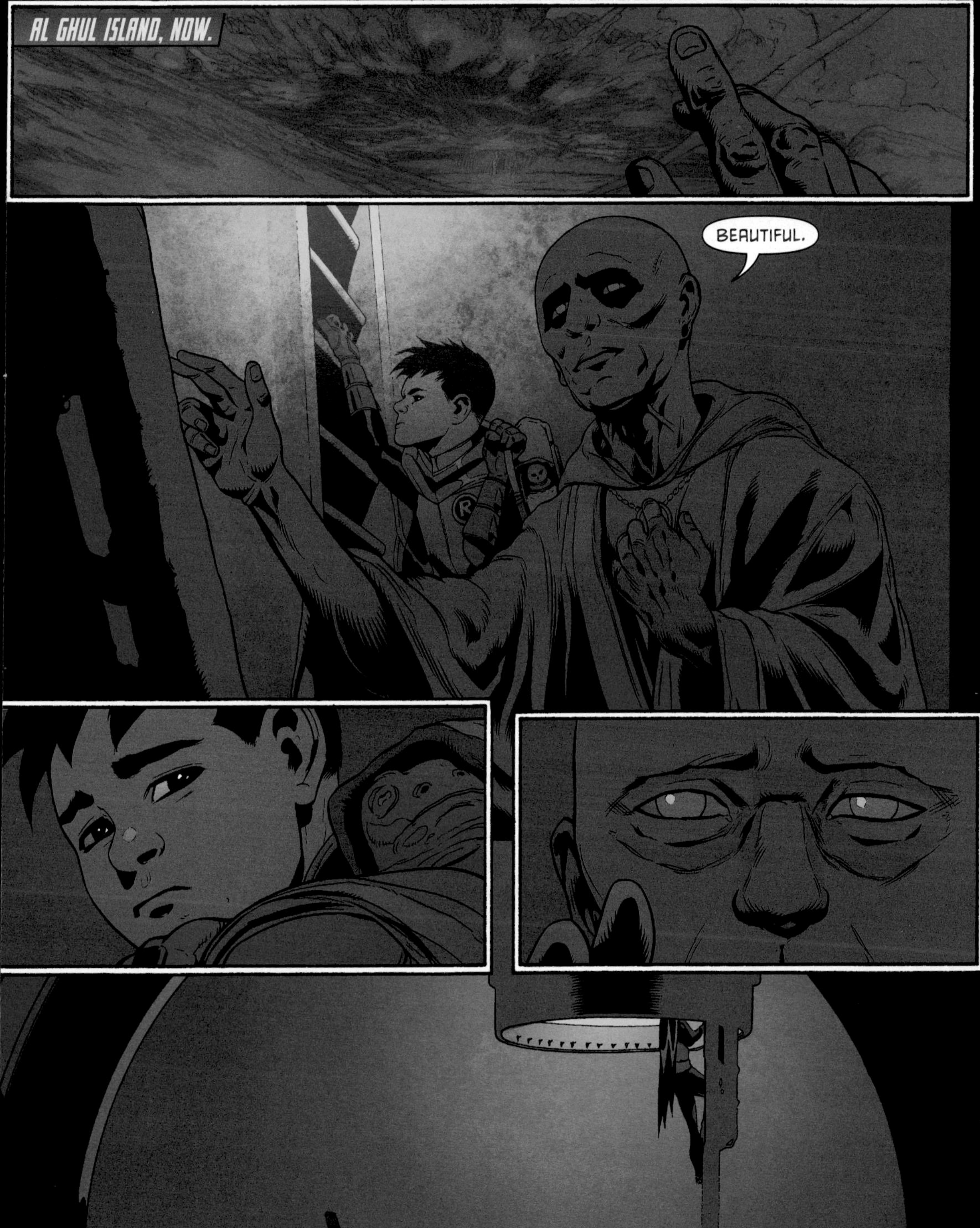
AL GHUL ISLAND, NOW.
BEAUTIFUL.

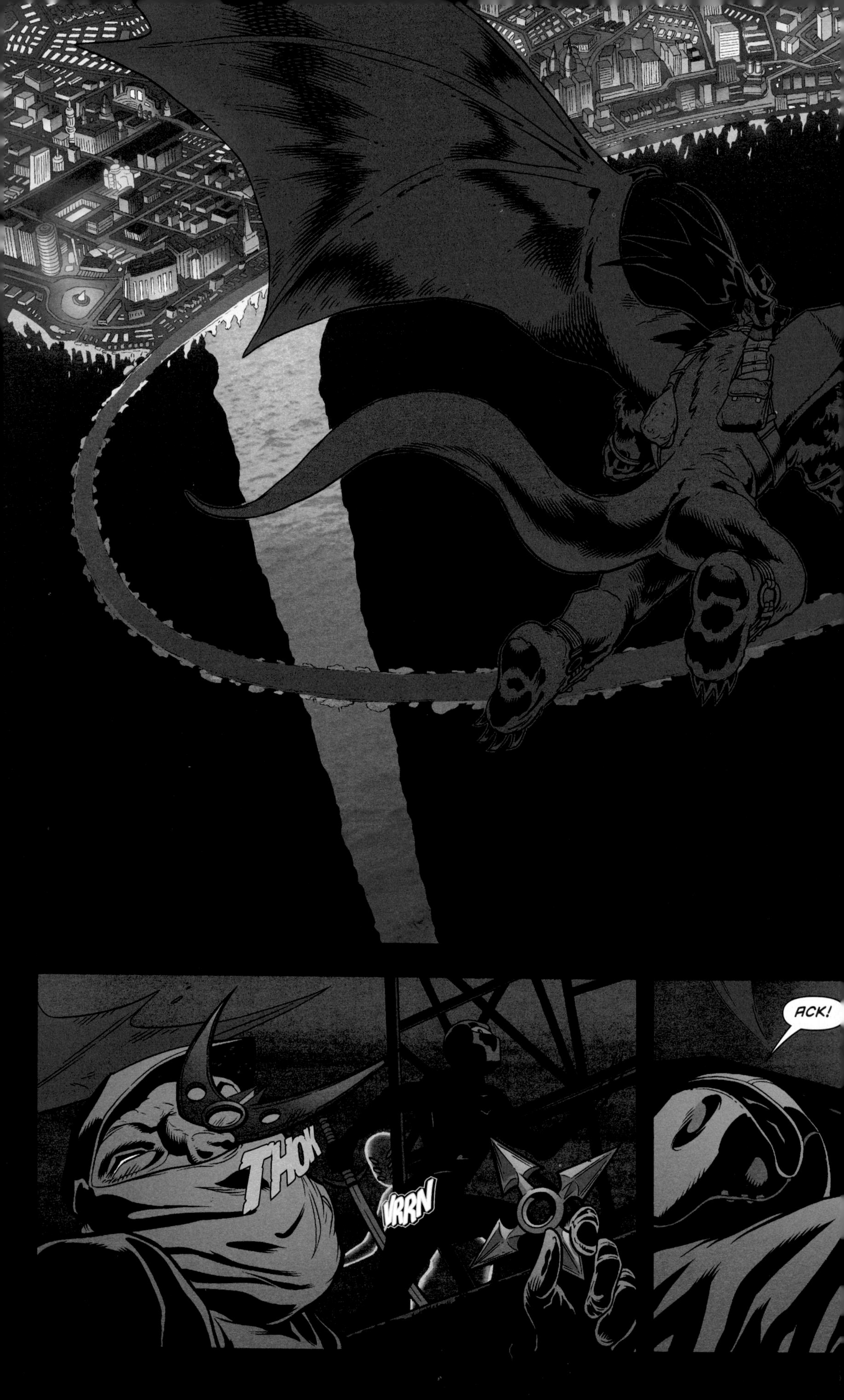
THOK
VRRN
ACK!

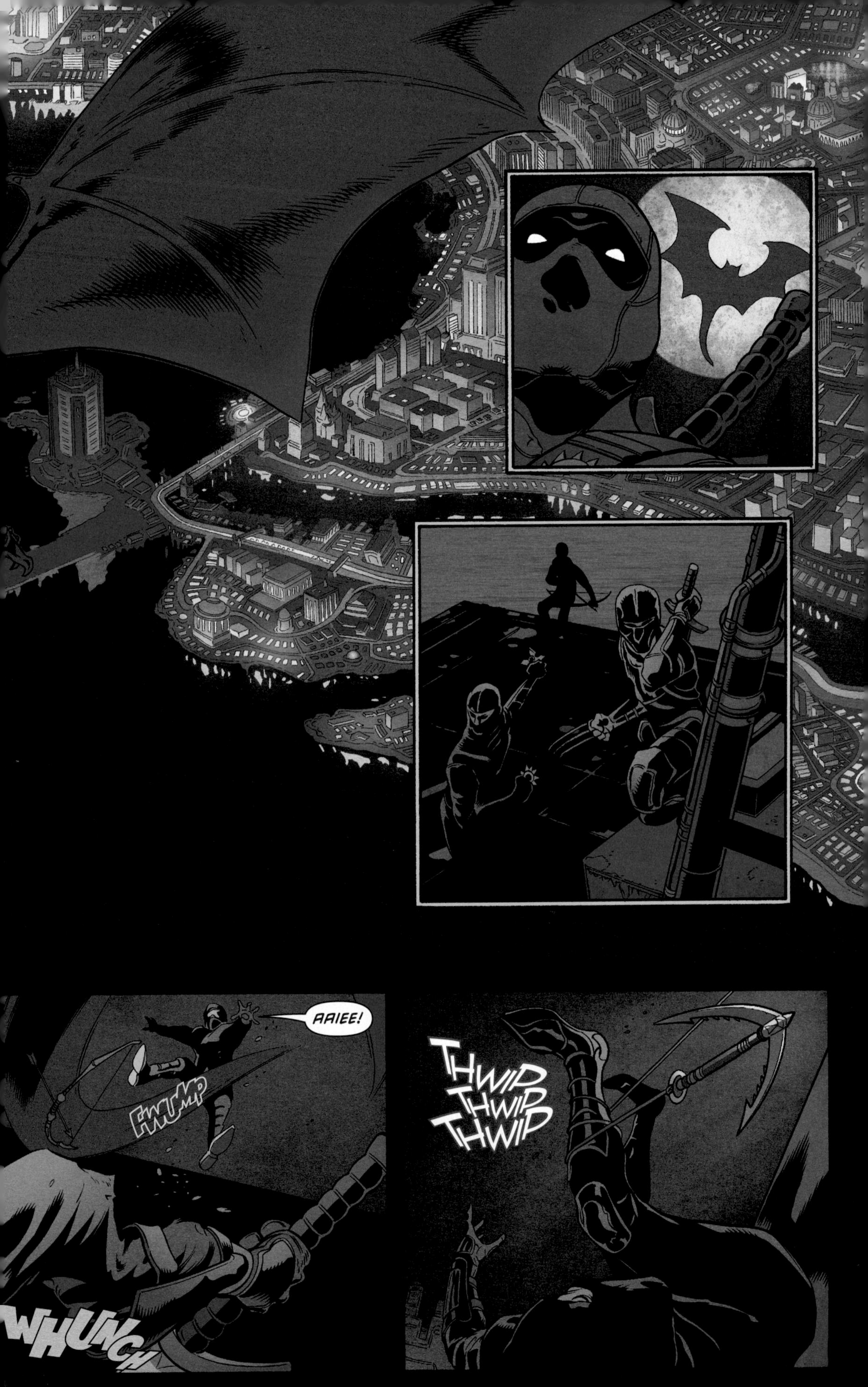
AAIEE!
FWUMP
WHUNCH
THWIP
THWIP
THWIP

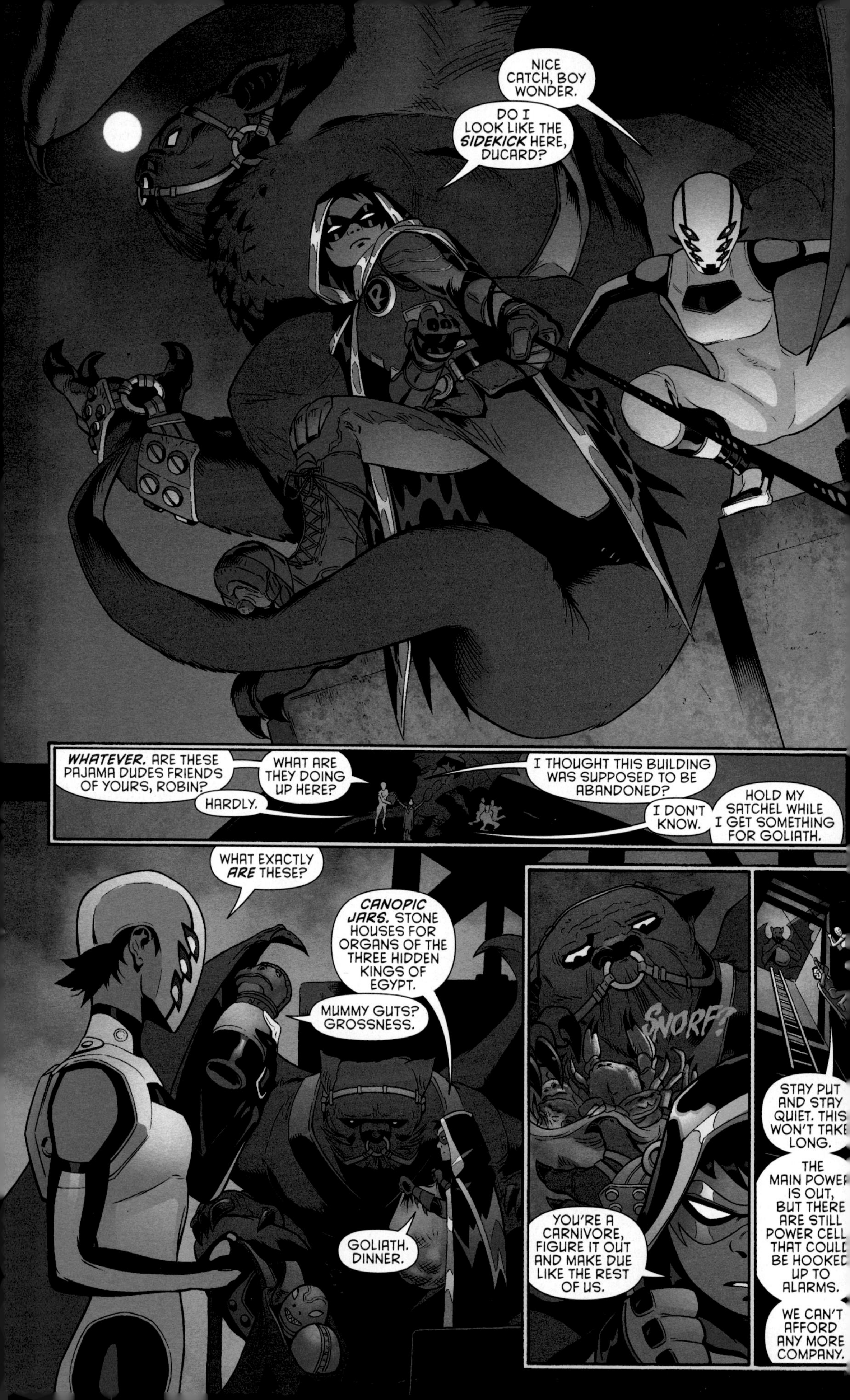
NICE CATCH, BOY WONDER.
DO I LOOK LIKE THE SIDEKICK HERE, DUCARD?
WHATEVER. ARE THESE PAJAMA DUDES FRIENDS OF YOURS, ROBIN?
HARDLY.
WHAT ARE THEY DOING UP HERE?
I THOUGHT THIS BUILDING WAS SUPPOSED TO BE ABANDONED?
I DON'T KNOW.
HOLD MY SATCHEL WHILE I GET SOMETHING FOR GOLIATH.
WHAT EXACTLY ARE THESE?
CANOPIC JARS. STONE HOUSES FOR ORGANS OF THE THREE HIDDEN KINGS OF EGYPT.
MUMMY GUTS? GROSSNESS.
GOLIATH. DINNER.
SNORF?
YOU'RE A CARNIVORE, FIGURE IT OUT AND MAKE DUE LIKE THE REST OF US.
STAY PUT AND STAY QUIET. THIS WON'T TAKE LONG.
THE MAIN POWER IS OUT, BUT THERE ARE STILL POWER CELL THAT COULD BE HOOKED UP TO ALARMS.
WE CAN'T AFFORD ANY MORE COMPANY.

THIS IS THE WEIRDEST, CREEPIEST BUILDING I'VE EVER BROKEN INTO, ROBIN.

IT'S NOT A BUILDING. IT'S A *TOMB*.

MUCH OF THE ANCIENT CITY OF ALEXANDRIA *SANK* BENEATH THE HARBOR DURING AN EARTHQUAKE.

ALEXANDRIA DOESN'T SOUND EGYPTIAN.

IT'S NAMED AFTER ALEXANDER THE GREAT, LIKE ME.

IT WAS THE INTELLECTUAL CENTER OF THE ANCIENT WORLD.

BUT ITS HOPE AND PROMISE WAS *WASHED AWAY* BY YEARS OF WARS AND BLOOD.

THE FIRST TIME I WAS HERE, THE RUINS UNDER THE BAY WERE INACCESSIBLE. FOR MOST.

MOST?

A LOCAL *PHILANTHROPIST*, RAISED ON TALES OF MIRACULOUS HEALING AND THE GLORY OF THE ORIGINAL CITY, DEVOTED HIS FORTUNE TO BRINGING A PIECE OF OF ANCIENT ALEXANDRIA BACK TO HELP THE MODERN PEOPLE.

HE UNCOVERED SECRETS ABOUT THREE KINGS AND A CULT OPERATING ALONGSIDE THE PHARAOHS OF OLD. A *CURSE* SOME SAID.

BUT HE STILL BELIEVED THIS WAS SACRED GROUND AND IT HELD THE *KEY* TO SOMETHING GOOD.

SO HE BUILT THIS MEDICAL *RESEARCH FACILITY* IN THE OUTER RING OF THE BUILDING TO HOUSE PATIENTS UNDERGOING EXPERIMENTAL TREATMENTS. HE SAVED MANY LIVES, ATTRIBUTING IT TO THE PROXIMITY OF THE TOMBS.

ONE OF THOSE LIVES WAS AN AL GHUL *SPY* WHO LEARNED ABOUT THIS INNER CORE AND THE SECRET HIDDEN BELOW.

HE TOOK THE INFORMATION BACK TO MY *GRANDFATHER*.

WHAT WAS THE SECRET?

NO ONE EVER GOT FAR ENOUGH TO FIND OUT.

THE ENTRANCE TO THE TOMB IS *BOOBY-TRAPPED* WITH DEVICES OF DEATH.

MANY OF HIS VOLUNTEERS TRIED TO GET THROUGH, BUT LOST THIER LIVES.

WHEN I GOT HERE, I FIGURED OUT THE TIMING AND WHERE NOT TO STEP. IT WAS CHILD'S PLAY.

WAY TO GO, *INDIANA*.

AFTER I FOUND THE *JARS*, I TOOK THEM AND LEFT.

AFTER THAT, THE PHILANTHROPIST BELIEVED THE AREA WAS *DESECRATED*.

HE LOST HIS VOLUNTEERS AND RAN OUT OF FUNDS.

HIS OPERATION WAS SHUT DOWN AND PUT INTO MOTHBALLS.

AND THE PATIENTS YOU DISPLACED?

SCATTERED TO FACE THEIR FATE.

AND THAT DIDN'T BOTHER YOU?

I'M HERE *NOW*, AREN'T I?

SO YOU GO BACK DOWN THROUGH THE TRAPS AND PUT THESE MUMMY GUTS BACK AND *THEN* WHAT?

THE POWER IS RESTORED? PEOPLE NEED *SCIENCE* NOT VOODOO.

AND THAT TAKES MONEY.

TONIGHT, AN *ANONYMOUS* DONOR WI CONTACT TH PHILAN- THROPIST' FOUNDATIC AND MAKE GENEROUS DONATION C *FIVE MILLIC* DOLLARS T RESTART TH RESEARCH HERE.

NOW KEEP QUIET AND FOCUS, GET EYES ON THE COMPUTERS AND HACK INTO THE OLD FINANCIALS FIRST WHILE I'M BELOW.

FINE. JUST GET US OUT OF HERE. I DON'T LIKE BEING UNDERWATER. FEELS LIKE DEATH IS WATCHING--

--WHAT'S THAT?!

KLANG KLANG KLANG

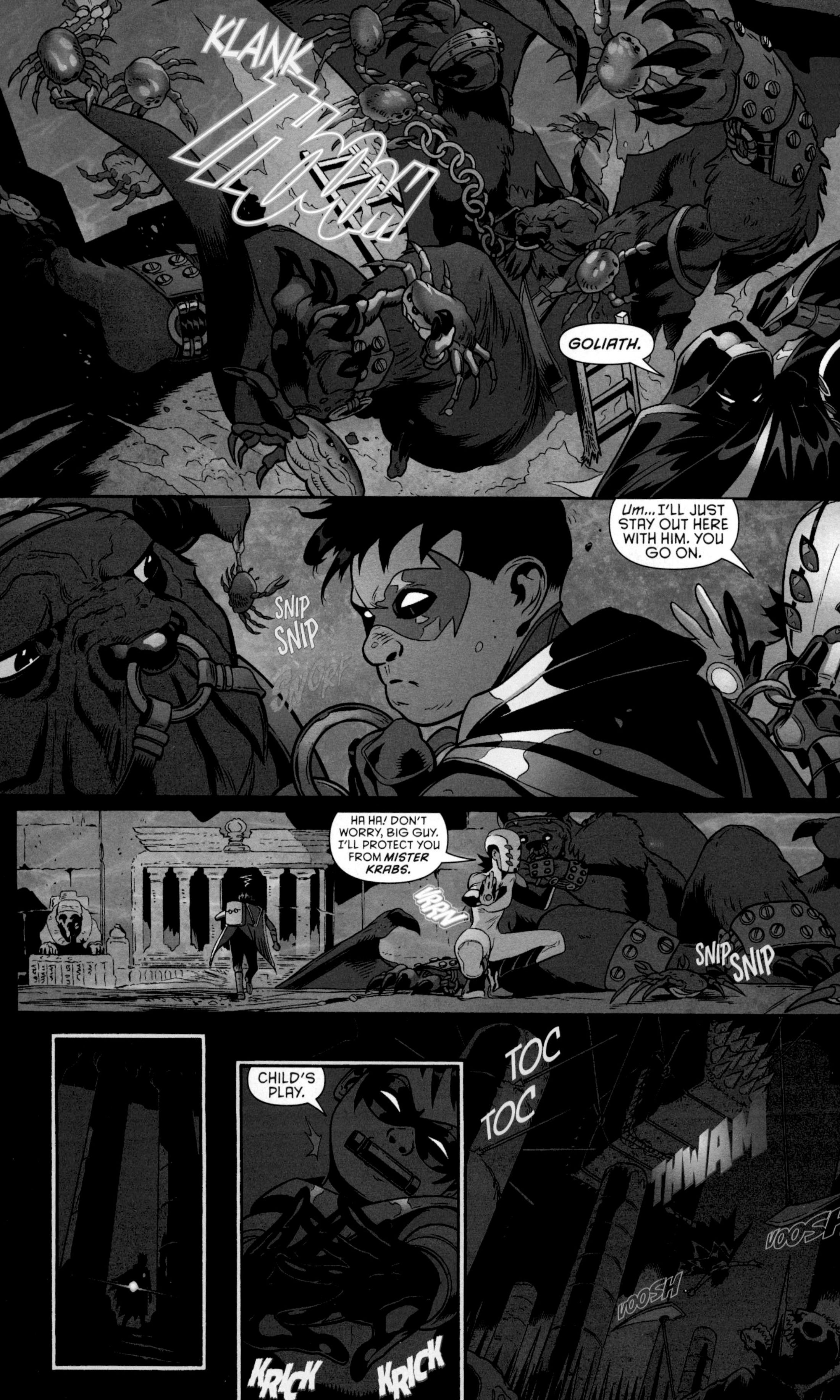
KLANK
THOOM
GOLIATH.
SNIP SNIP
SNORF
Um... I'LL JUST STAY OUT HERE WITH HIM. YOU GO ON.
HA HA! DON'T WORRY, BIG GUY. I'LL PROTECT YOU FROM MISTER KRABS.
VRRN
SNIP SNIP
CHILD'S PLAY.
TOC
TOC
THWAM
VOOSH
VOOSH
KRICK
KRICK

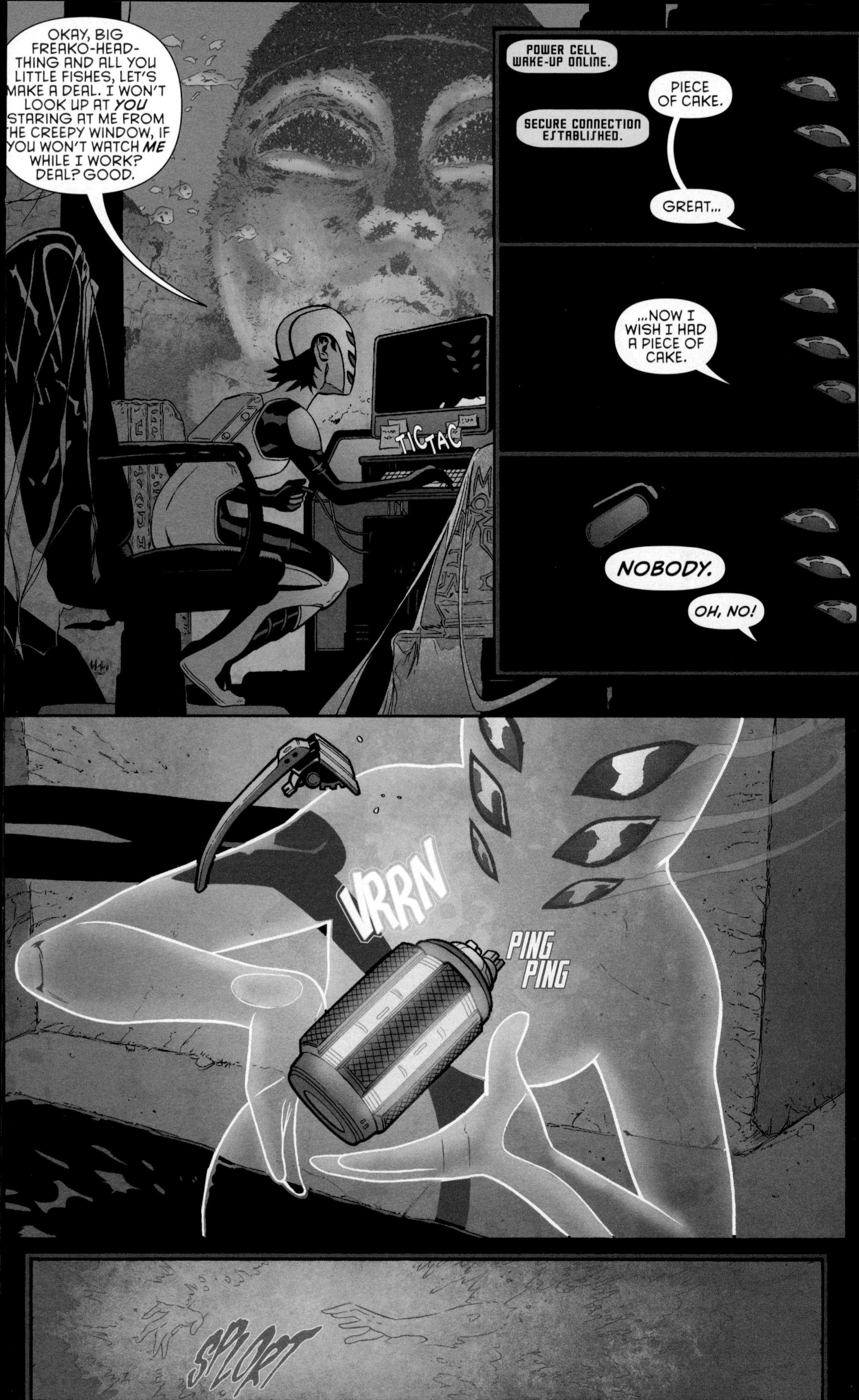
OKAY, BIG FREAKO-HEAD-THING AND ALL YOU LITTLE FISHES, LET'S MAKE A DEAL. I WON'T LOOK UP AT *YOU* STARING AT ME FROM THE CREEPY WINDOW, IF YOU WON'T WATCH *ME* WHILE I WORK? DEAL? GOOD.
TIC TAC
POWER CELL WAKE-UP ONLINE.
PIECE OF CAKE.
SECURE CONNECTION ESTABLISHED.
GREAT...
...NOW I WISH I HAD A PIECE OF CAKE.
NOBODY.
OH, NO!
VRRN
PING PING
SPLORT

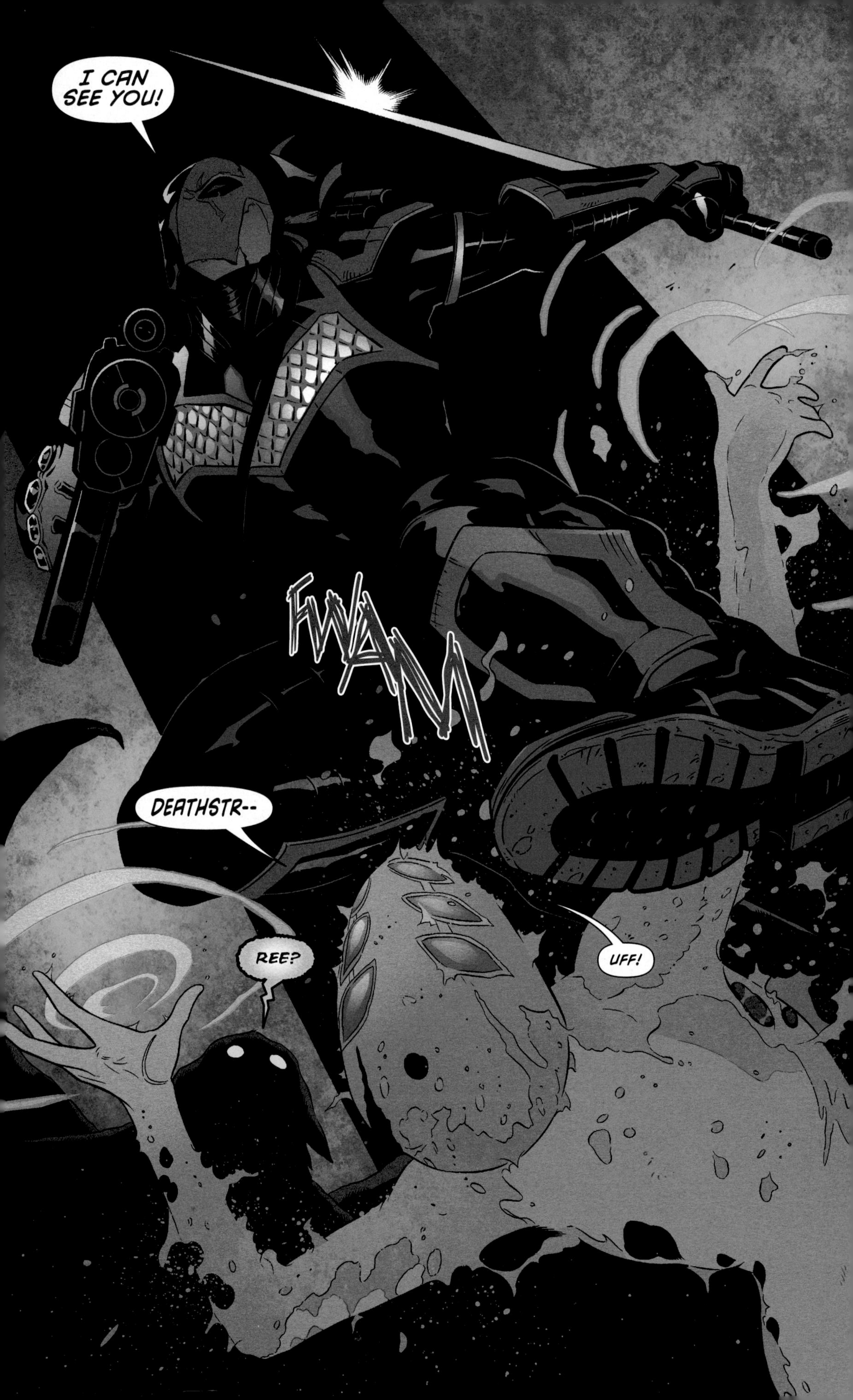
I CAN SEE YOU!
FWAM
DEATHSTR--
REE?
UFF!

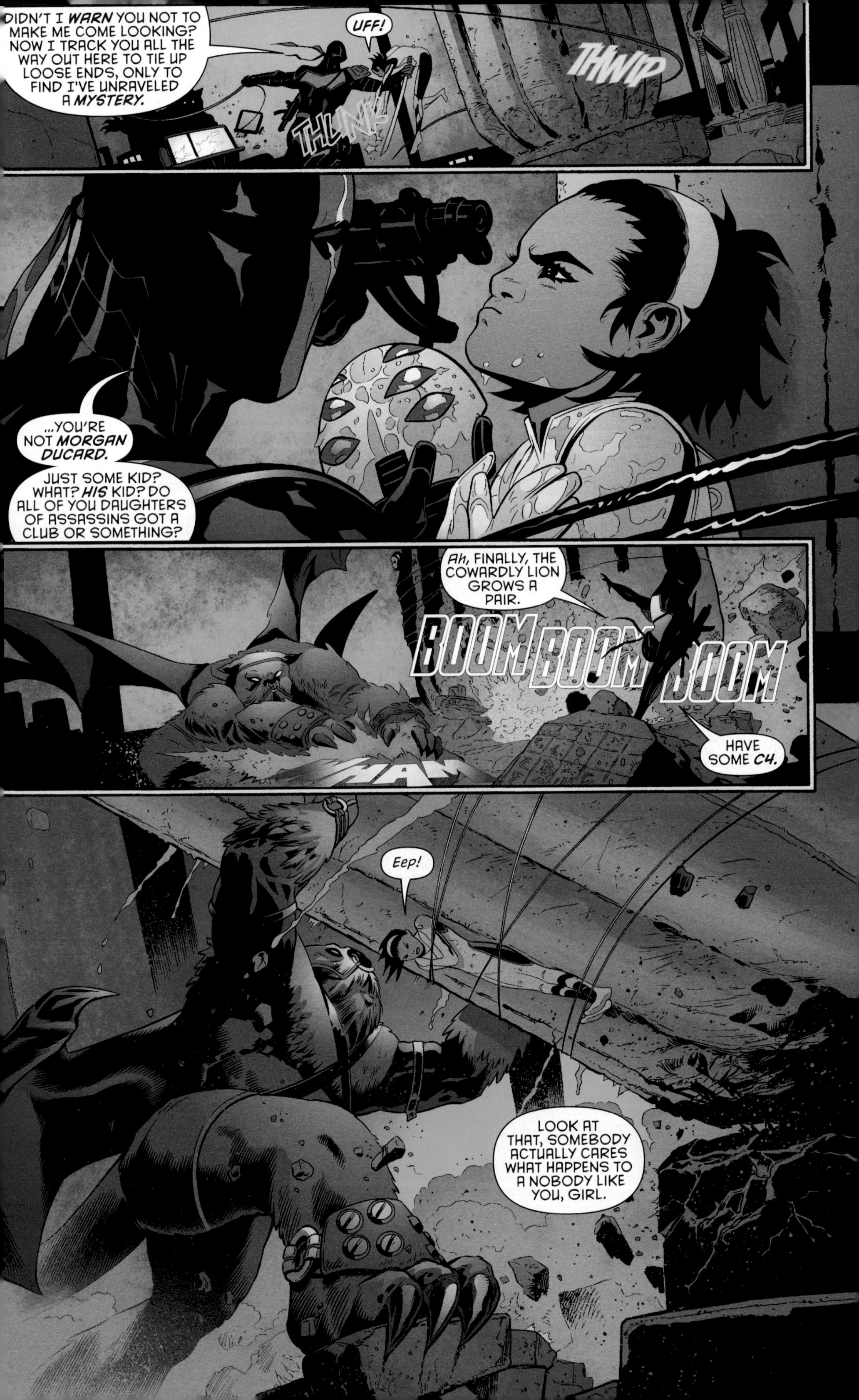

DIDN'T I WARN YOU NOT TO MAKE ME COME LOOKING? NOW I TRACK YOU ALL THE WAY OUT HERE TO TIE UP LOOSE ENDS, ONLY TO FIND I'VE UNRAVELED A MYSTERY.
UFF!
THWIP
THUNK
...YOU'RE NOT MORGAN DUCARD.
JUST SOME KID? WHAT? HIS KID? DO ALL OF YOU DAUGHTERS OF ASSASSINS GOT A CLUB OR SOMETHING?
Ah, FINALLY, THE COWARDLY LION GROWS A PAIR.
BOOM BOOM BOOM
HAVE SOME C4.
WHAM
Eep!
LOOK AT THAT, SOMEBODY ACTUALLY CARES WHAT HAPPENS TO A NOBODY LIKE YOU, GIRL.

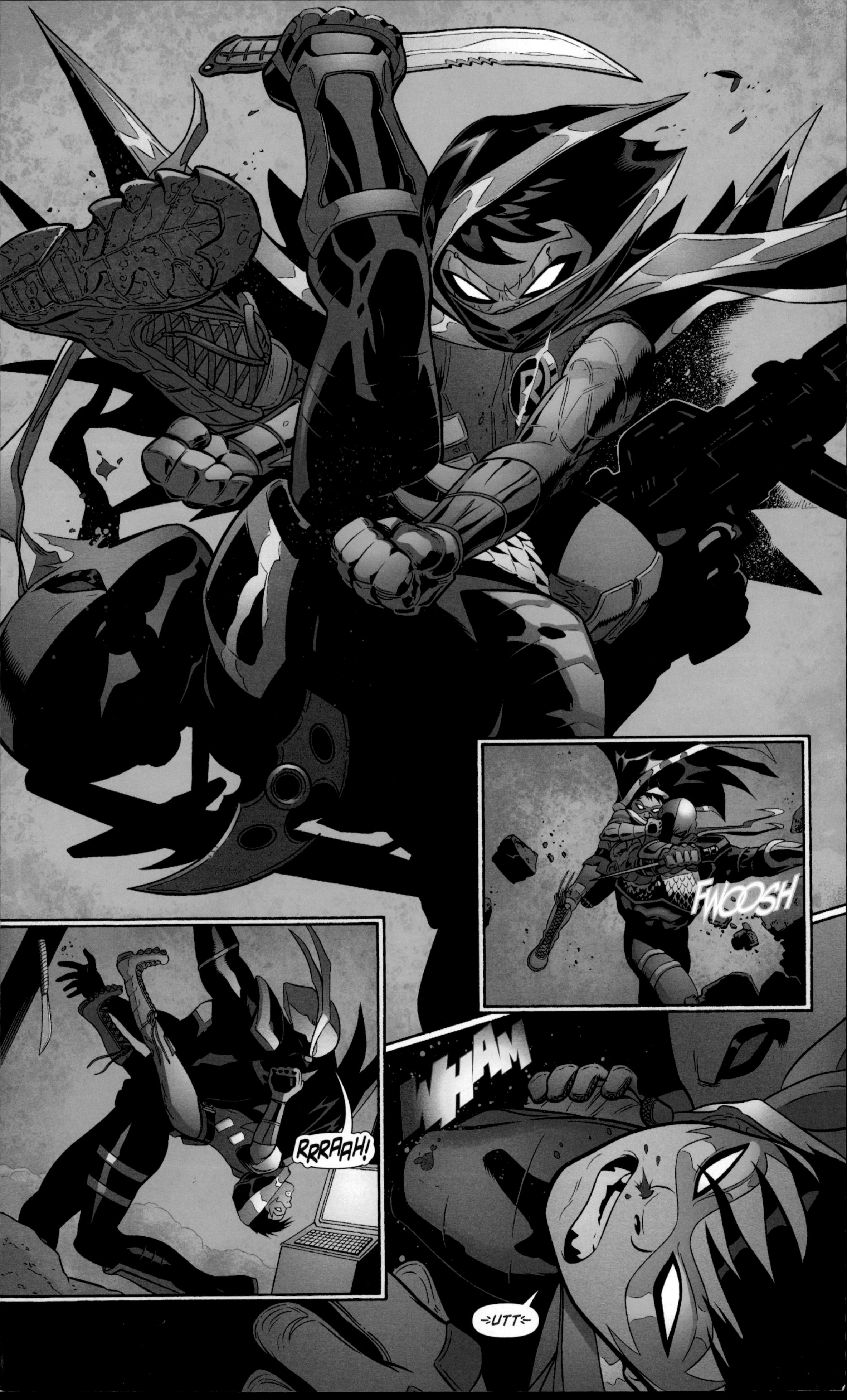
FWOOSH
RRRAAH!
WHAM
UTT

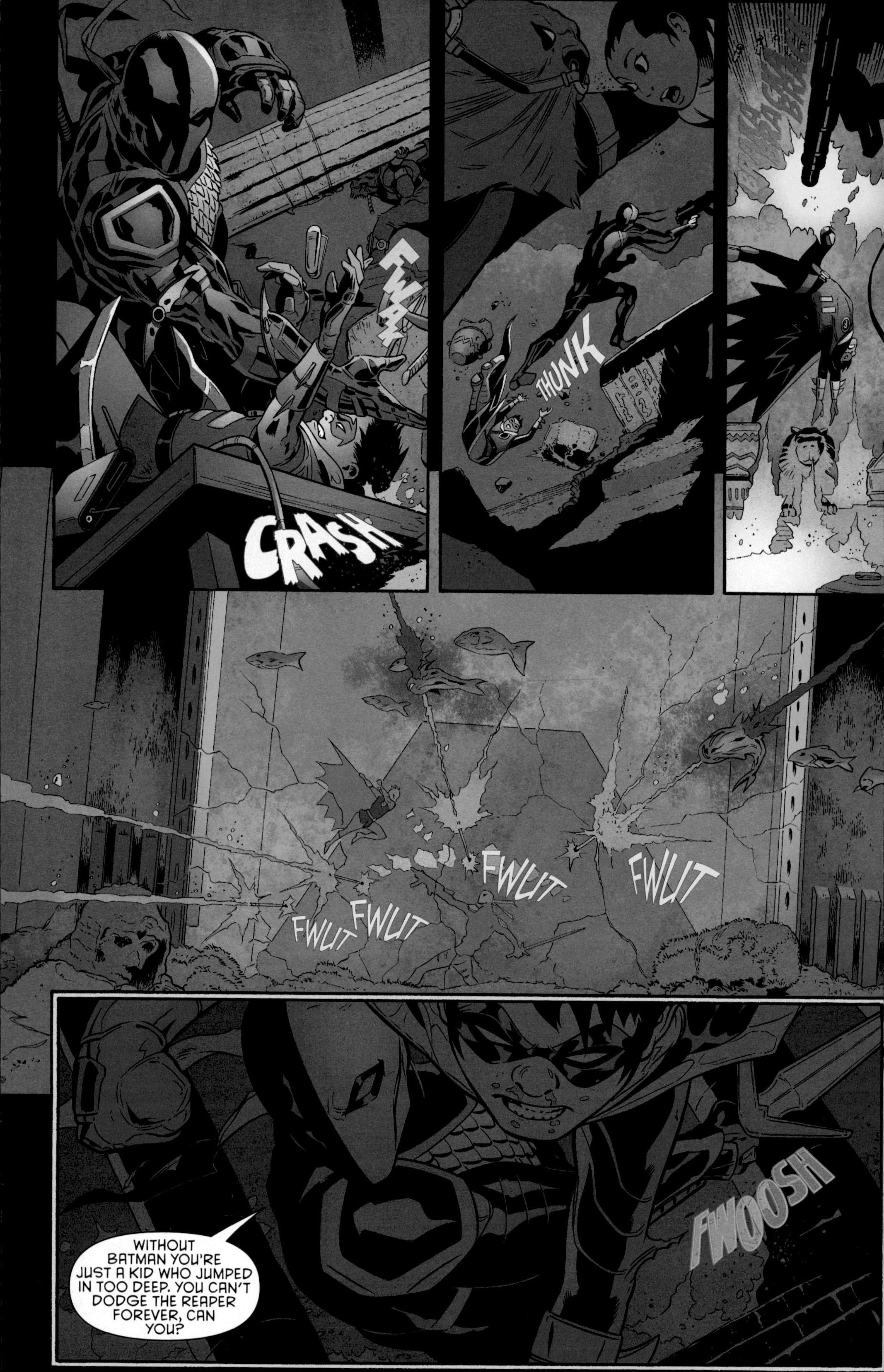
FWAAAK
THUNK
CRASH
FWUT
FWUT
FWUT
FWUT
WITHOUT BATMAN YOU'RE JUST A KID WHO JUMPED IN TOO DEEP. YOU CAN'T DODGE THE REAPER FOREVER, CAN YOU?
FWOOSH

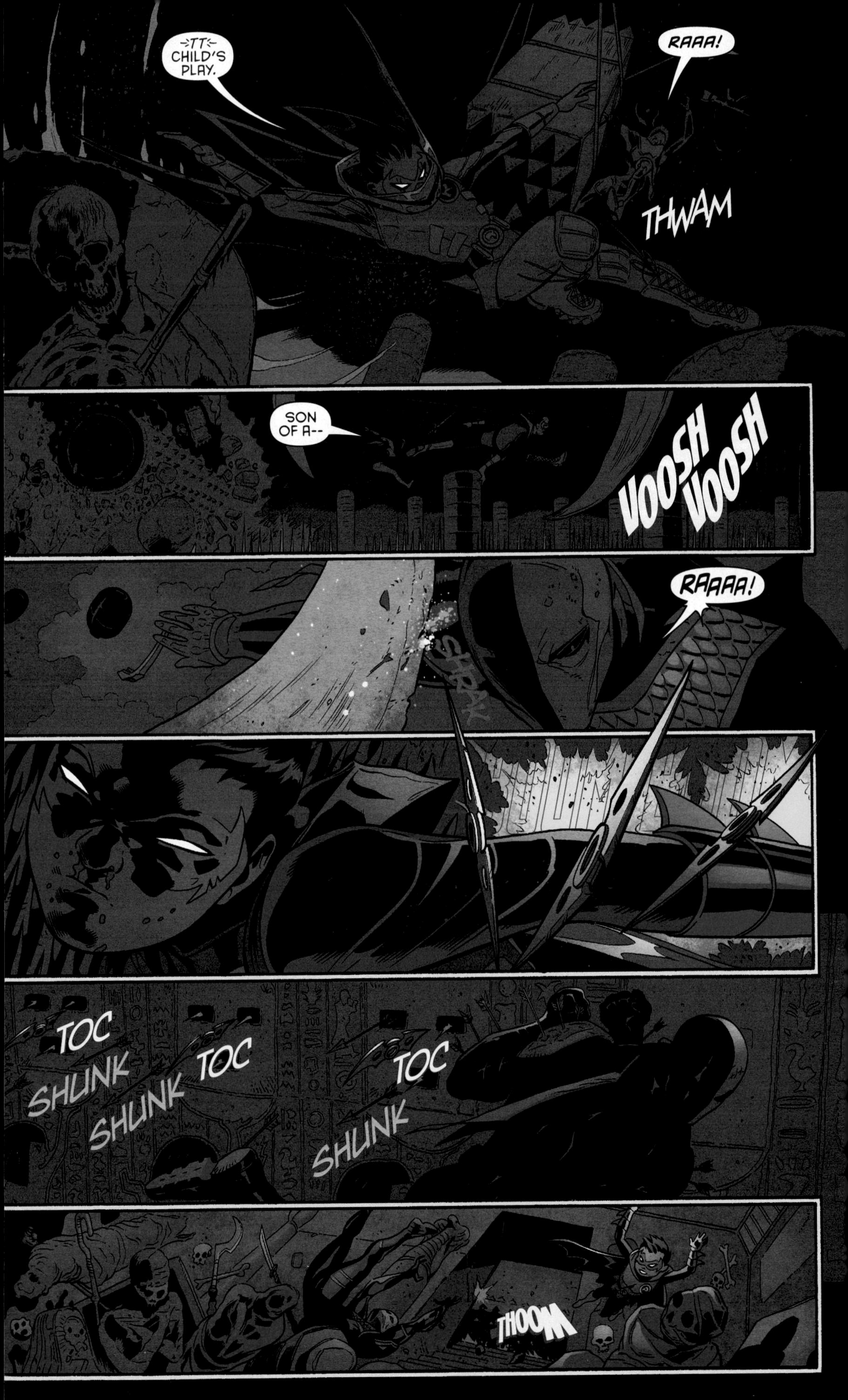
TT
CHILD'S PLAY.
RAAA!
THWAM
SON OF A--
VOOSH
VOOSH
RAAAA!
TOC
SHUNK
SHUNK
TOC
TOC
SHUNK
THOOM

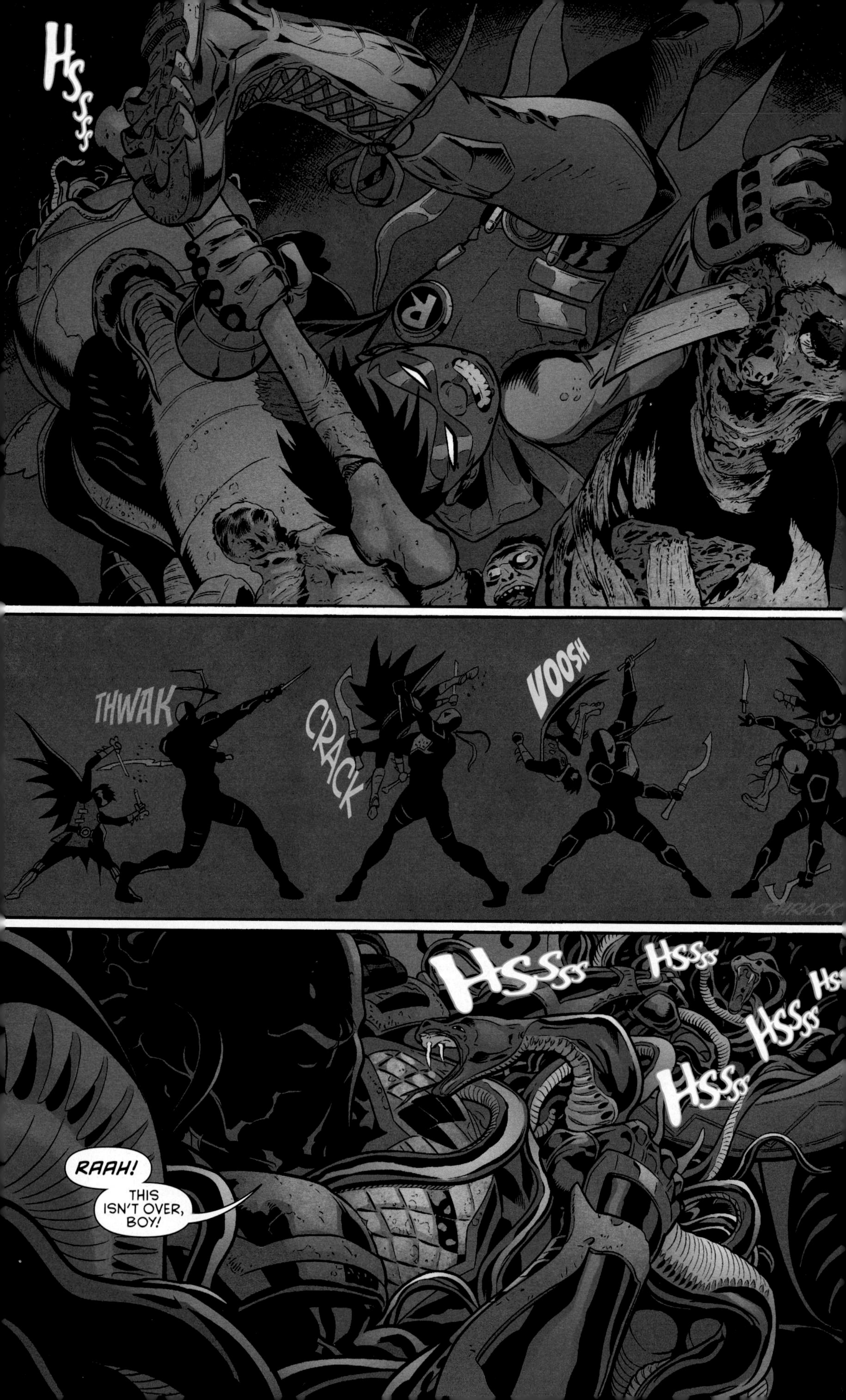
HSSSS
THWAK
CRACK
VOOSH
SHRACK
HSSSS
HSSSS
HSSSS
HSSSS
RAAH!
THIS ISN'T OVER, BOY!

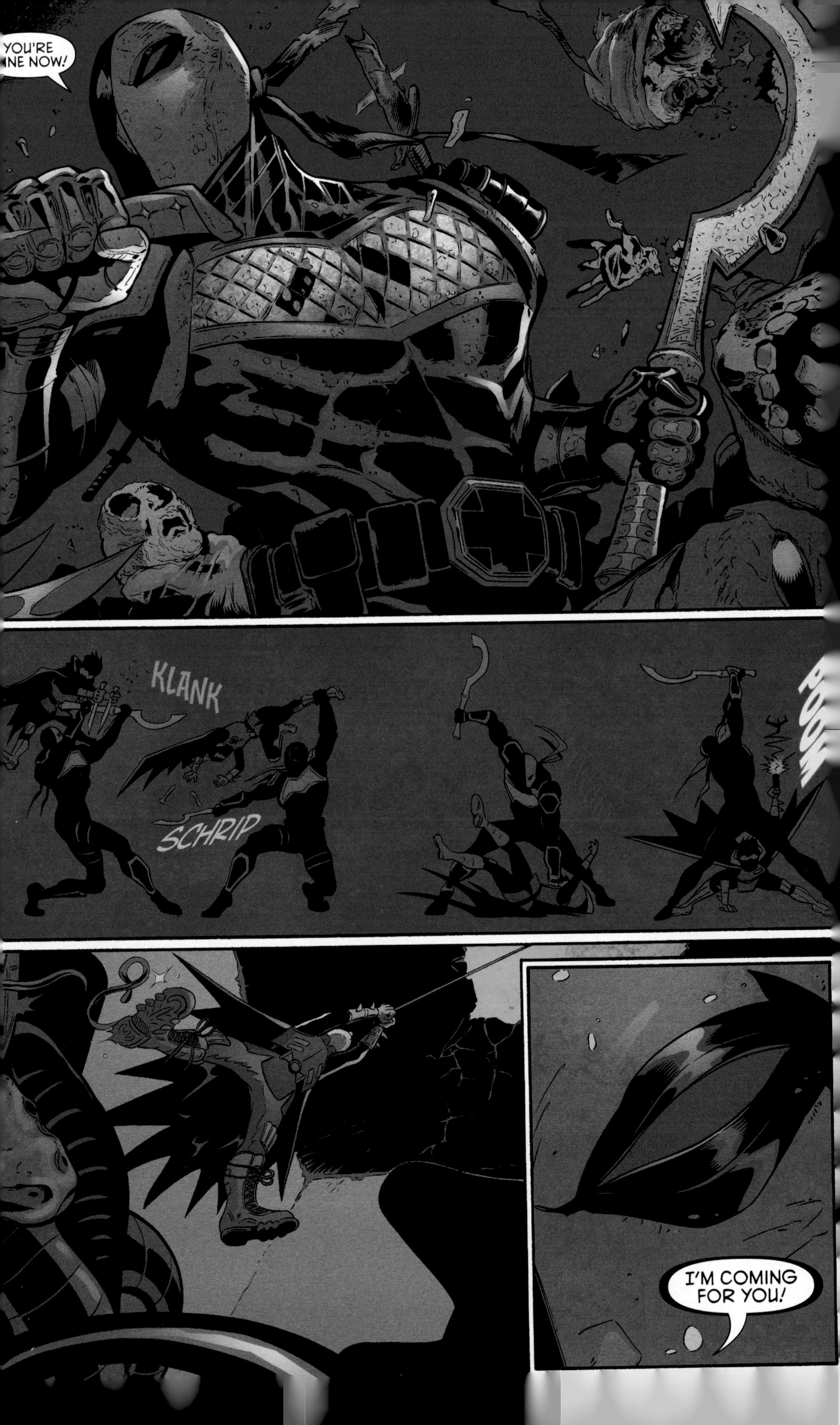

YOU'RE
NE NOW!
KLANK
SCHRIP
POOM
I'M COMING FOR YOU!

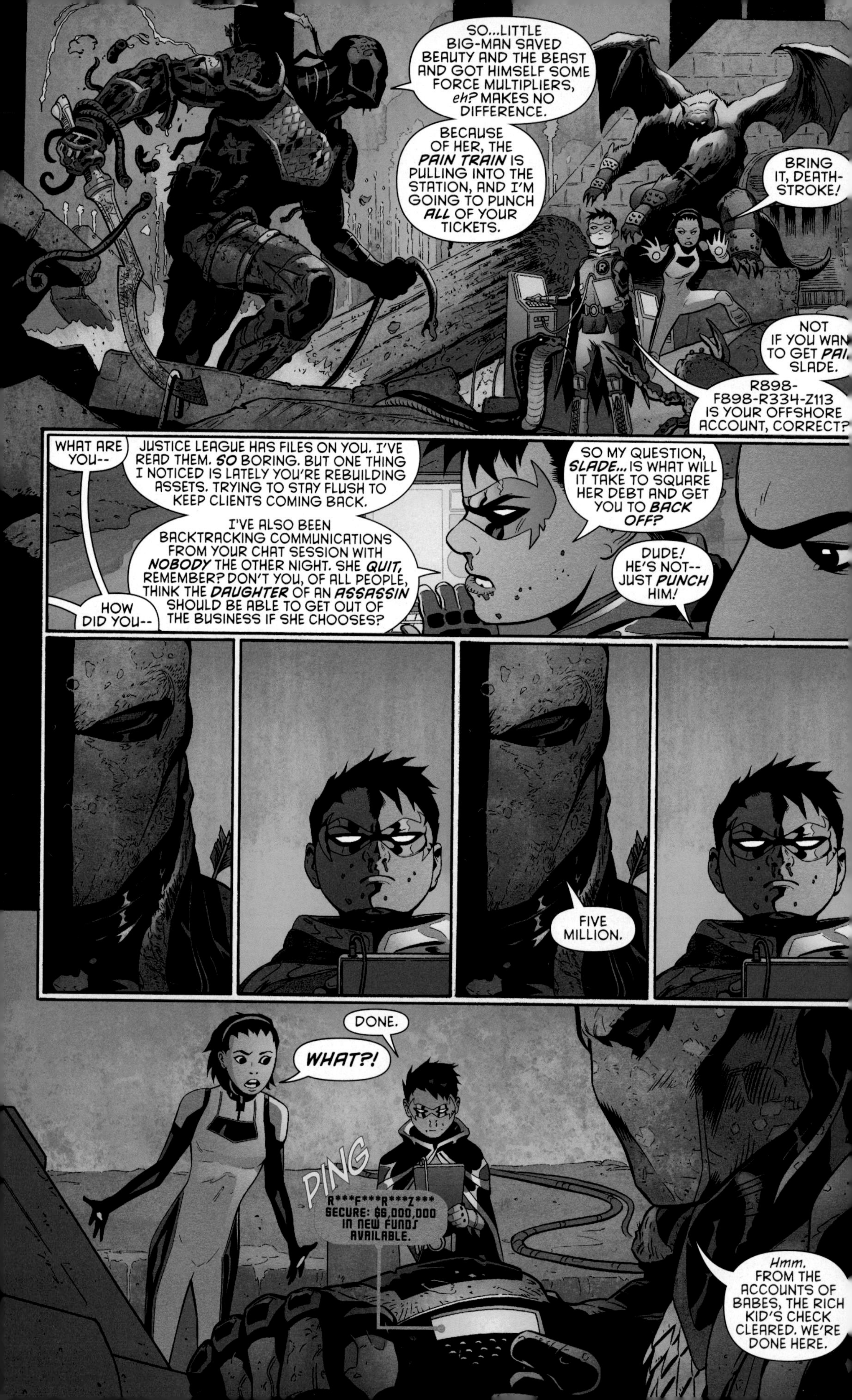
SO...LITTLE BIG-MAN SAVED BEAUTY AND THE BEAST AND GOT HIMSELF SOME FORCE MULTIPLIERS, *eh?* MAKES NO DIFFERENCE.
BECAUSE OF HER, THE *PAIN TRAIN* IS PULLING INTO THE STATION, AND I'M GOING TO PUNCH *ALL* OF YOUR TICKETS.
BRING IT, DEATH-STROKE!
NOT IF YOU WAN TO GET PAI SLADE.
R898-F898-R334-Z113 IS YOUR OFFSHORE ACCOUNT, CORRECT?
WHAT ARE YOU--
JUSTICE LEAGUE HAS FILES ON YOU. I'VE READ THEM. *SO* BORING. BUT ONE THING I NOTICED IS LATELY YOU'RE REBUILDING ASSETS. TRYING TO STAY FLUSH TO KEEP CLIENTS COMING BACK.
HOW DID YOU--
I'VE ALSO BEEN BACKTRACKING COMMUNICATIONS FROM YOUR CHAT SESSION WITH *NOBODY* THE OTHER NIGHT. SHE *QUIT,* REMEMBER? DON'T YOU, OF ALL PEOPLE, THINK THE *DAUGHTER* OF AN *ASSASSIN* SHOULD BE ABLE TO GET OUT OF THE BUSINESS IF SHE CHOOSES?
SO MY QUESTION, *SLADE...* IS WHAT WILL IT TAKE TO SQUARE HER DEBT AND GET YOU TO *BACK OFF?*
DUDE! HE'S NOT-- JUST *PUNCH* HIM!
FIVE MILLION.
DONE.
WHAT?!
PING
R****F****R****Z*** SECURE: $6,000,000 IN NEW FUNDS AVAILABLE.
Hmm. FROM THE ACCOUNTS OF BABES, THE RICH KID'S CHECK CLEARED. WE'RE DONE HERE.

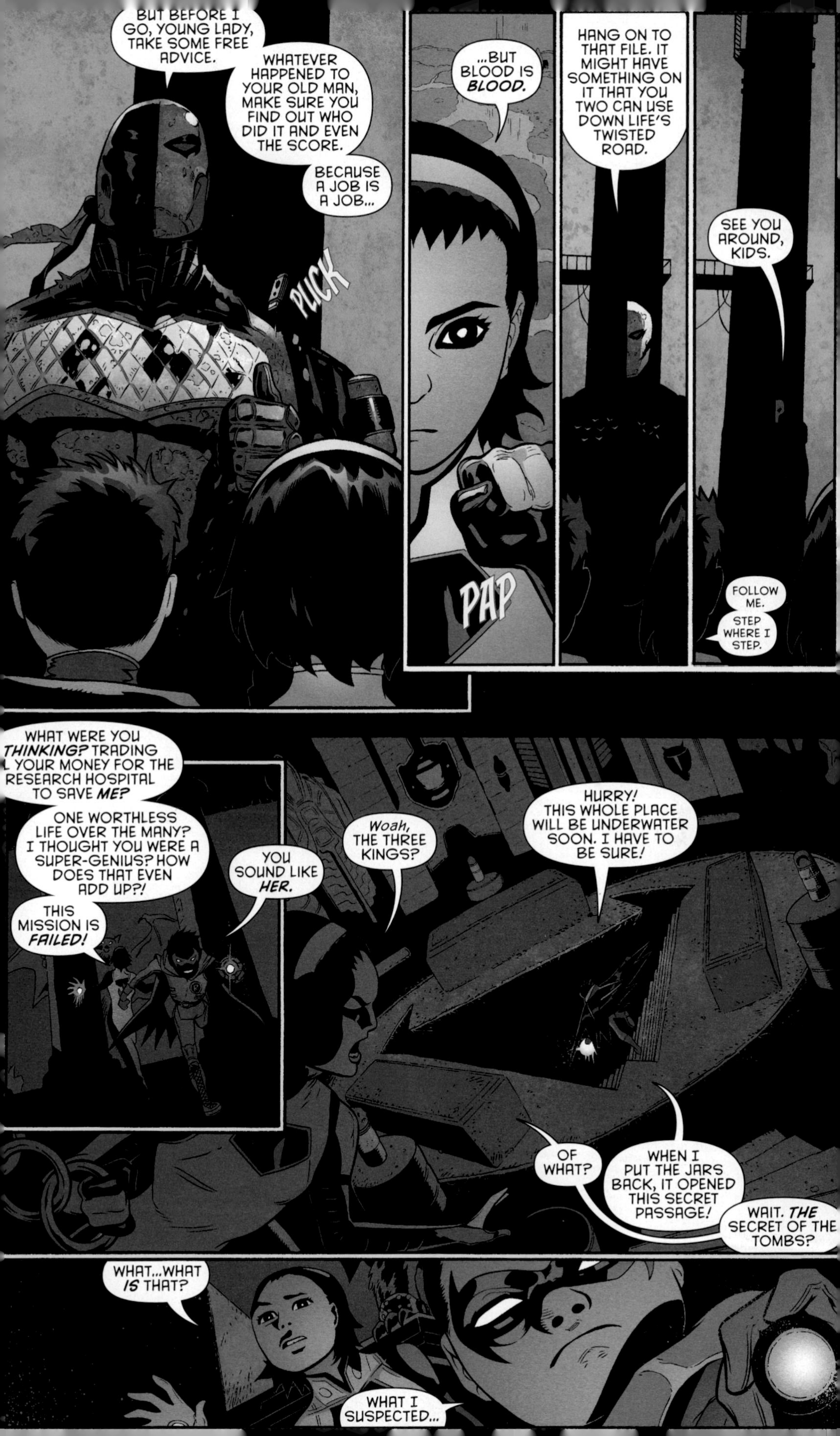
BUT BEFORE I GO, YOUNG LADY, TAKE SOME FREE ADVICE.
WHATEVER HAPPENED TO YOUR OLD MAN, MAKE SURE YOU FIND OUT WHO DID IT AND EVEN THE SCORE.
BECAUSE A JOB IS A JOB...
PLICK
...BUT BLOOD IS *BLOOD.*
PAP
HANG ON TO THAT FILE. IT MIGHT HAVE SOMETHING ON IT THAT YOU TWO CAN USE DOWN LIFE'S TWISTED ROAD.
SEE YOU AROUND, KIDS.
FOLLOW ME.
STEP WHERE I STEP.
WHAT WERE YOU *THINKING?* TRADING L YOUR MONEY FOR THE RESEARCH HOSPITAL TO SAVE *ME?*
ONE WORTHLESS LIFE OVER THE MANY? I THOUGHT YOU WERE A SUPER-GENIUS? HOW DOES THAT EVEN ADD UP?!
THIS MISSION IS *FAILED!*
YOU SOUND LIKE *HER.*
Woah, THE THREE KINGS?
HURRY! THIS WHOLE PLACE WILL BE UNDERWATER SOON. I HAVE TO BE SURE!
OF WHAT?
WHEN I PUT THE JARS BACK, IT OPENED THIS SECRET PASSAGE!
WAIT. *THE* SECRET OF THE TOMBS?
WHAT...WHAT *IS* THAT?
WHAT I SUSPECTED...

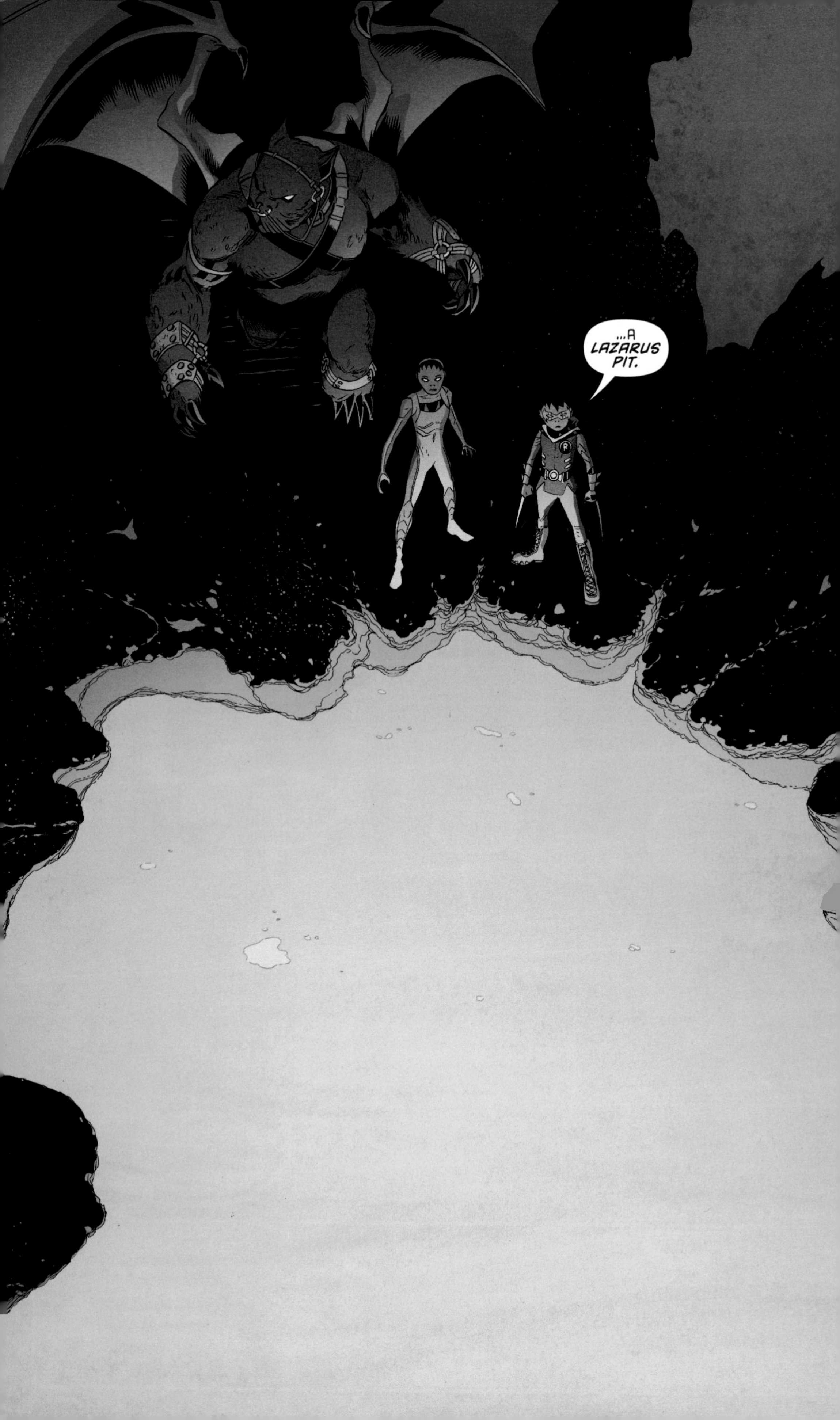
...A LAZARUS PIT.

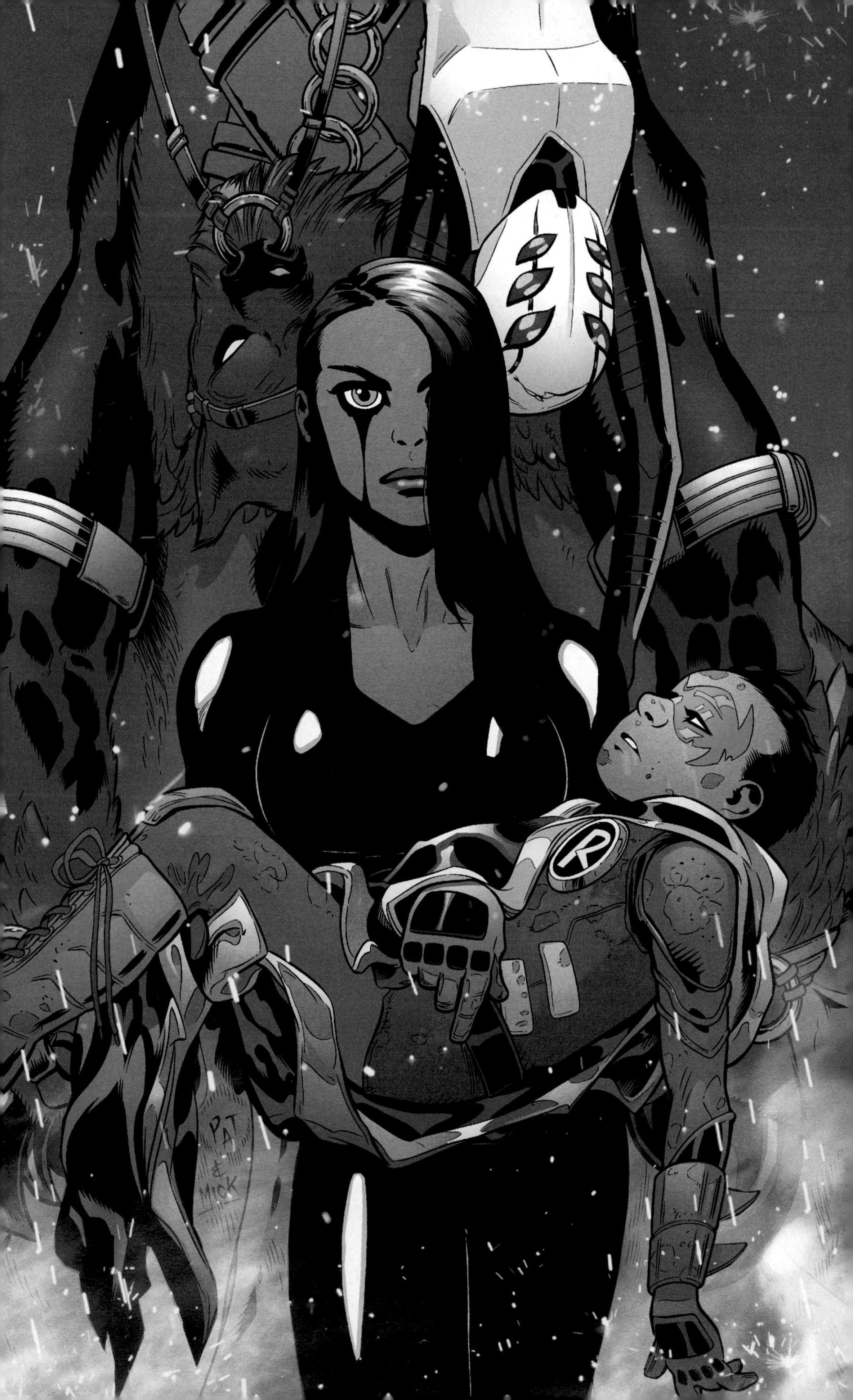
PAT & MICK

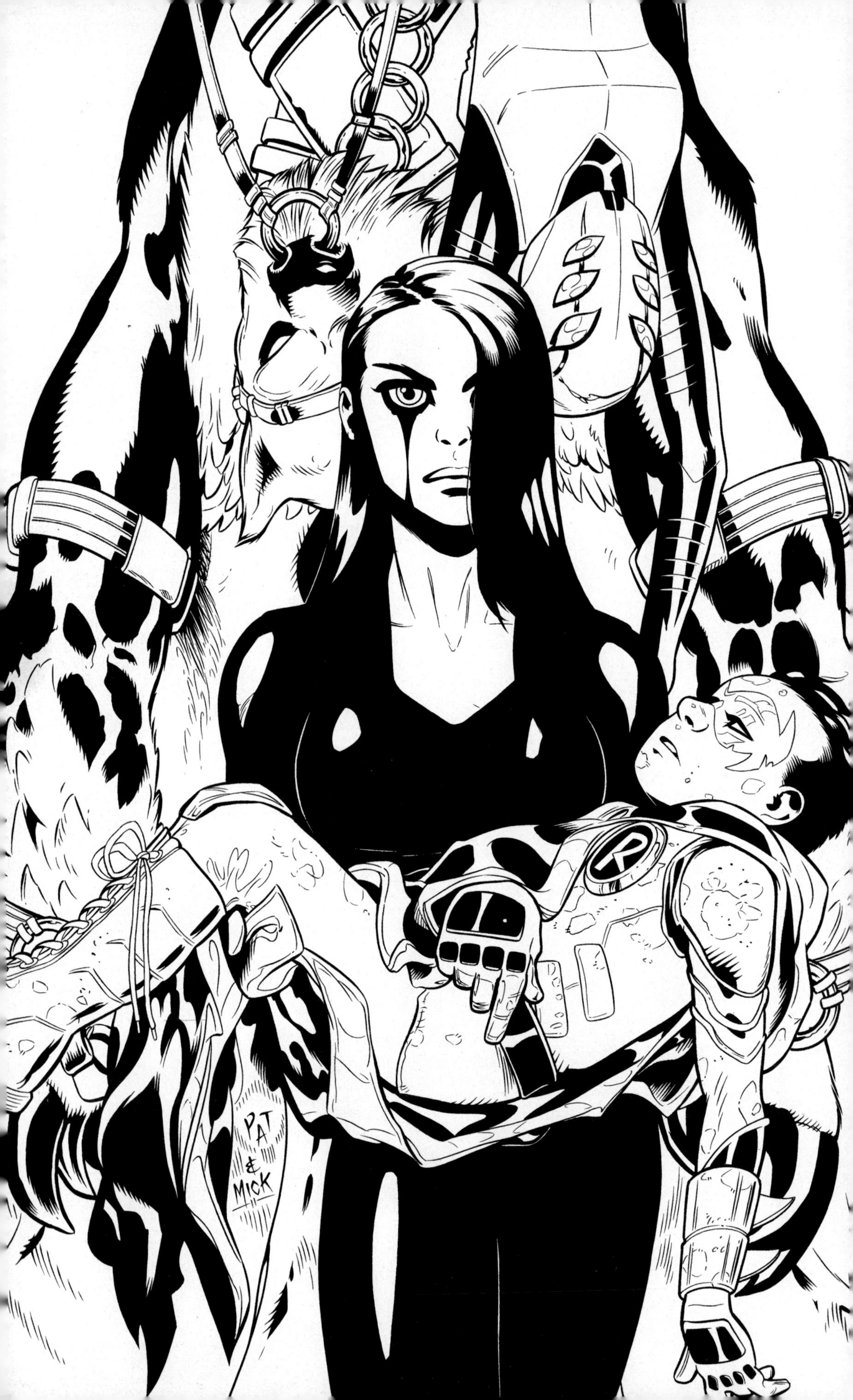
PAT & MICK

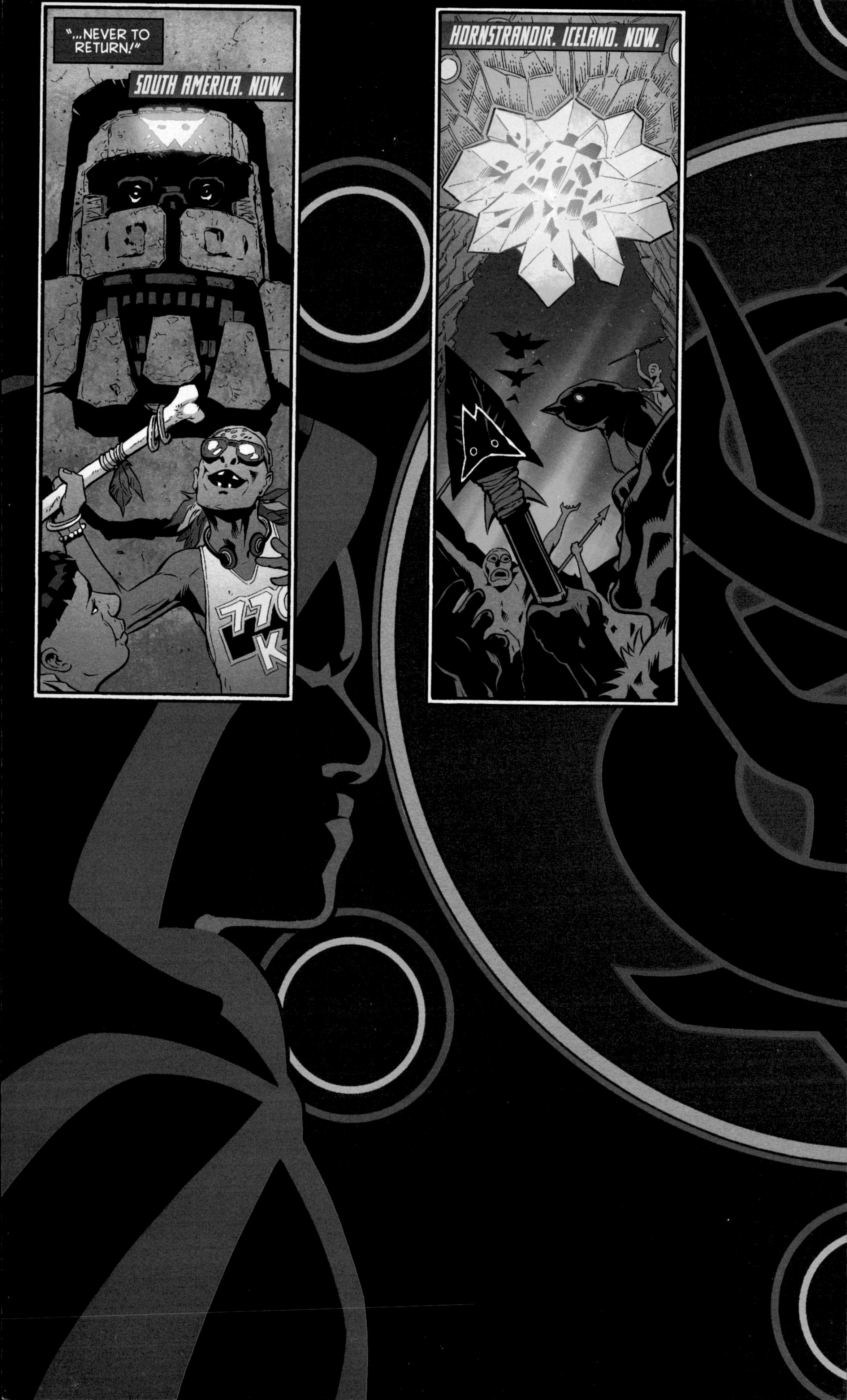
"...NEVER TO RETURN!"
SOUTH AMERICA. NOW.
HORNSTRANDIR. ICELAND. NOW.

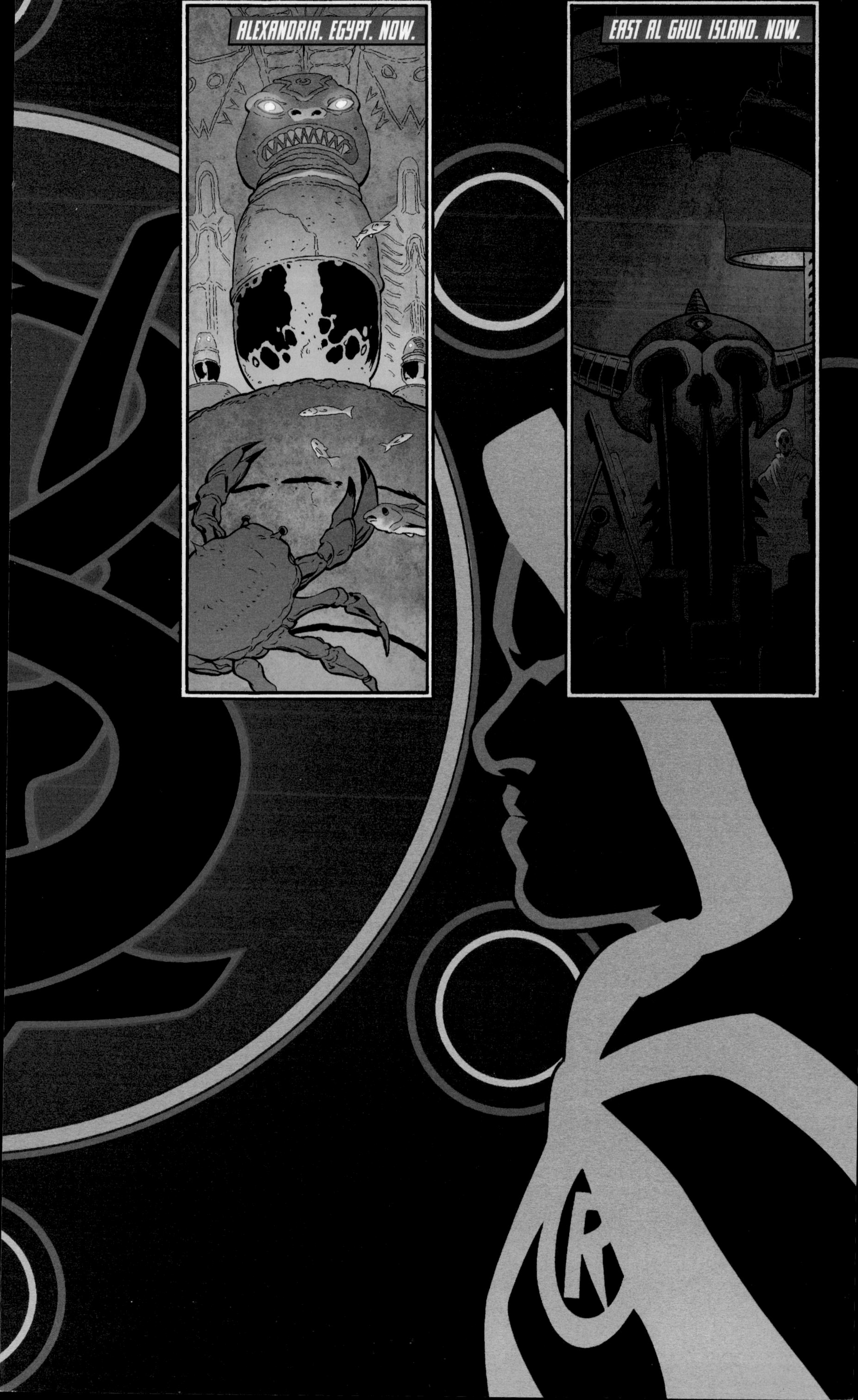
ALEXANDRIA. EGYPT. NOW.
EAST AL GHUL ISLAND. NOW.

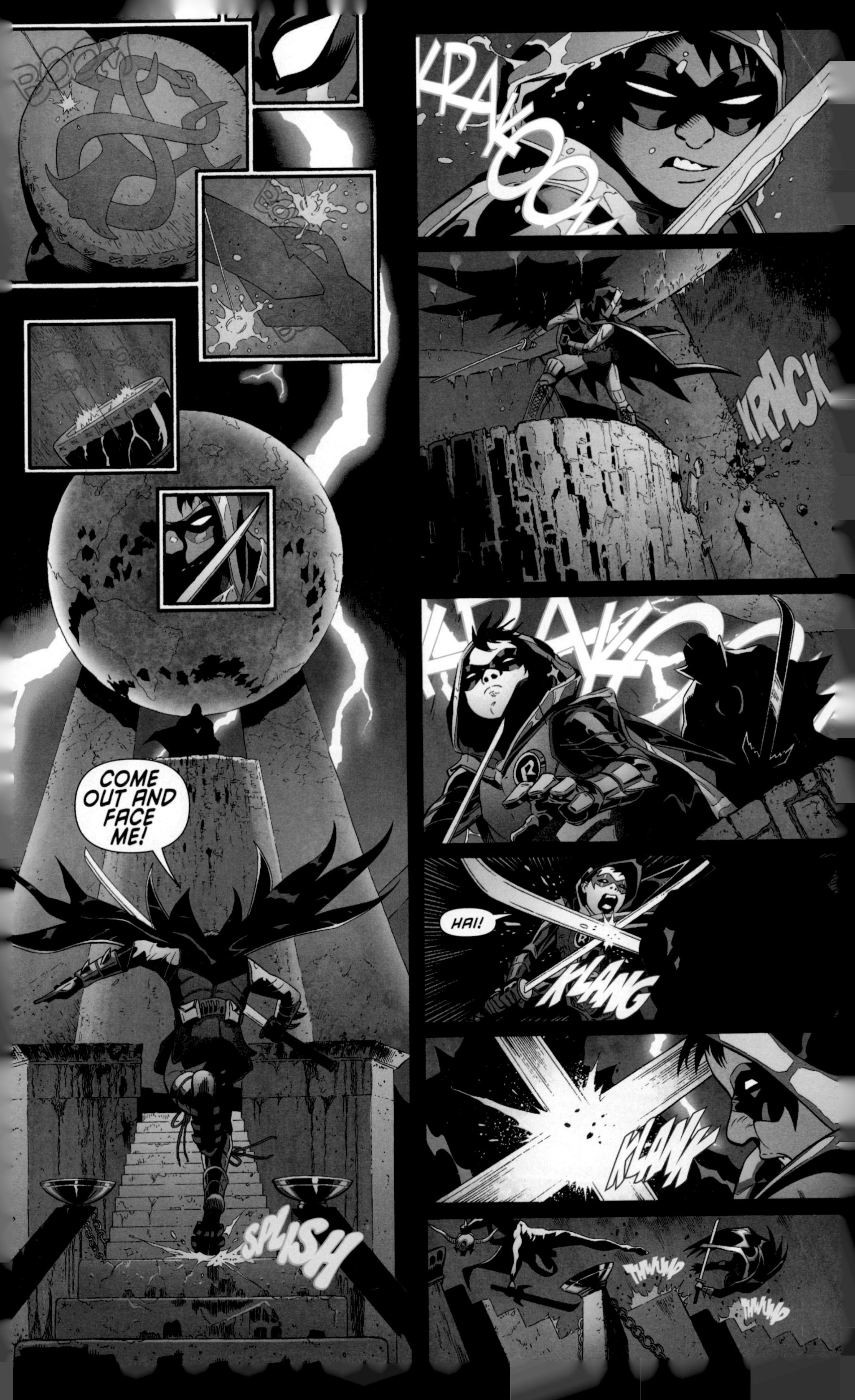
BOOM
COME OUT AND FACE ME!
SPLISH
KRAKOOM
KRACK
HAI!
KLANG
KLANK
THWUMP
THWUMP

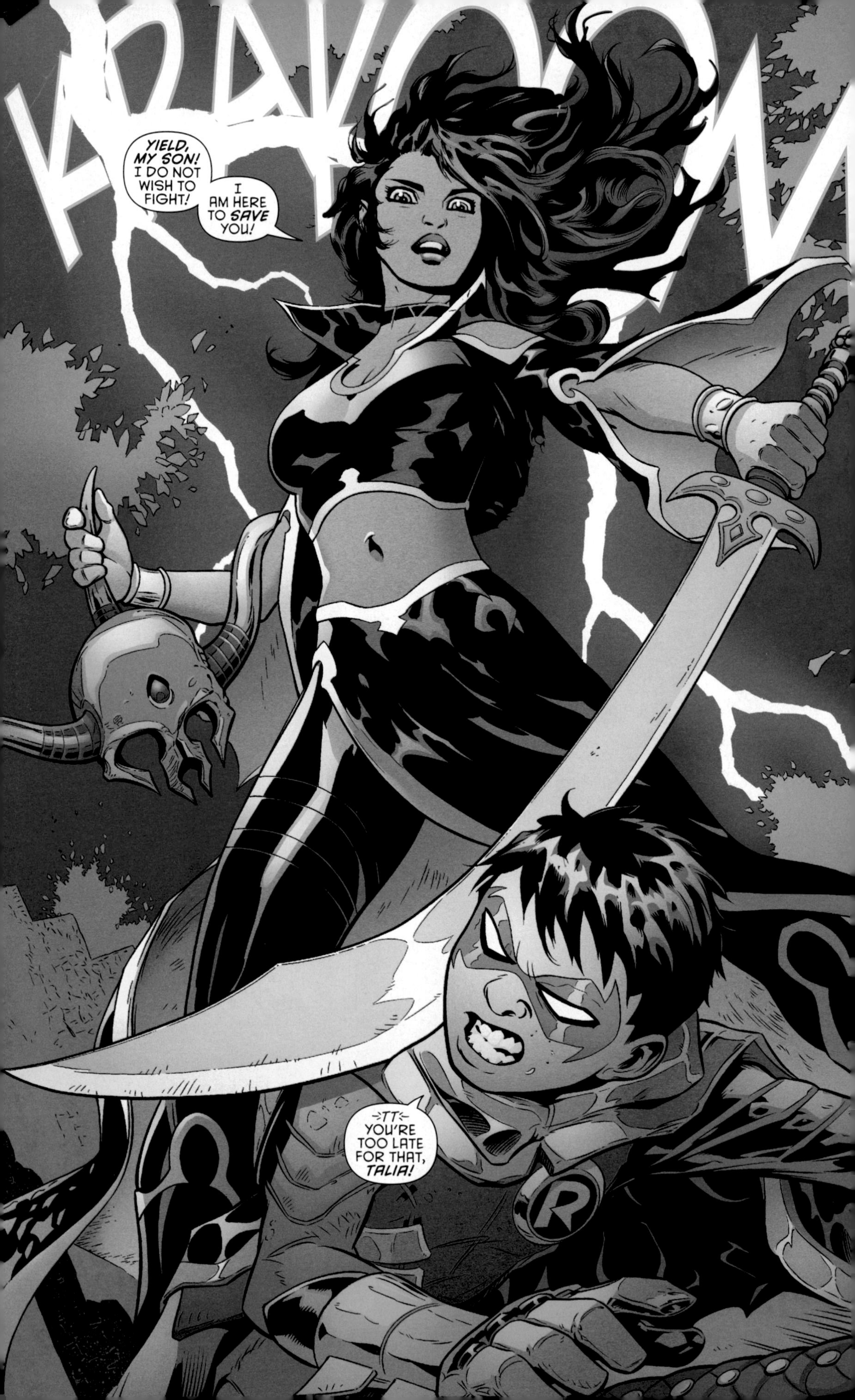
YIELD, MY SON! I DO NOT WISH TO FIGHT!
I AM HERE TO SAVE YOU!
-TT- YOU'RE TOO LATE FOR THAT, TALIA!

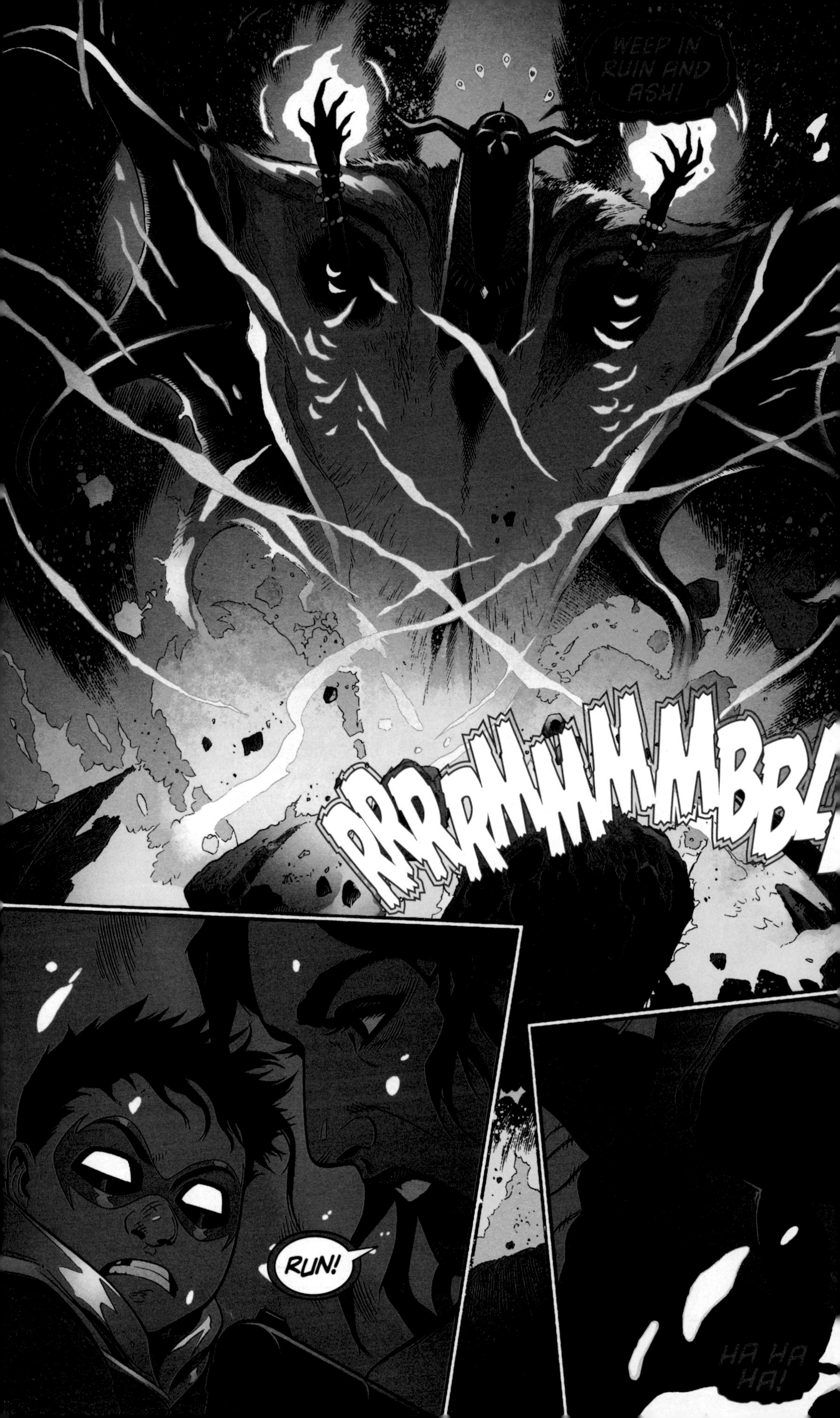
WEEP IN RUIN AND ASH!
RRRRMMMMMBBL
RUN!
HA HA HA!

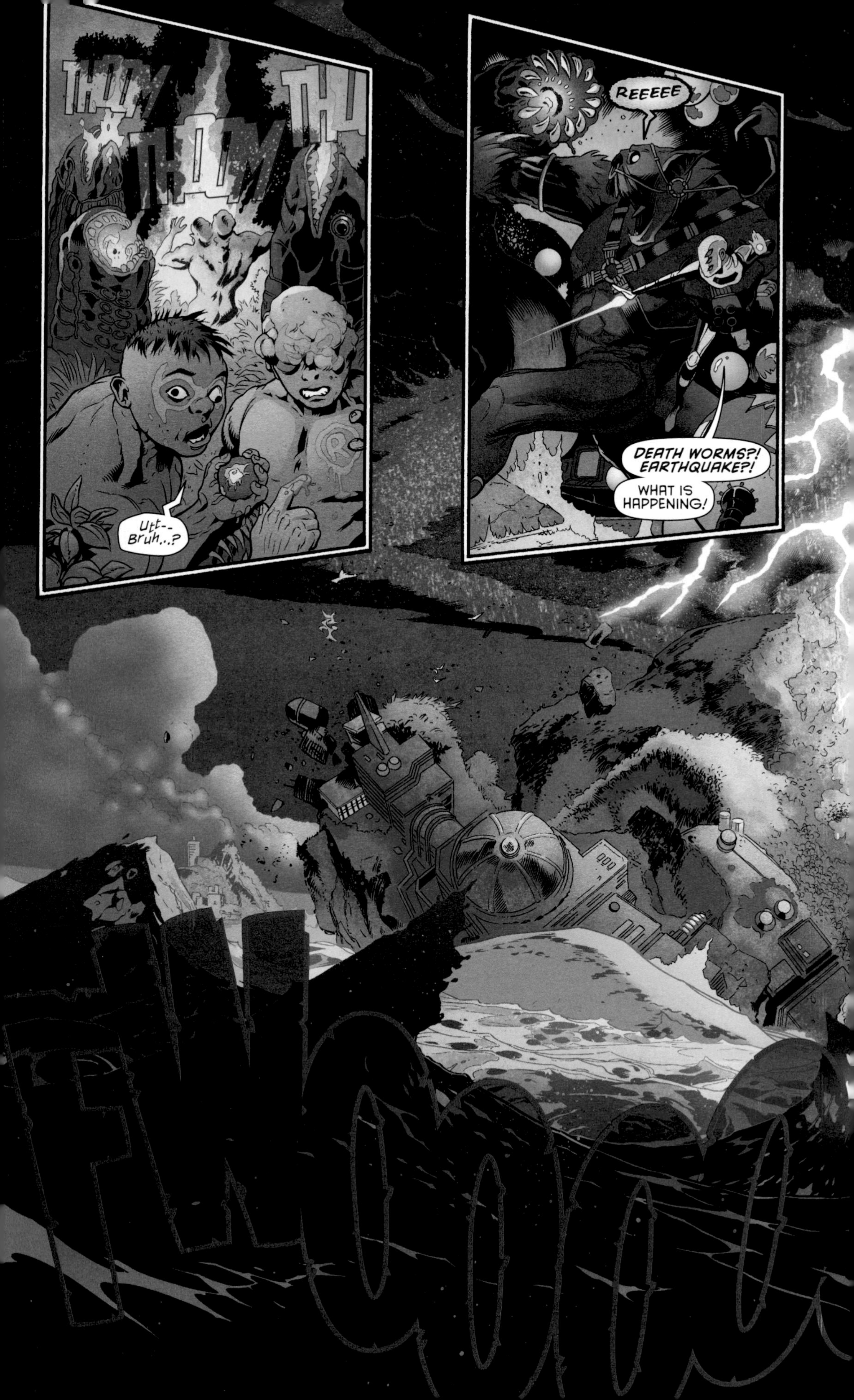
THUM
THUM
THU
Utt--
Bruh...?
REEEEE
DEATH WORMS?! EARTHQUAKE?!
WHAT IS HAPPENING!
FWOOOOO

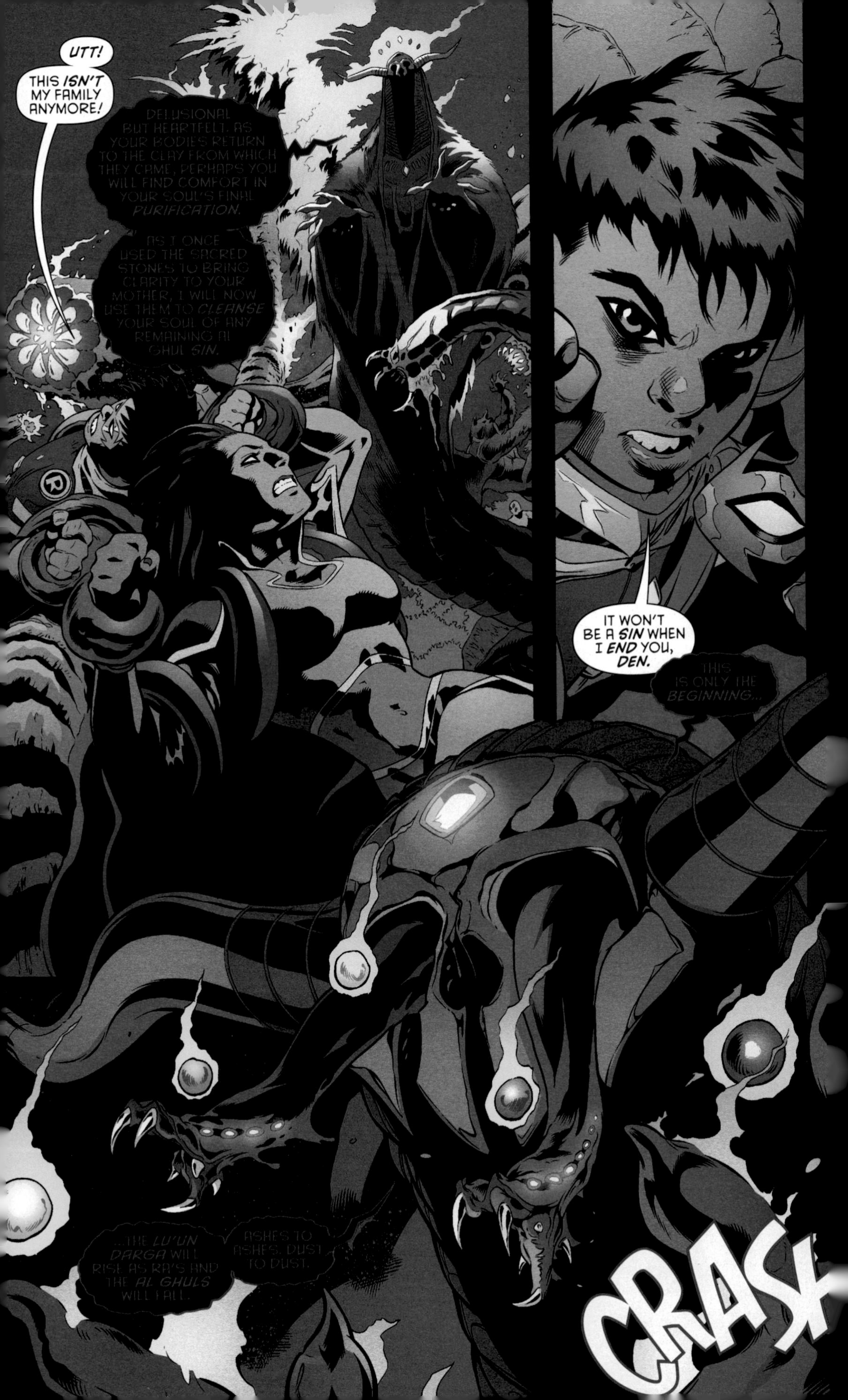
UTT!
THIS ISN'T MY FAMILY ANYMORE!
DELUSIONAL BUT HEARTFELT. AS YOUR BODIES RETURN TO THE CLAY FROM WHICH THEY CAME, PERHAPS YOU WILL FIND COMFORT IN YOUR SOUL'S FINAL PURIFICATION.
AS I ONCE USED THE SACRED STONES TO BRING CLARITY TO YOUR MOTHER, I WILL NOW USE THEM TO CLEANSE YOUR SOUL OF ANY REMAINING AL GHUL SIN.
IT WON'T BE A SIN WHEN I END YOU, DEN.
THIS IS ONLY THE BEGINNING...
...THE LU'UN DARGA WILL RISE AS RA'S AND THE AL GHULS WILL FALL.
ASHES TO ASHES. DUST TO DUST.
CRASH

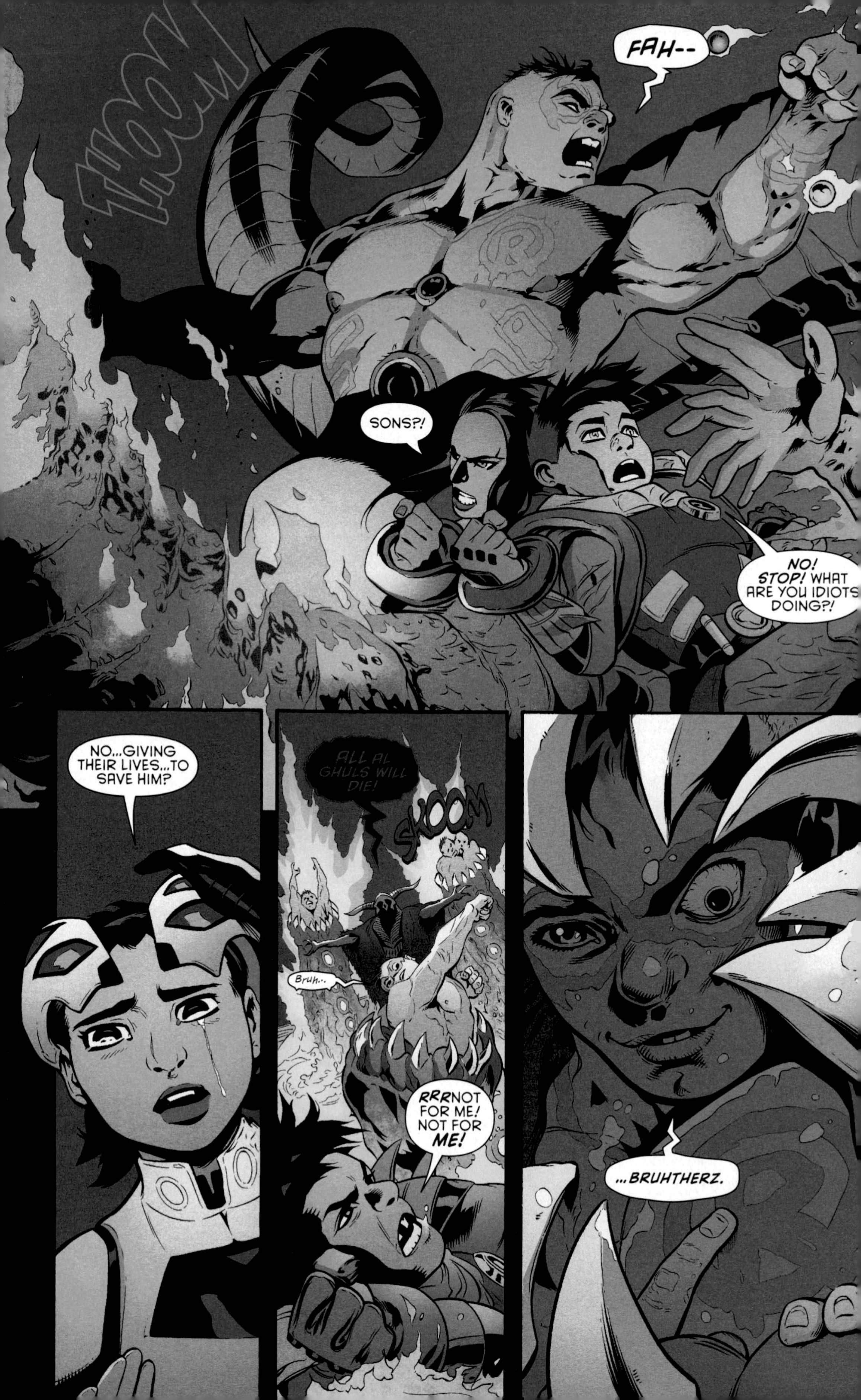
FAH--
SONS?!
NO! STOP! WHAT ARE YOU IDIOTS DOING?!
NO...GIVING THEIR LIVES...TO SAVE HIM?
ALL AL GHULS WILL DIE!
SKOOM
Bruh..
RRRNOT FOR ME! NOT FOR ME!
...BRUHTHERZ.

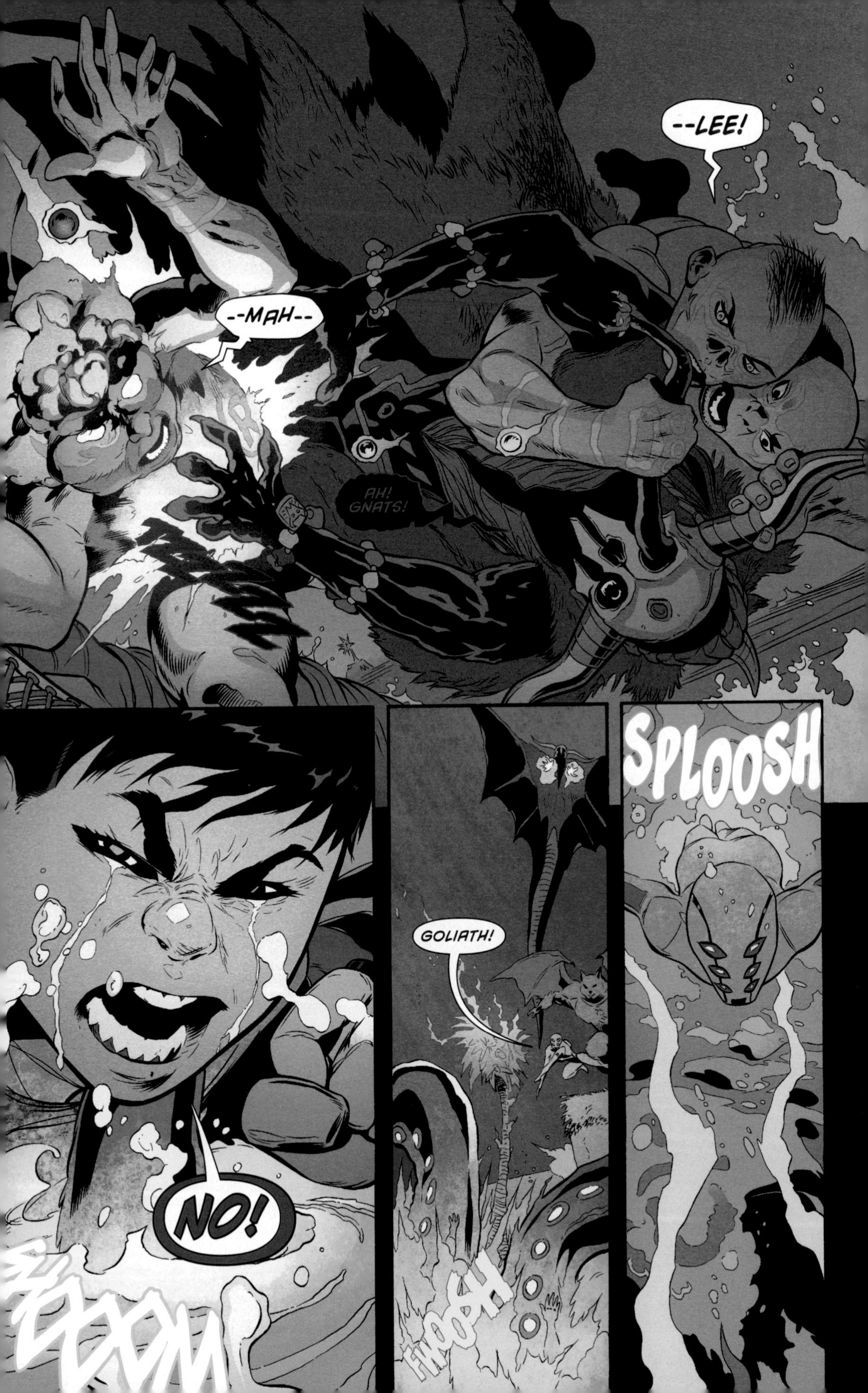
--MAH--
--LEE!
AH! GNATS!
NO!
GOLIATH!
FWOOSH
SPLOOSH

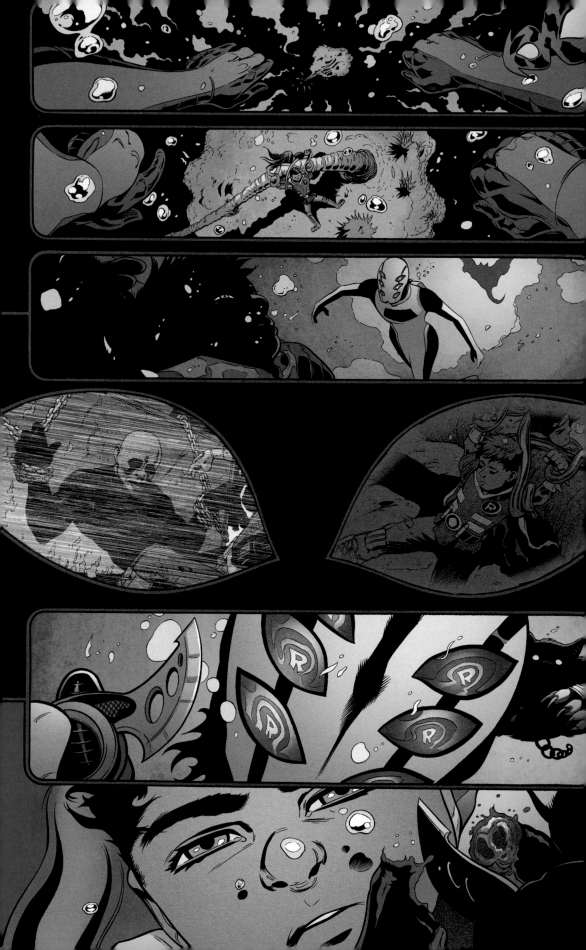

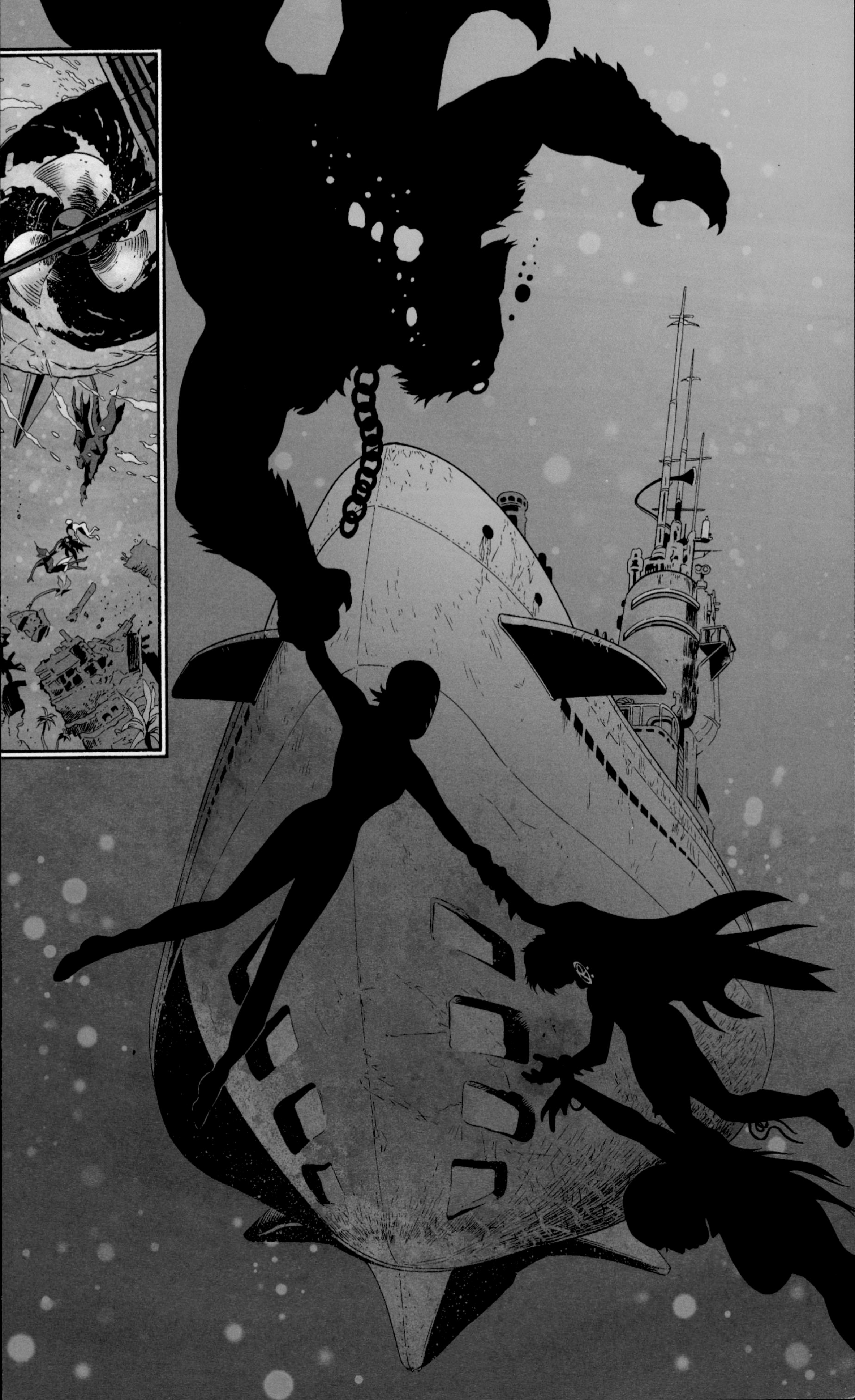

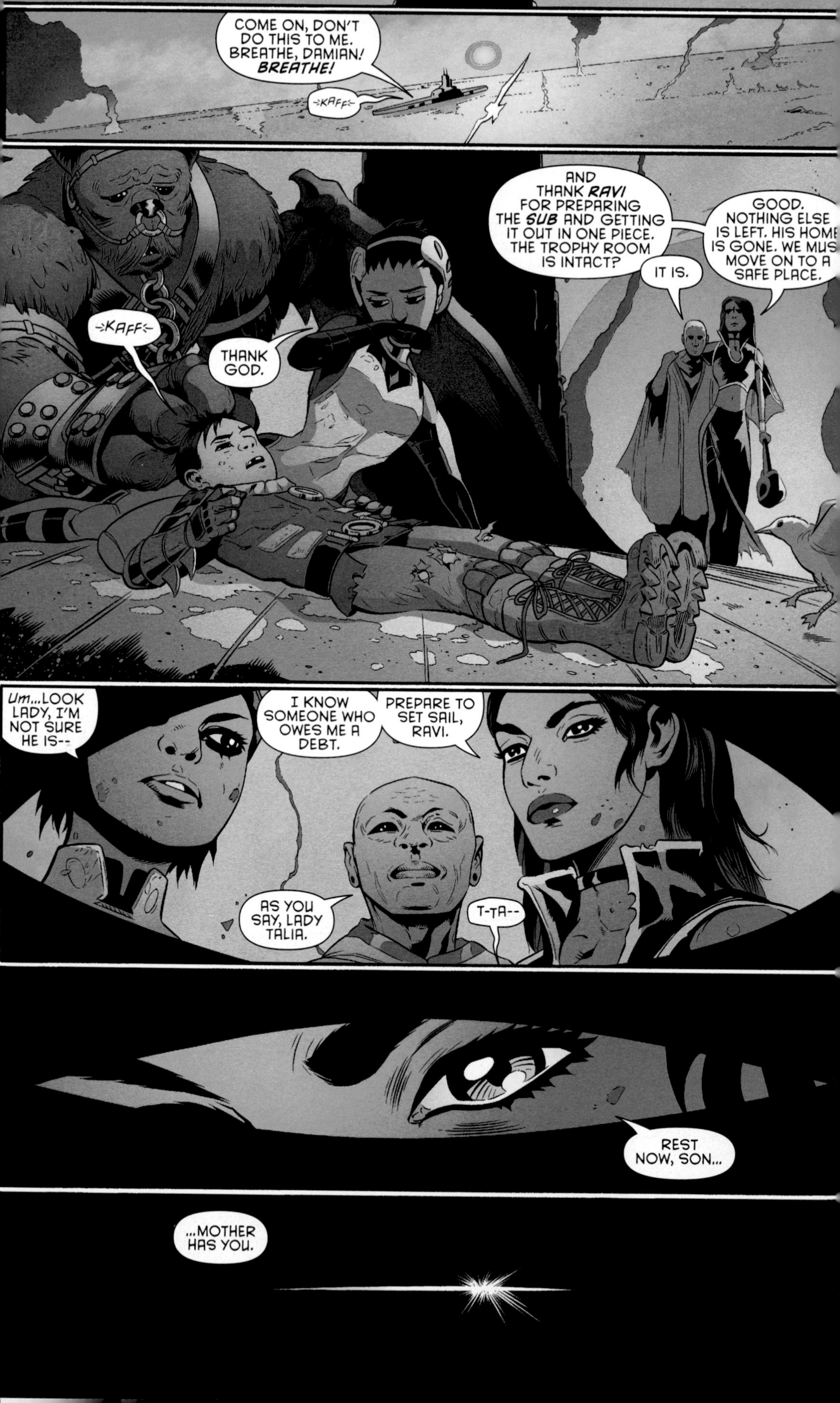

COME ON, DON'T DO THIS TO ME. BREATHE, DAMIAN! **BREATHE!**
KAFF
KAFF
THANK GOD.
AND THANK *RAVI* FOR PREPARING THE *SUB* AND GETTING IT OUT IN ONE PIECE. THE TROPHY ROOM IS INTACT?
IT IS.
GOOD. NOTHING ELSE IS LEFT. HIS HOME IS GONE. WE MUS MOVE ON TO A SAFE PLACE.
Um...LOOK LADY, I'M NOT SURE HE IS--
I KNOW SOMEONE WHO OWES ME A DEBT.
PREPARE TO SET SAIL, RAVI.
AS YOU SAY, LADY TALIA.
T-TA--
REST NOW, SON...
...MOTHER HAS YOU.

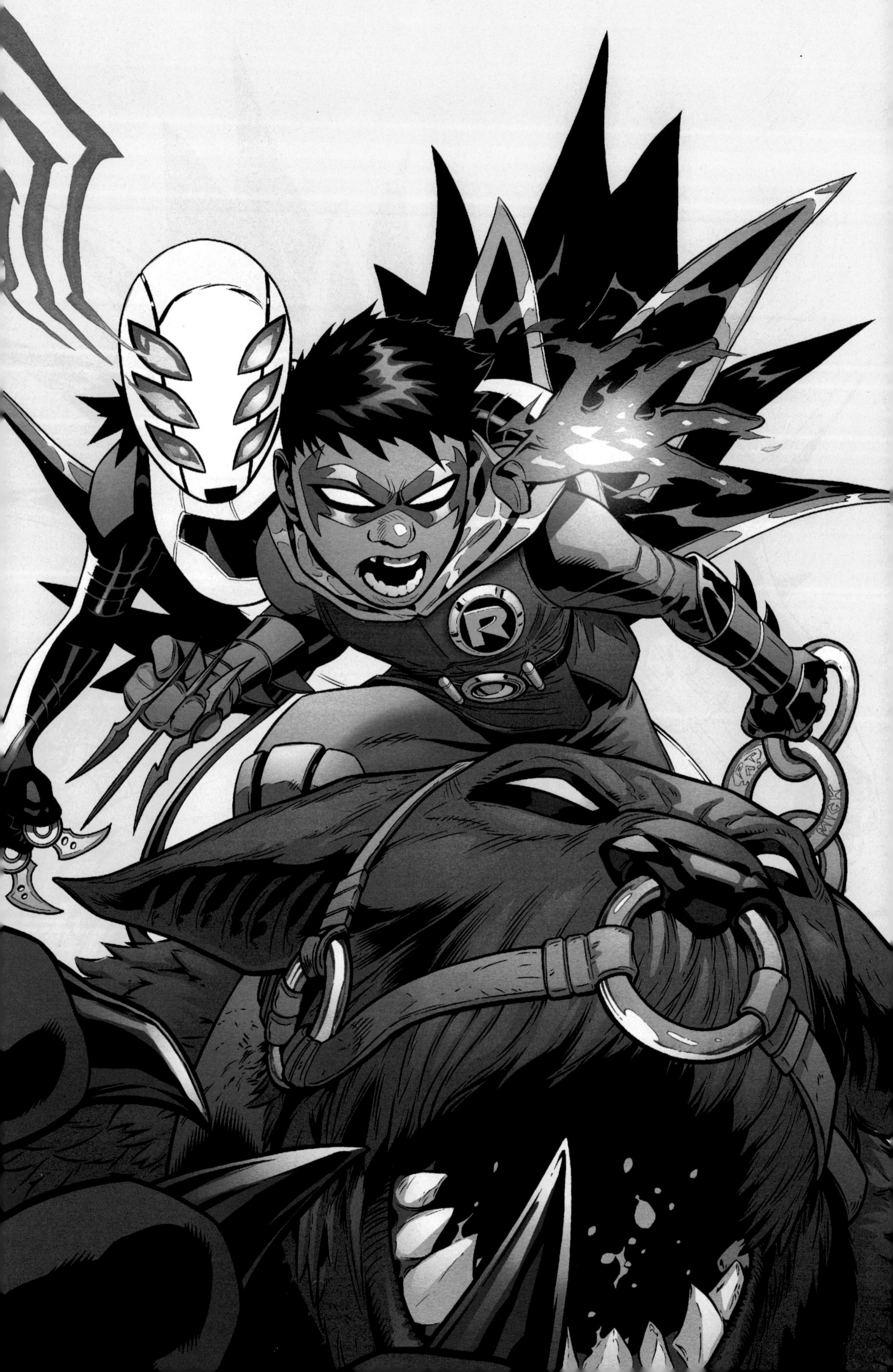

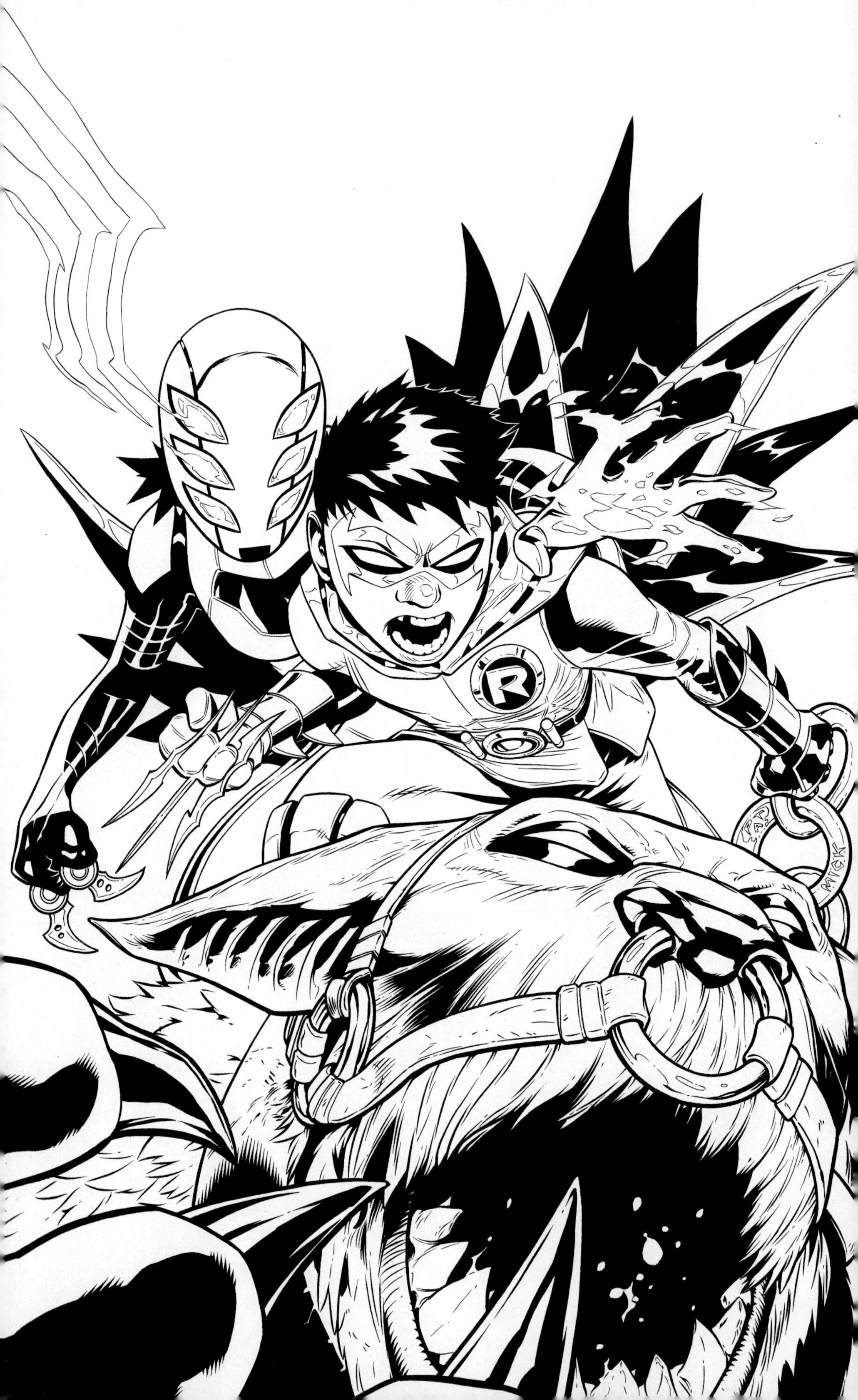

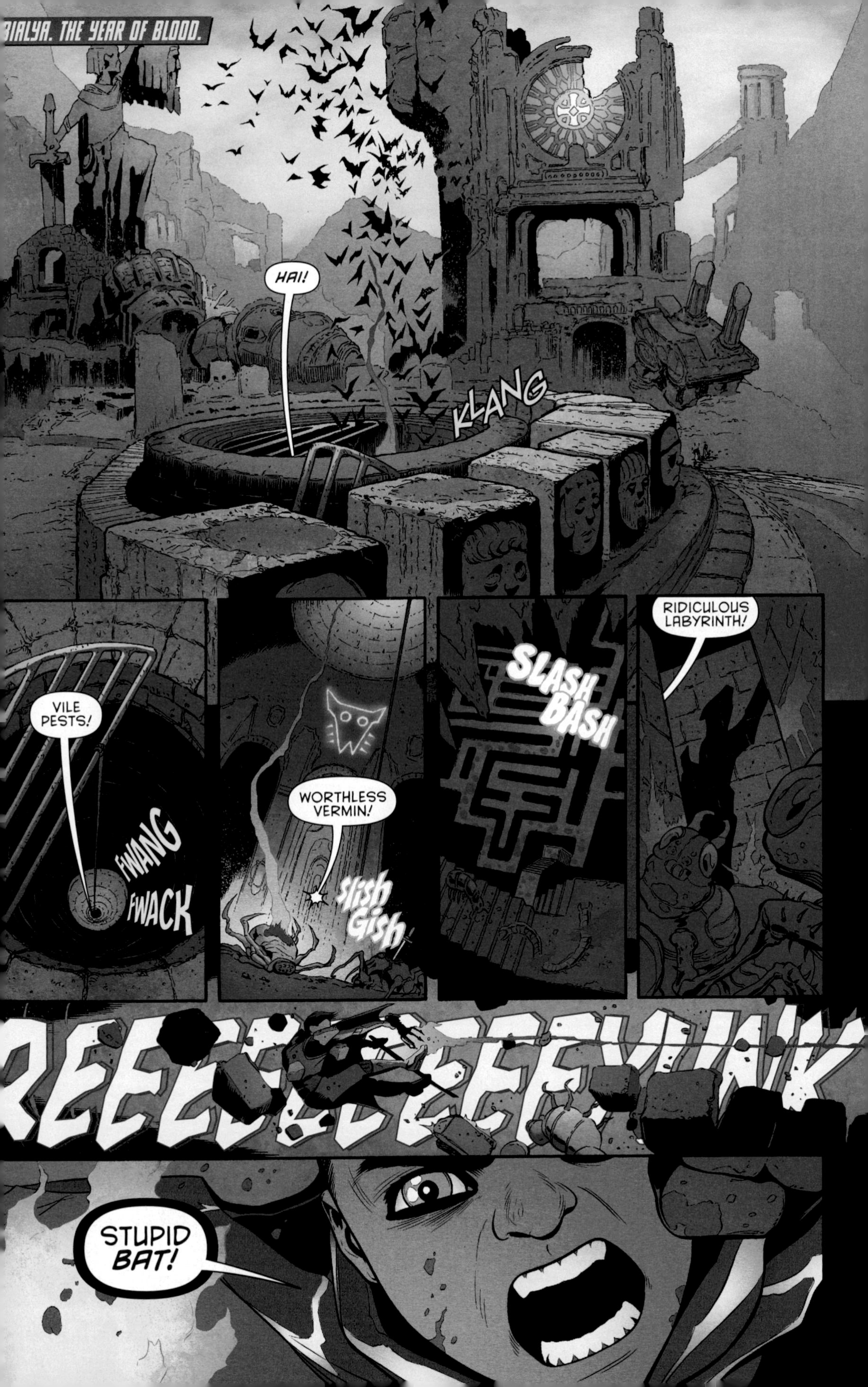

BIALYA. THE YEAR OF BLOOD.
HAI!
KLANG
VILE PESTS!
FWANG
FWACK
WORTHLESS VERMIN!
slish
Gish
SLASH
BASH
RIDICULOUS LABYRINTH!
STUPID BAT!

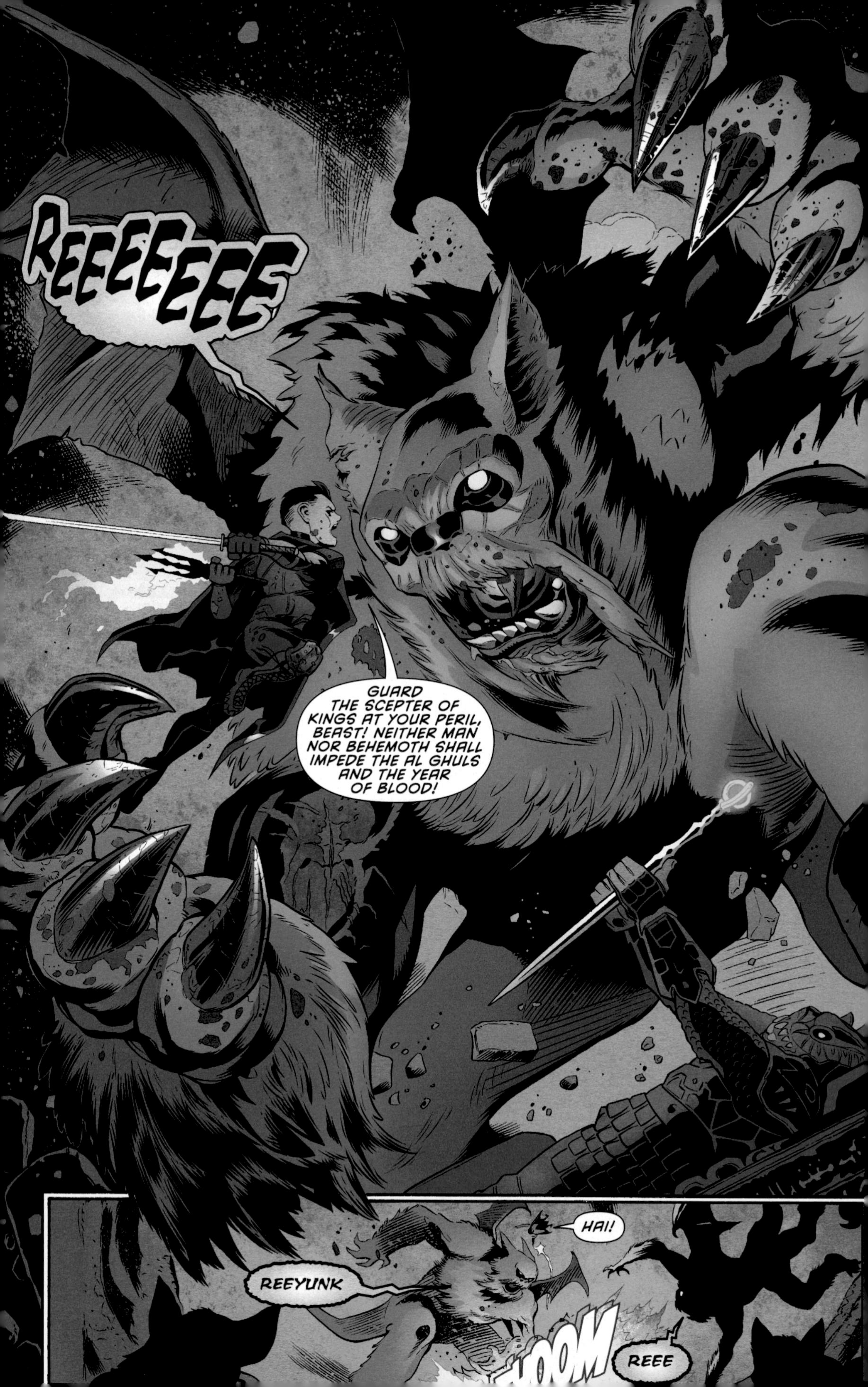
REEEEEEEE
GUARD THE SCEPTER OF KINGS AT YOUR PERIL, BEAST! NEITHER MAN NOR BEHEMOTH SHALL IMPEDE THE AL GHULS AND THE YEAR OF BLOOD!
HAI!
REEYUNK
REEE

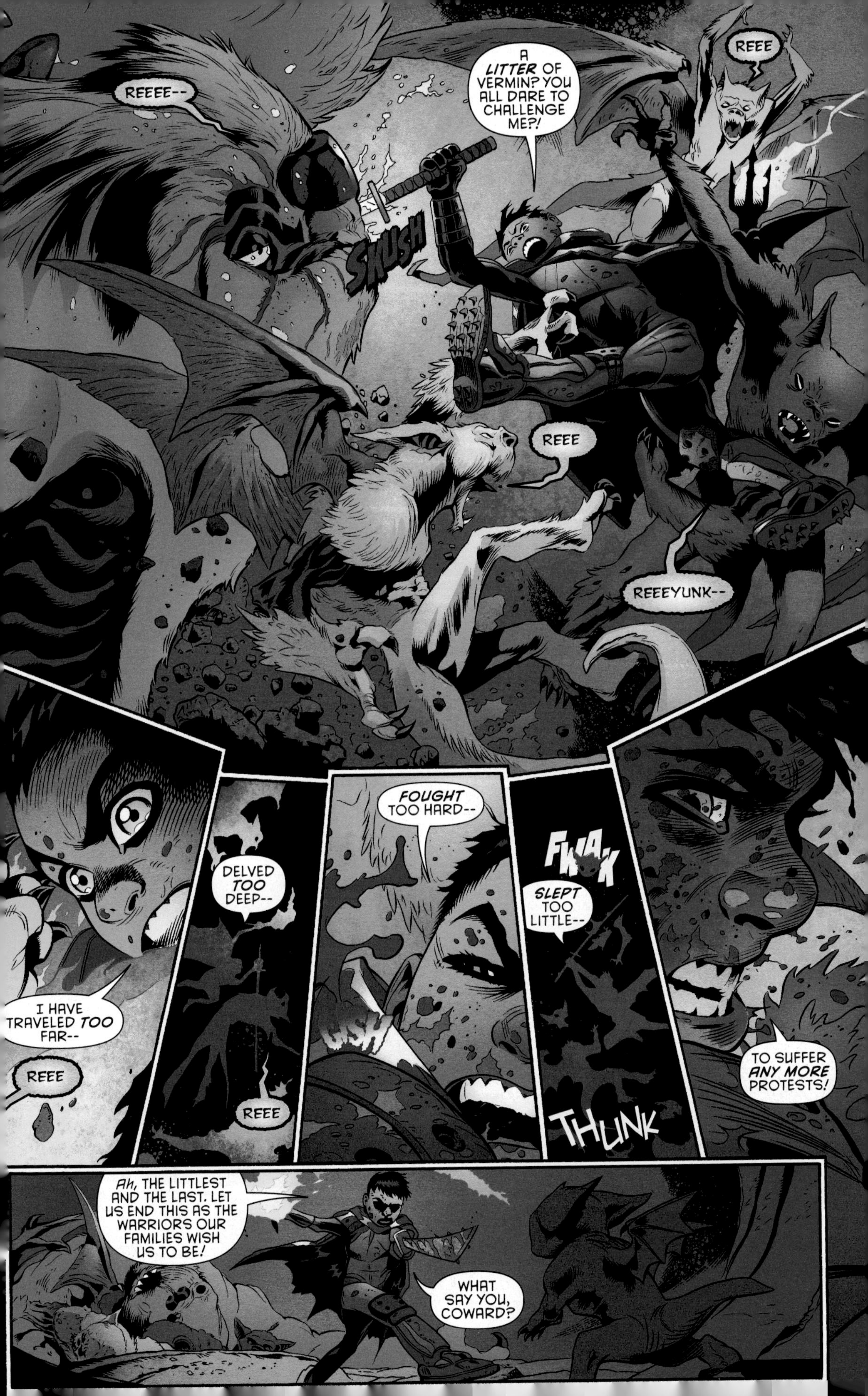
REEEE--
A LITTER OF VERMIN? YOU ALL DARE TO CHALLENGE ME?!
REEE
SKUSH
REEE
REEEYUNK--
I HAVE TRAVELED TOO FAR--
REEE
DELVED TOO DEEP--
REEE
FOUGHT TOO HARD--
SLEPT TOO LITTLE--
THUNK
TO SUFFER ANY MORE PROTESTS!
Ah, THE LITTLEST AND THE LAST. LET US END THIS AS THE WARRIORS OUR FAMILIES WISH US TO BE!
WHAT SAY YOU, COWARD?

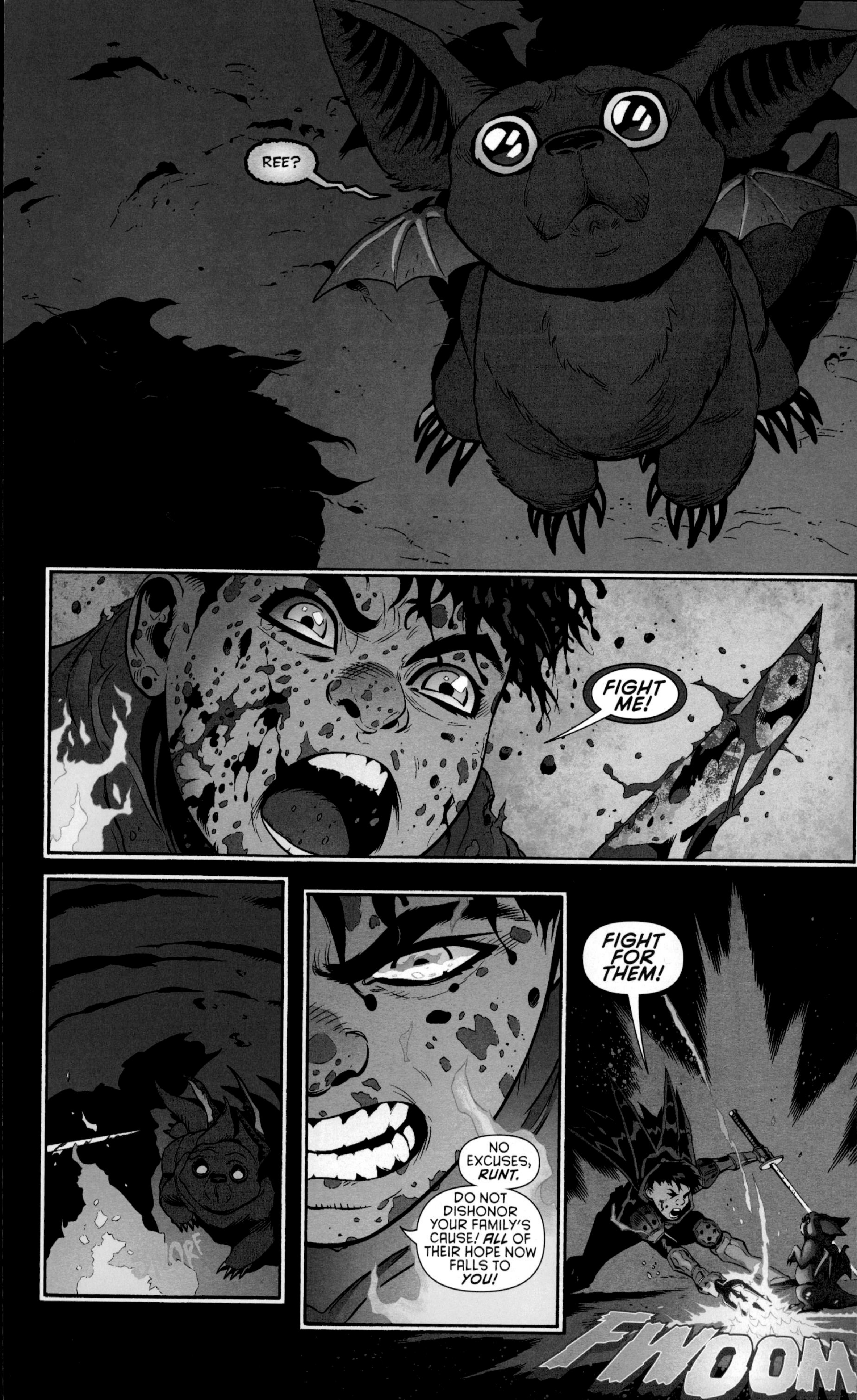
REE?
FIGHT ME!
FIGHT FOR THEM!
NO EXCUSES, RUNT.
DO NOT DISHONOR YOUR FAMILY'S CAUSE! ALL OF THEIR HOPE NOW FALLS TO YOU!
FWOOM

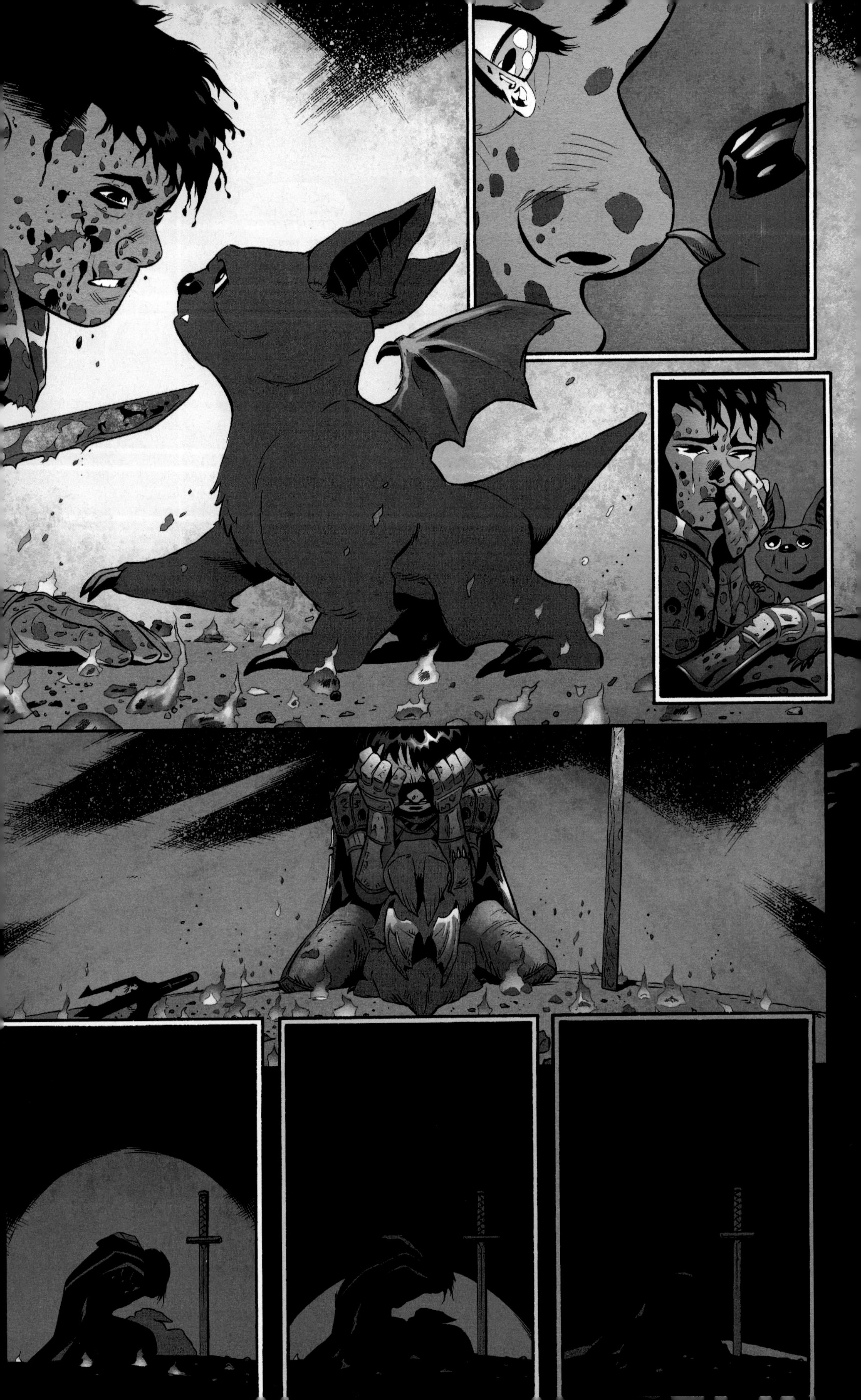

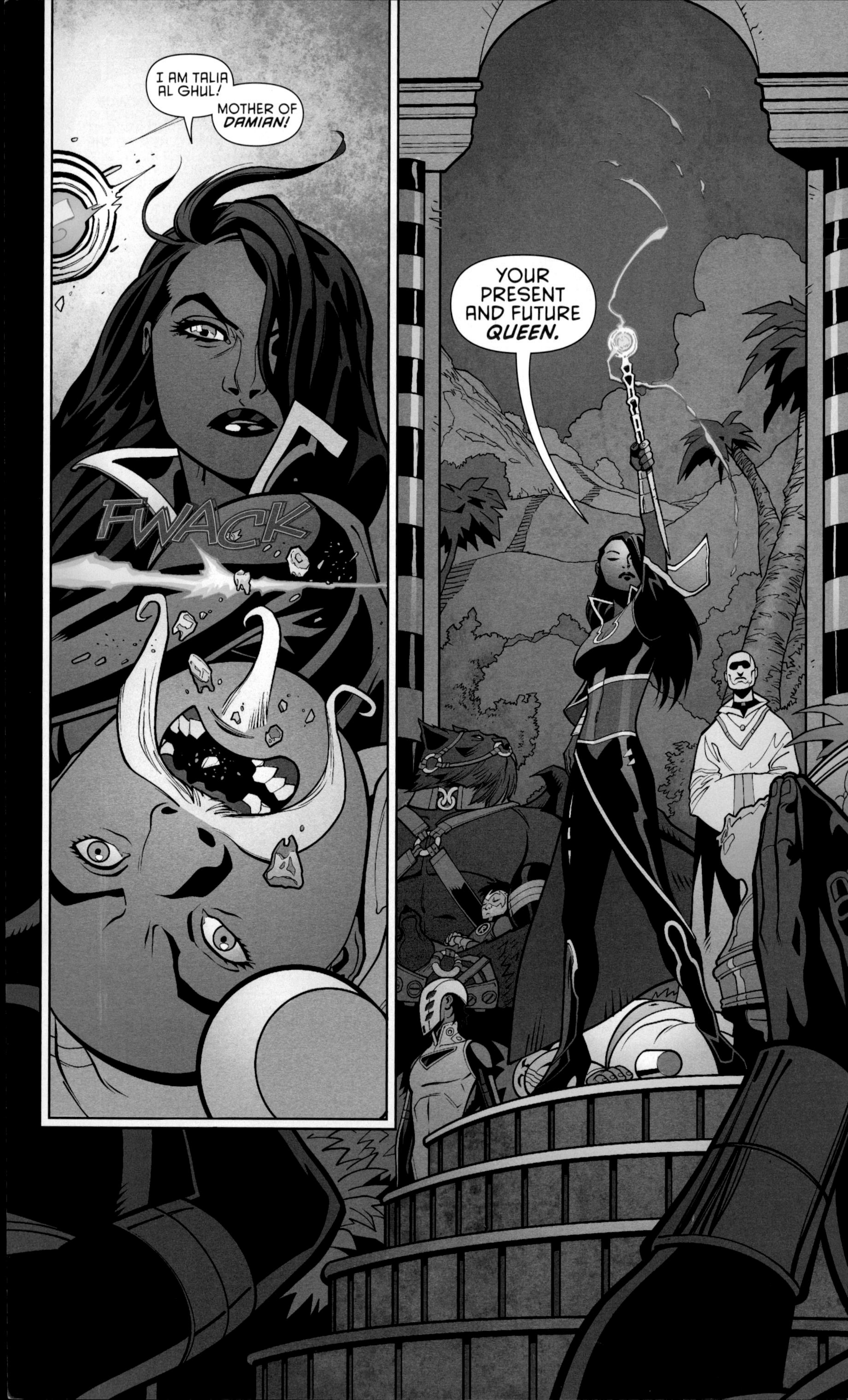
I AM TALIA AL GHUL!
MOTHER OF DAMIAN!
FWACK
YOUR PRESENT AND FUTURE QUEEN.

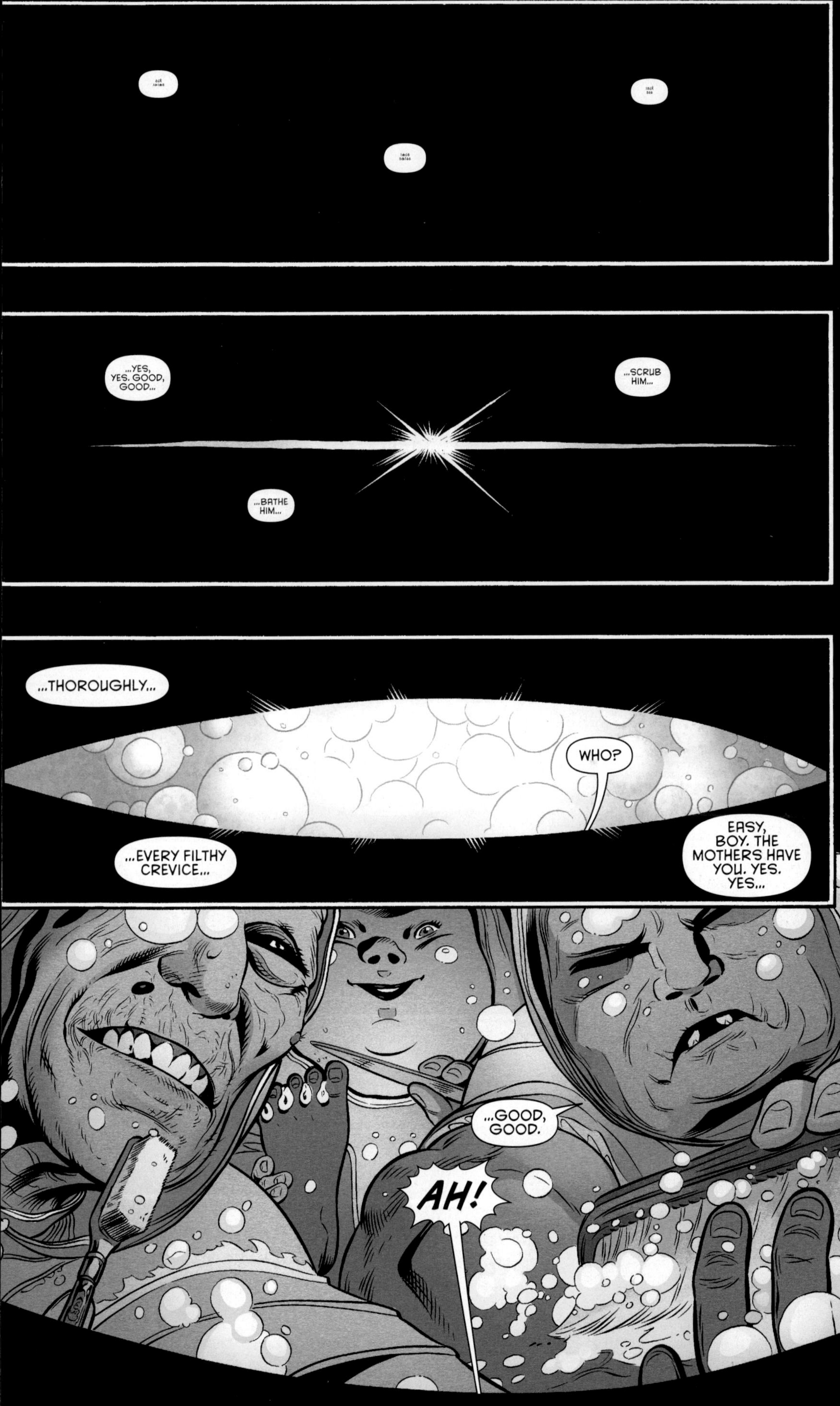
...YES, YES. GOOD, GOOD...
...SCRUB HIM...
...BATHE HIM...
...THOROUGHLY...
WHO?
...EVERY FILTHY CREVICE...
EASY, BOY. THE MOTHERS HAVE YOU. YES. YES...
...GOOD, GOOD.
AH!

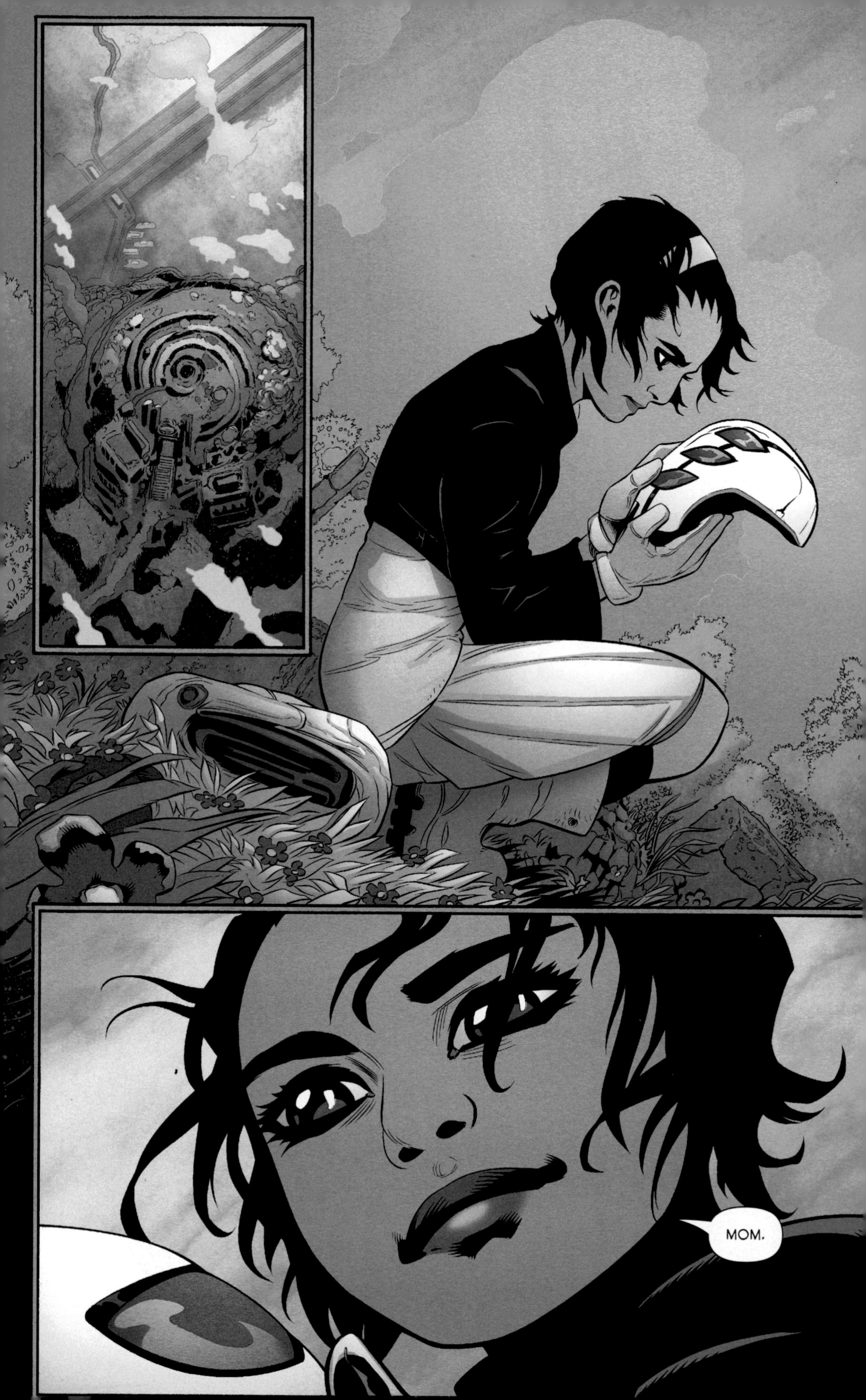
MOM.

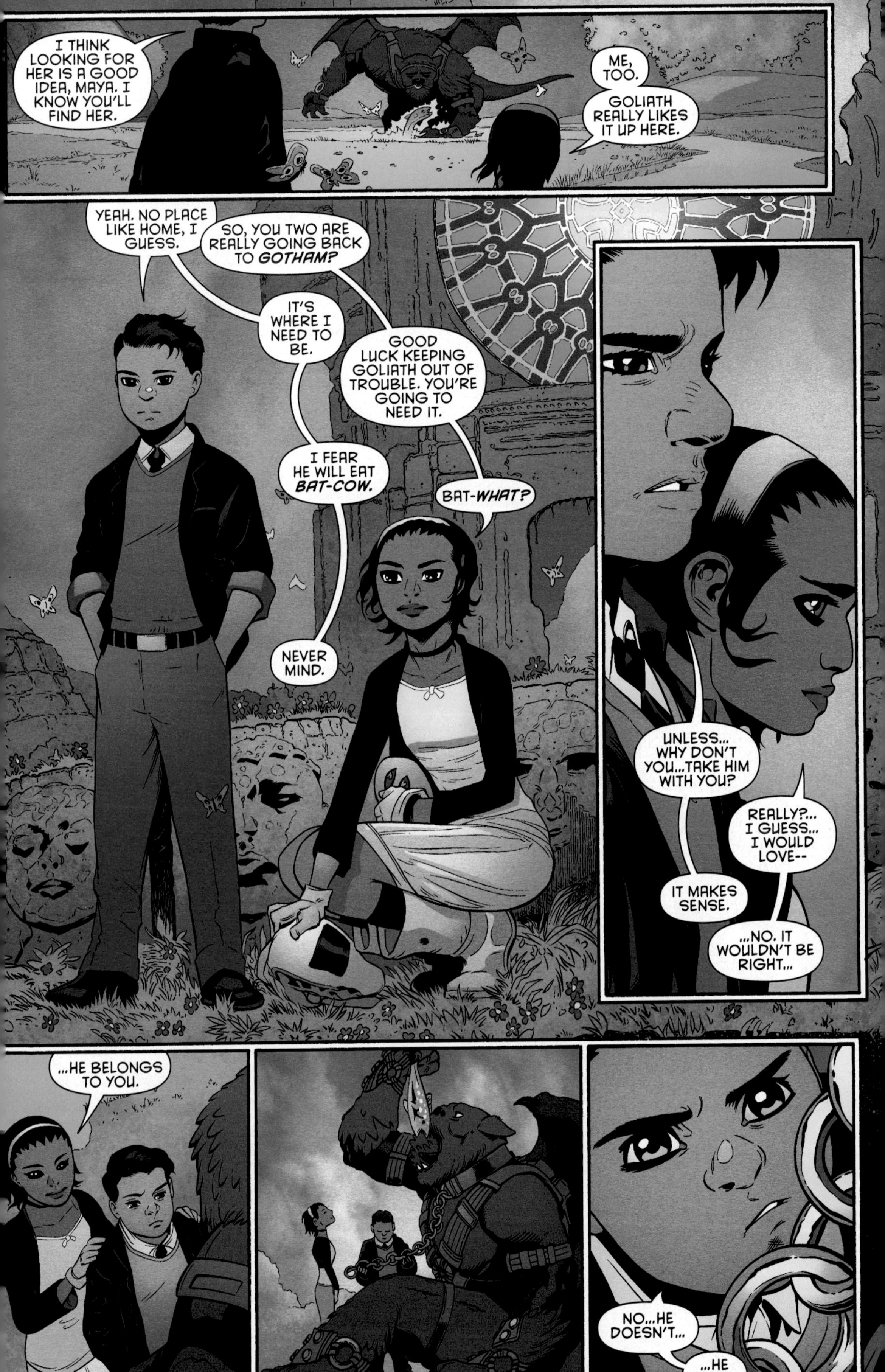

I THINK LOOKING FOR HER IS A GOOD IDEA, MAYA. I KNOW YOU'LL FIND HER.
ME, TOO.
GOLIATH REALLY LIKES IT UP HERE.
YEAH. NO PLACE LIKE HOME, I GUESS.
SO, YOU TWO ARE REALLY GOING BACK TO GOTHAM?
IT'S WHERE I NEED TO BE.
GOOD LUCK KEEPING GOLIATH OUT OF TROUBLE. YOU'RE GOING TO NEED IT.
I FEAR HE WILL EAT BAT-COW.
BAT-WHAT?
NEVER MIND.
UNLESS... WHY DON'T YOU...TAKE HIM WITH YOU?
REALLY?... I GUESS... I WOULD LOVE--
IT MAKES SENSE.
...NO. IT WOULDN'T BE RIGHT...
...HE BELONGS TO YOU.
NO...HE DOESN'T...
...HE NEVER DID.

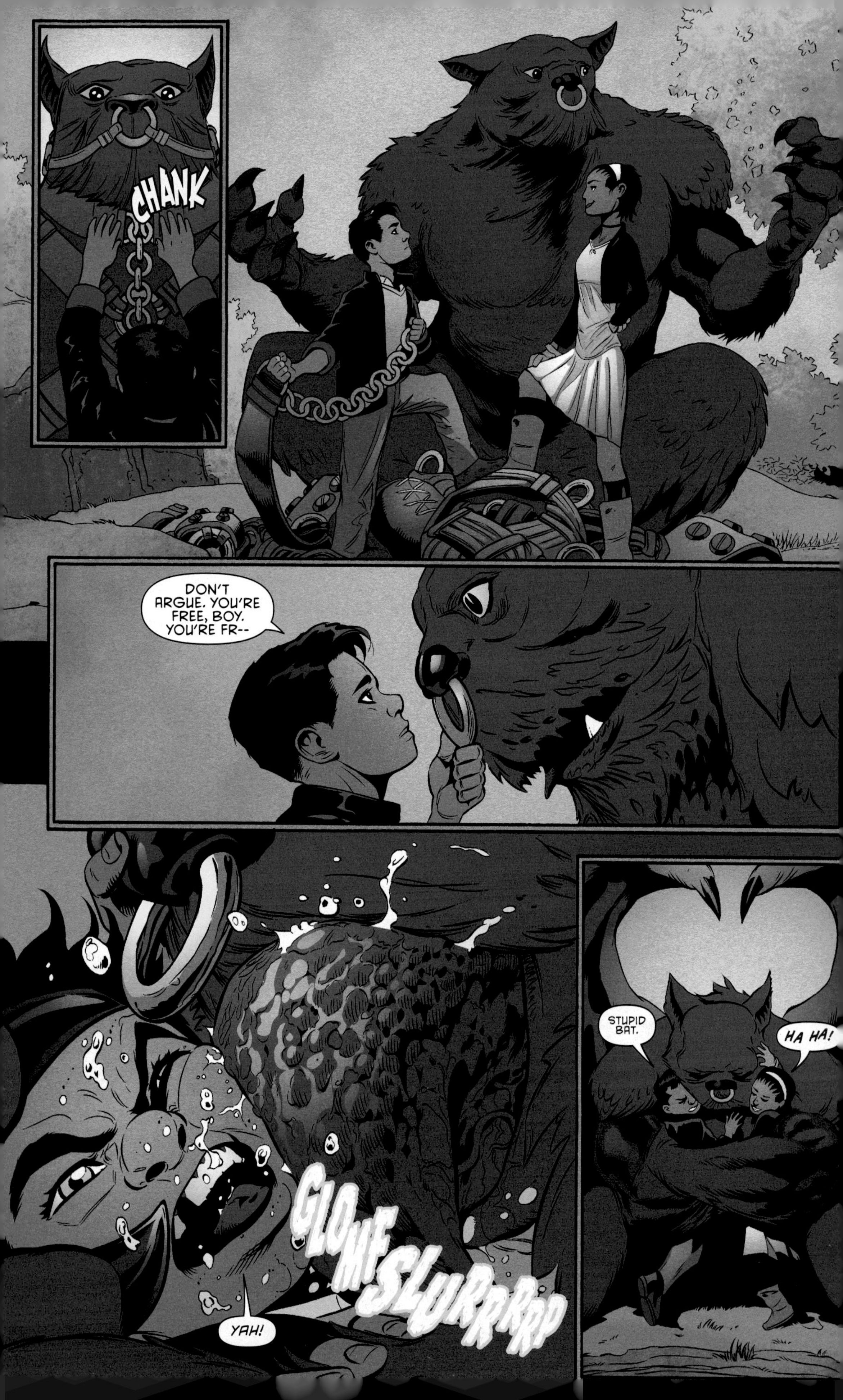
CHANK
DON'T ARGUE. YOU'RE FREE, BOY. YOU'RE FR--
GLOMF SLURRRRP
YAH!
STUPID BAT.
HA HA!

MOTHER WILL BE FURIOUS WHEN SHE FINDS OUT. BE CAREFUL.

WE HAVE SURVIVED THE *AL GHULS* THIS LONG. I WILL REPORT TO YOU WHAT I CAN WHILE YOU ARE AWAY.

GOOD.

THIS NOTE TO THE ARENA AFTER YOU'VE ESCORTED MAYA BACK TO HER SHIP. UNDERSTOOD?

FAREWELL, LORD DAMIAN.

HE WILL BE QUITE AT HOME UP HERE, LORD DAMIAN.

KEEP EACH OTHER SAFE, RAVI.

IT IS WHAT WE DO. YOUR BAGS ARE WELL STOCKED WITH FOOD AND REPAIRED SUPPLIES FOR YOUR LONG JOURNEYS.

YOUR INEXPERIENCE ON THIS NEW PATH WILL REQUIRE GUIDANCE, MAYA. SHOULD YOU NEED HELP--

GAG ME, DUDE.

->TT<-

BUT, THANKS. I WILL.

TAKE CARE OF YOURSELF OUT THERE, DAMIAN.

"MOTHER..."

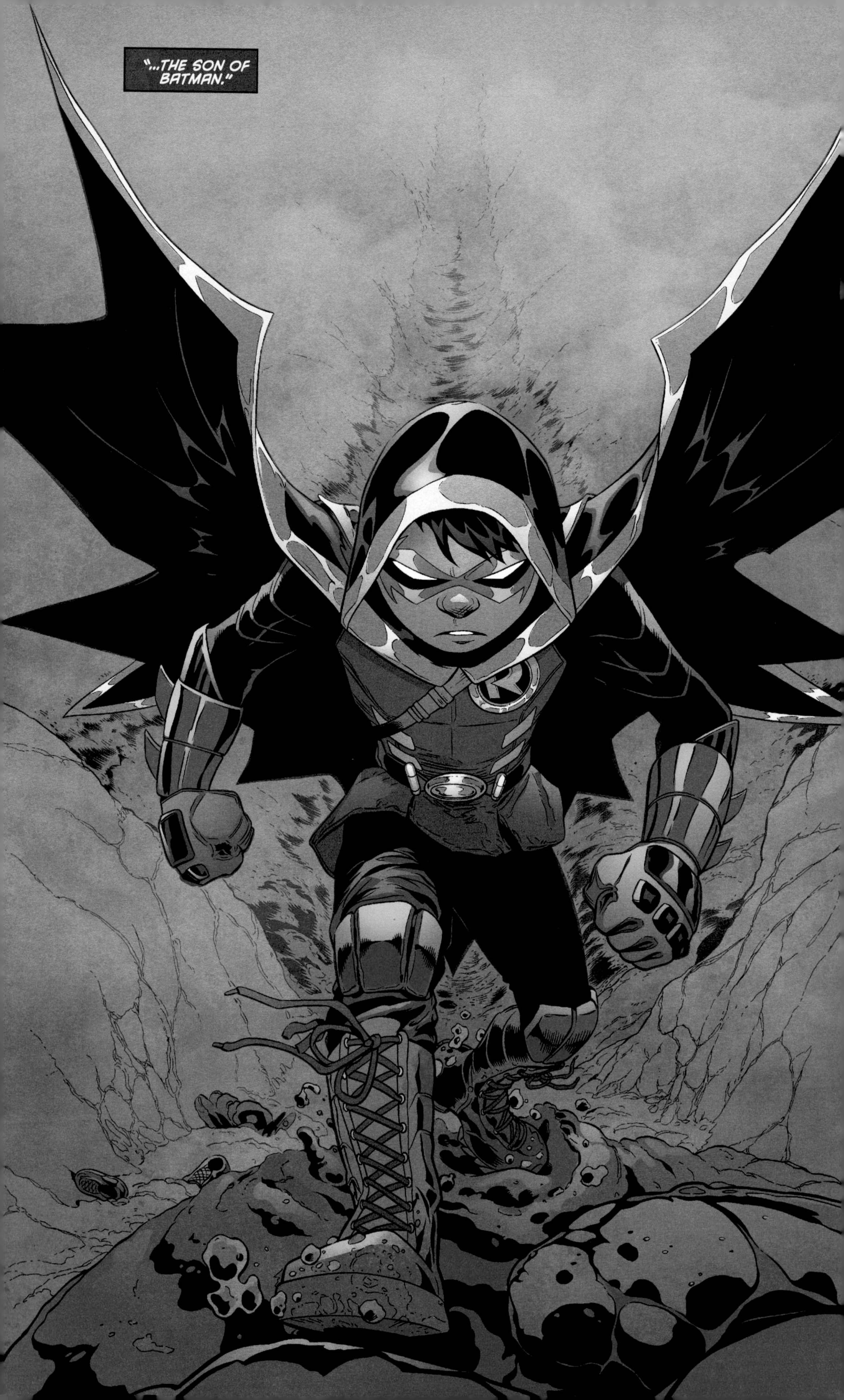
"...THE SON OF BATMAN."

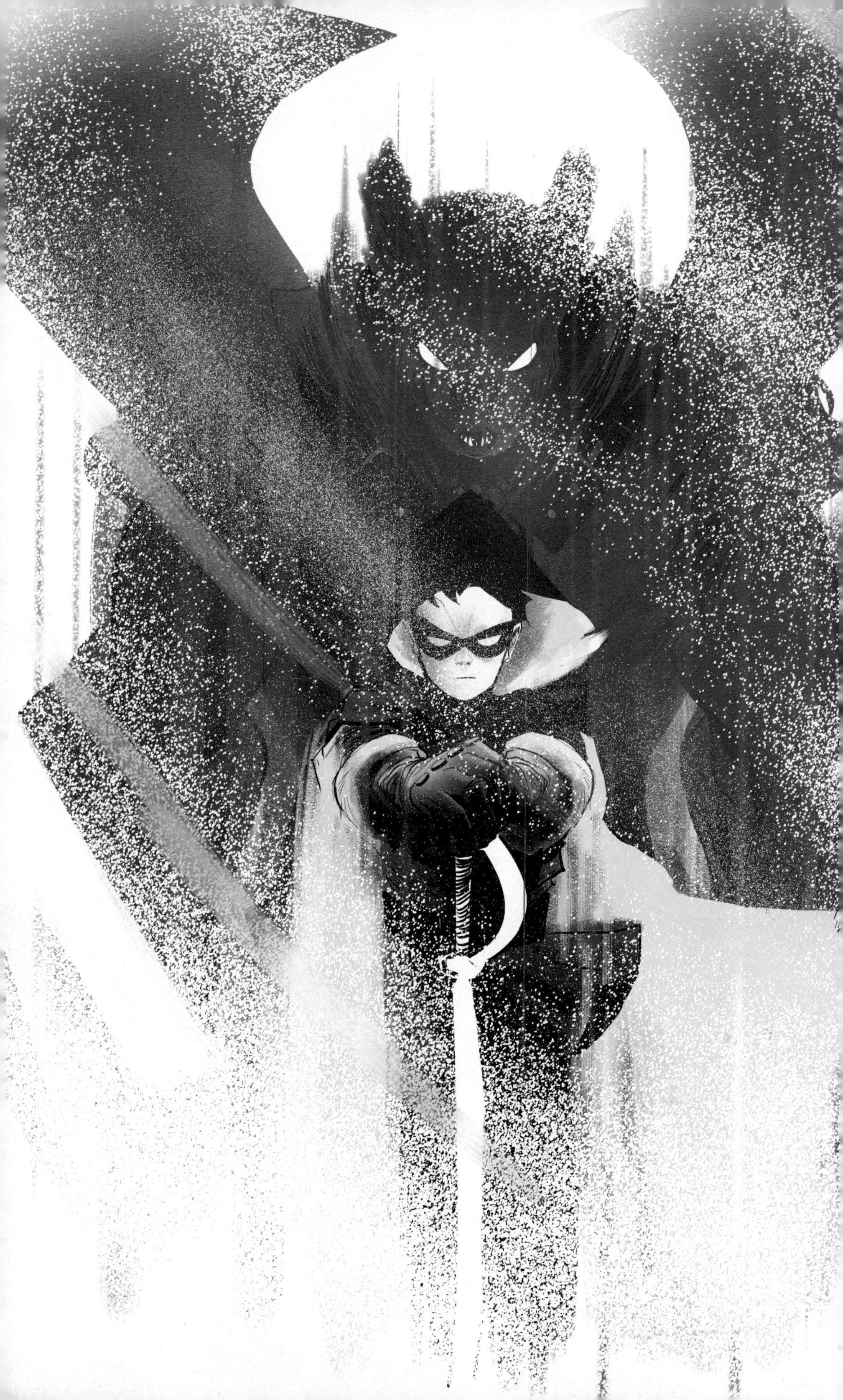

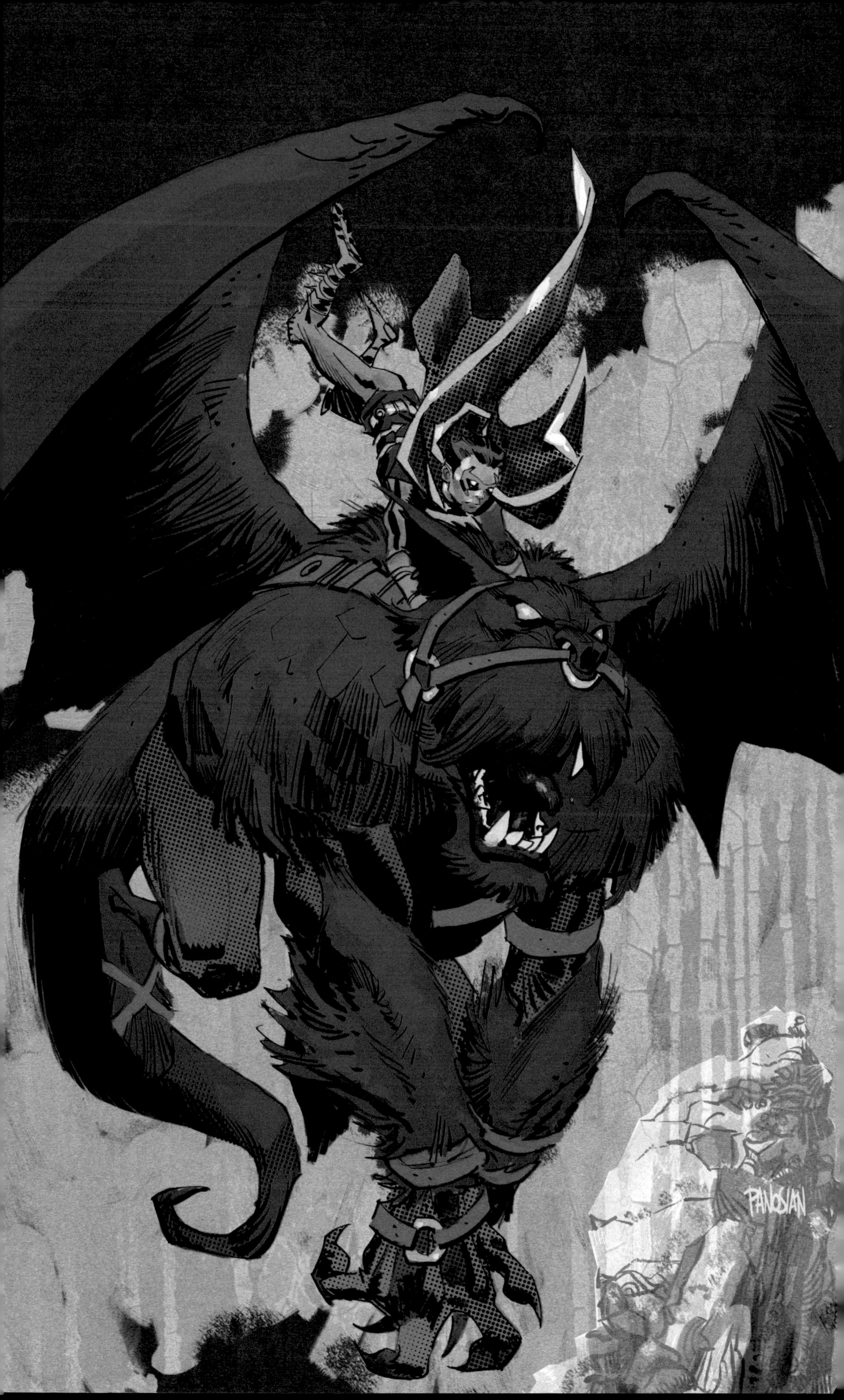
PANOSIAN

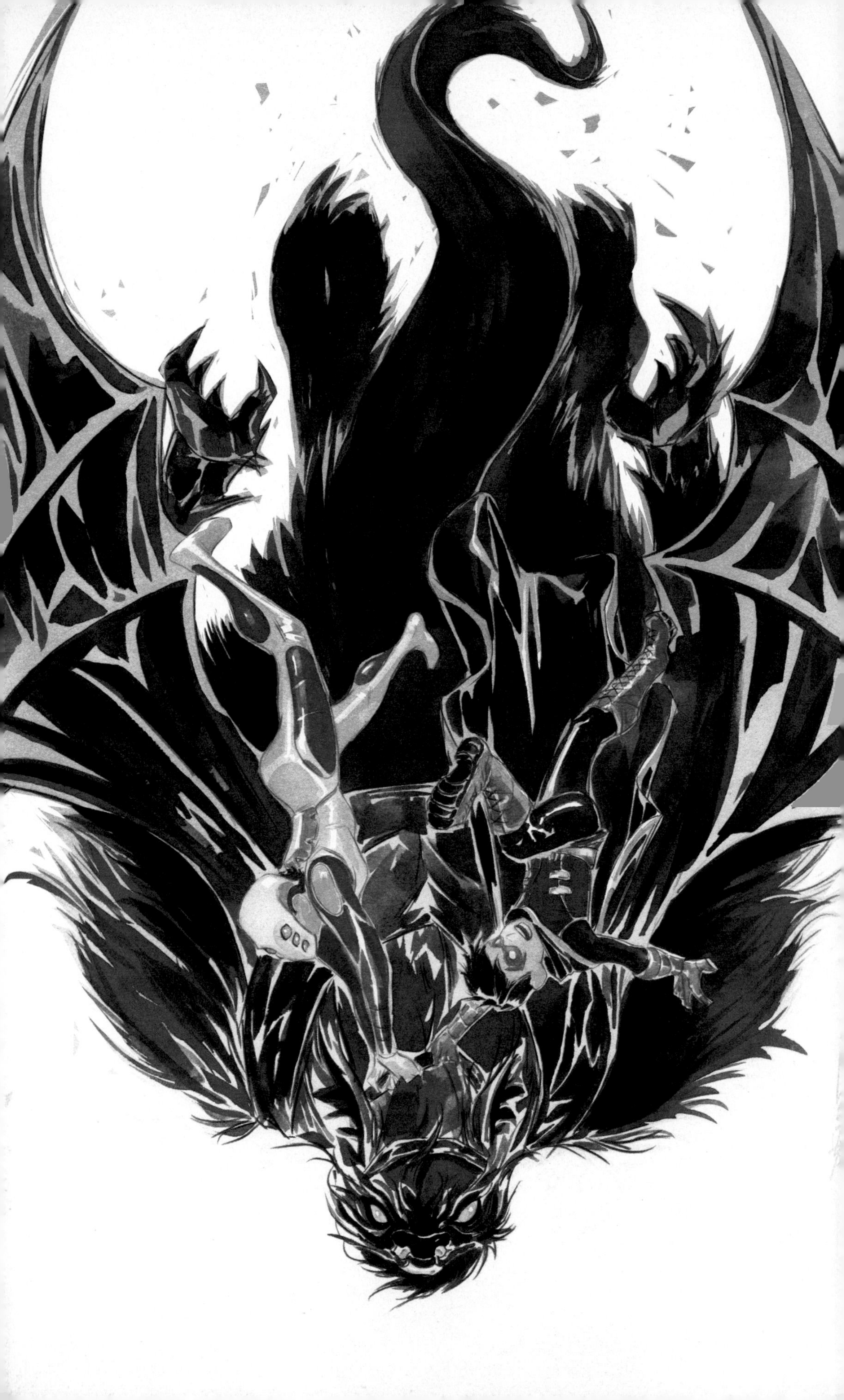

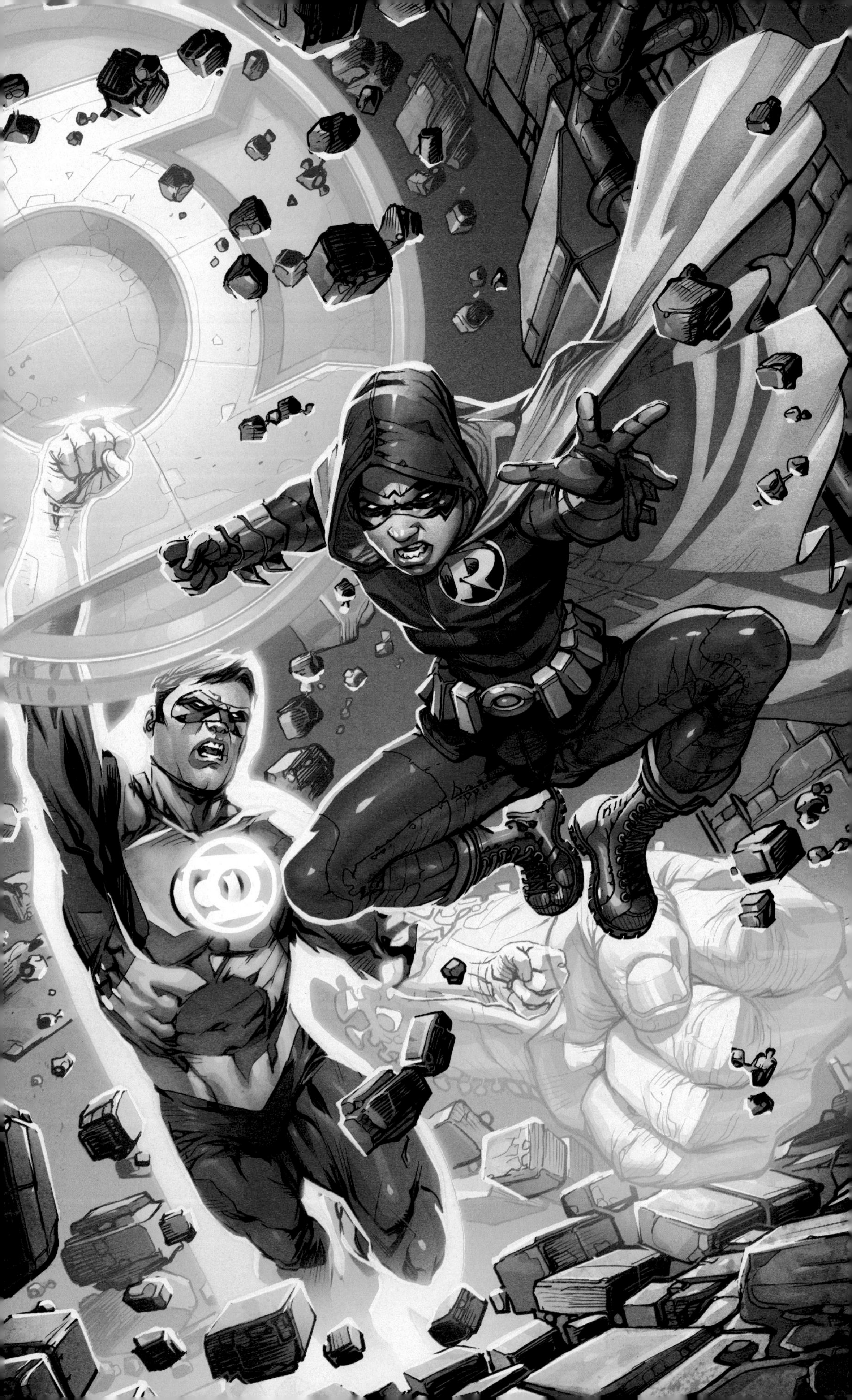

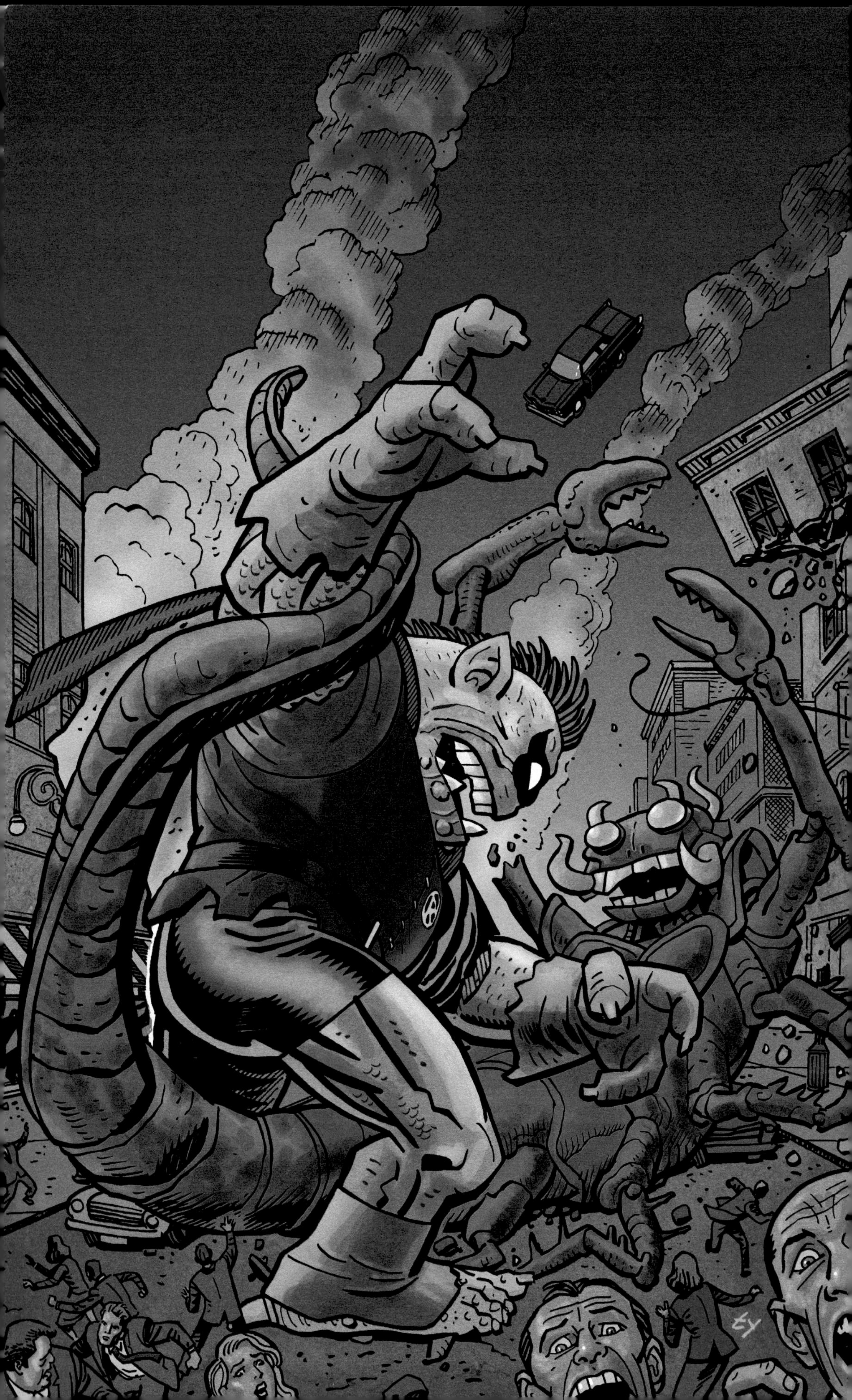

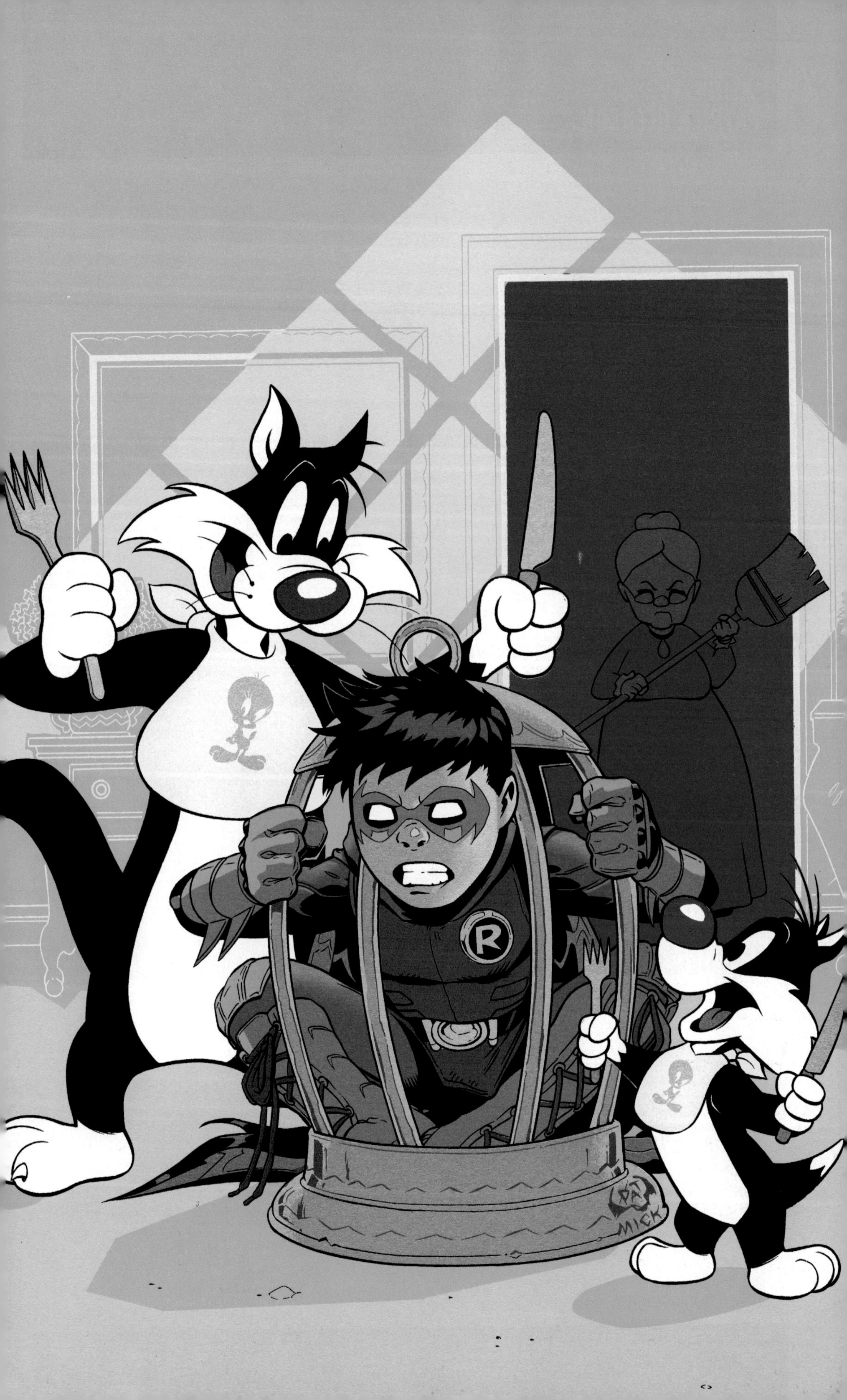

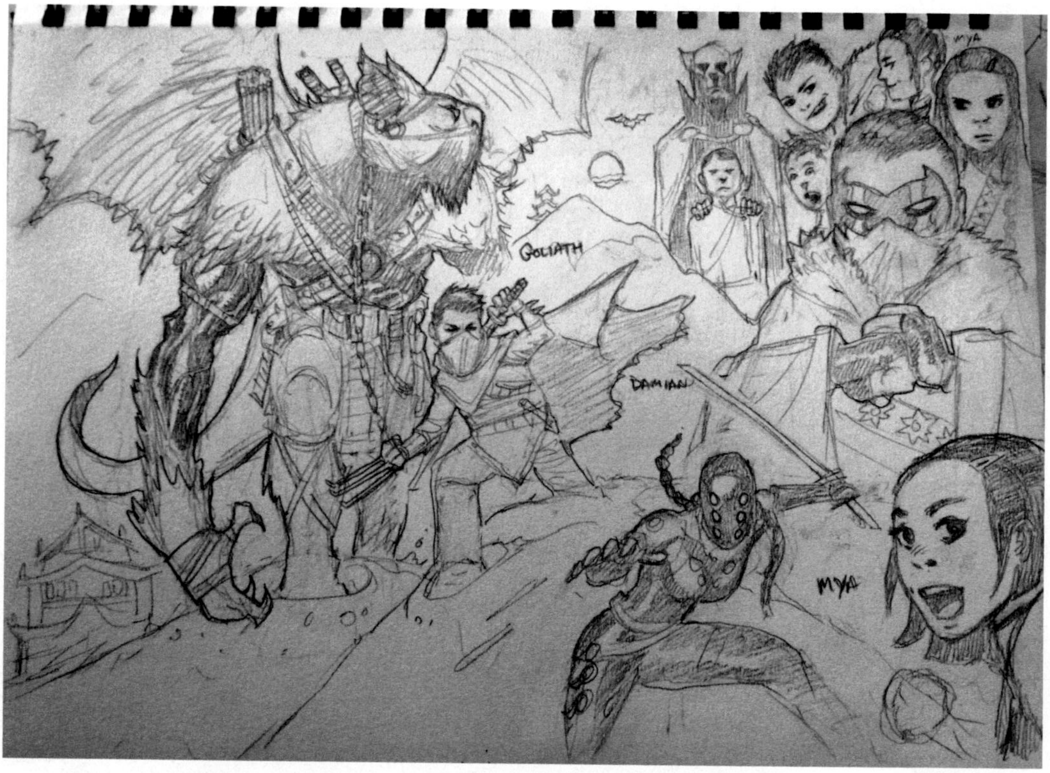
MYA
GOLIATH
DAMIAN
MYA

SNORF

REE?

BABY GOLIATH
PATCHEASU

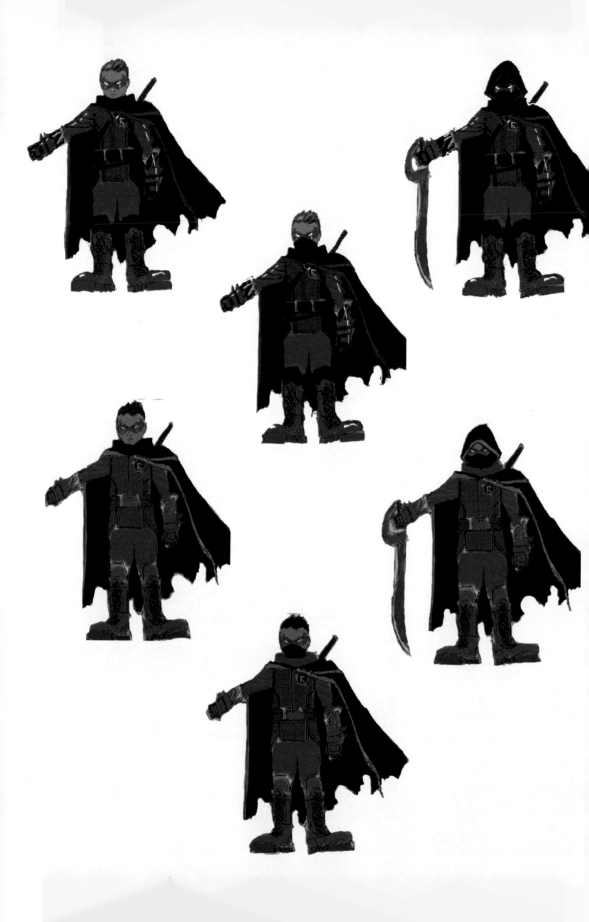

TALIA
AL
GHUL

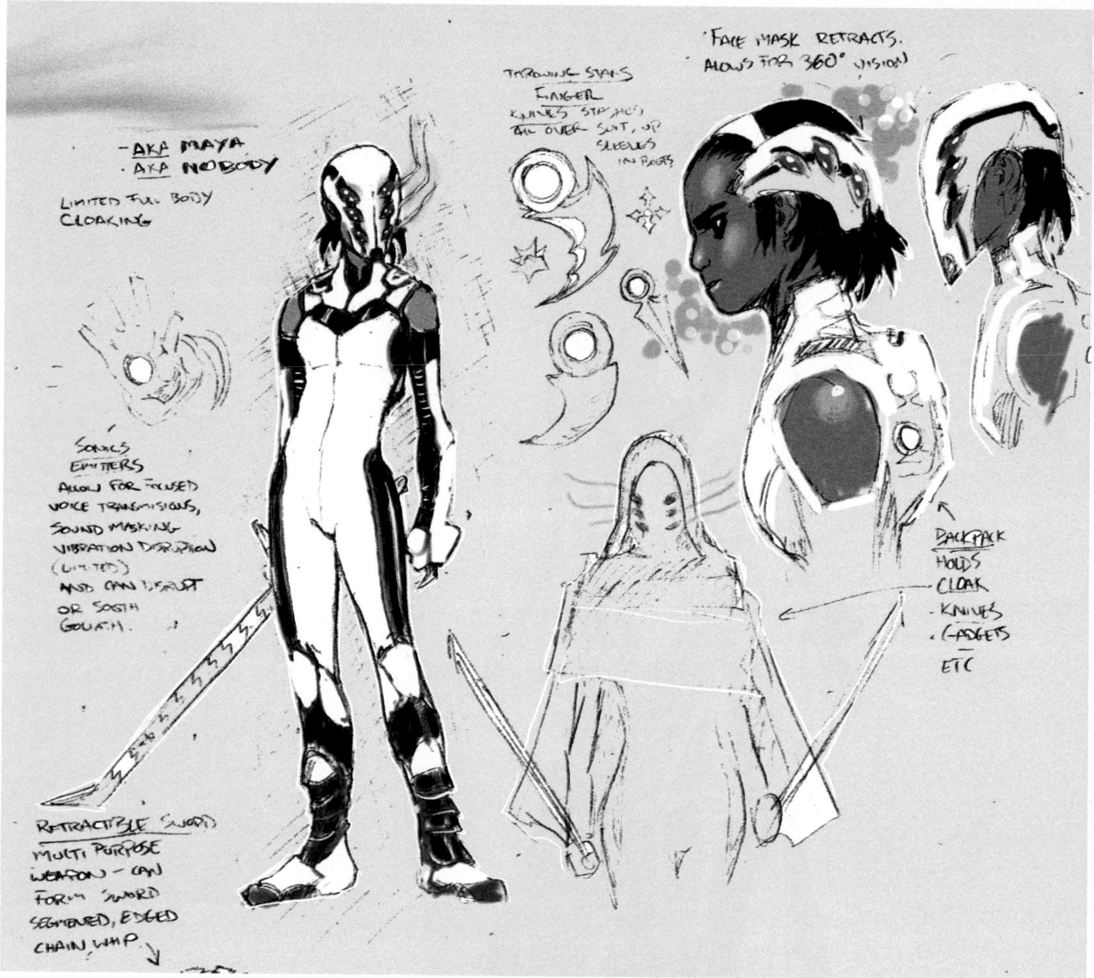

- AKA MAYA
· AKA NOBODY
LIMITED FULL BODY CLOAKING
SONICS EMITTERS ALLOW FOR FOCUSED VOICE TRANSMISIONS, SOUND MASKING VIBRATION DISRUPTION (LIMITED) AND CAN DISRUPT OR SOOTH GOLIATH.
THROWING STARS
DAGGER
KNIVES STASHED ALL OVER SUIT, UP SLEEVES IN BOOTS
FACE MASK RETRACTS. ALOWS FOR 360° VISION
BACKPACK HOLDS
- CLOAK
- KNIVES
- GADGETS
ETC
RETRACTIBLE SWORD
MULTI PURPOSE WEAPON - CAN FORM SWORD SEGMENTED, EDGED CHAIN WHIP.

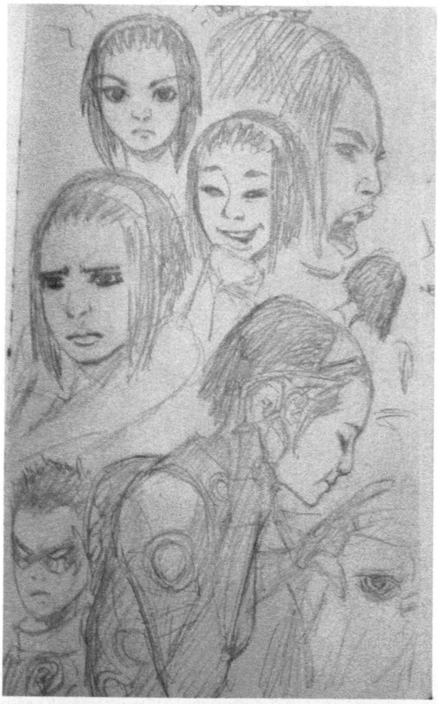

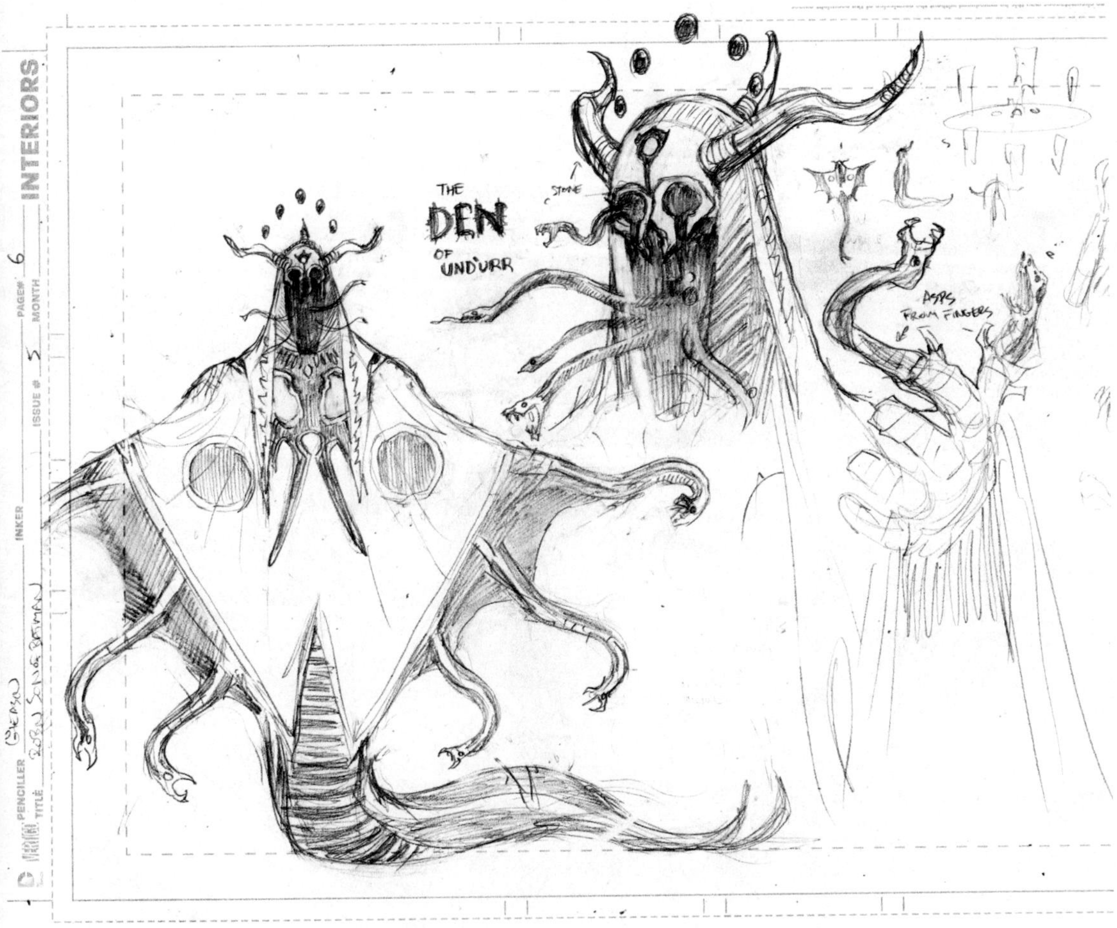
INTERIORS
PAGE# 6
ISSUE # 5
MONTH
INKER
PENCILLER Gleason
TITLE Robin Son of Batman
THE DEN OF UND'URR
STONE
ASPS FROM FINGERS

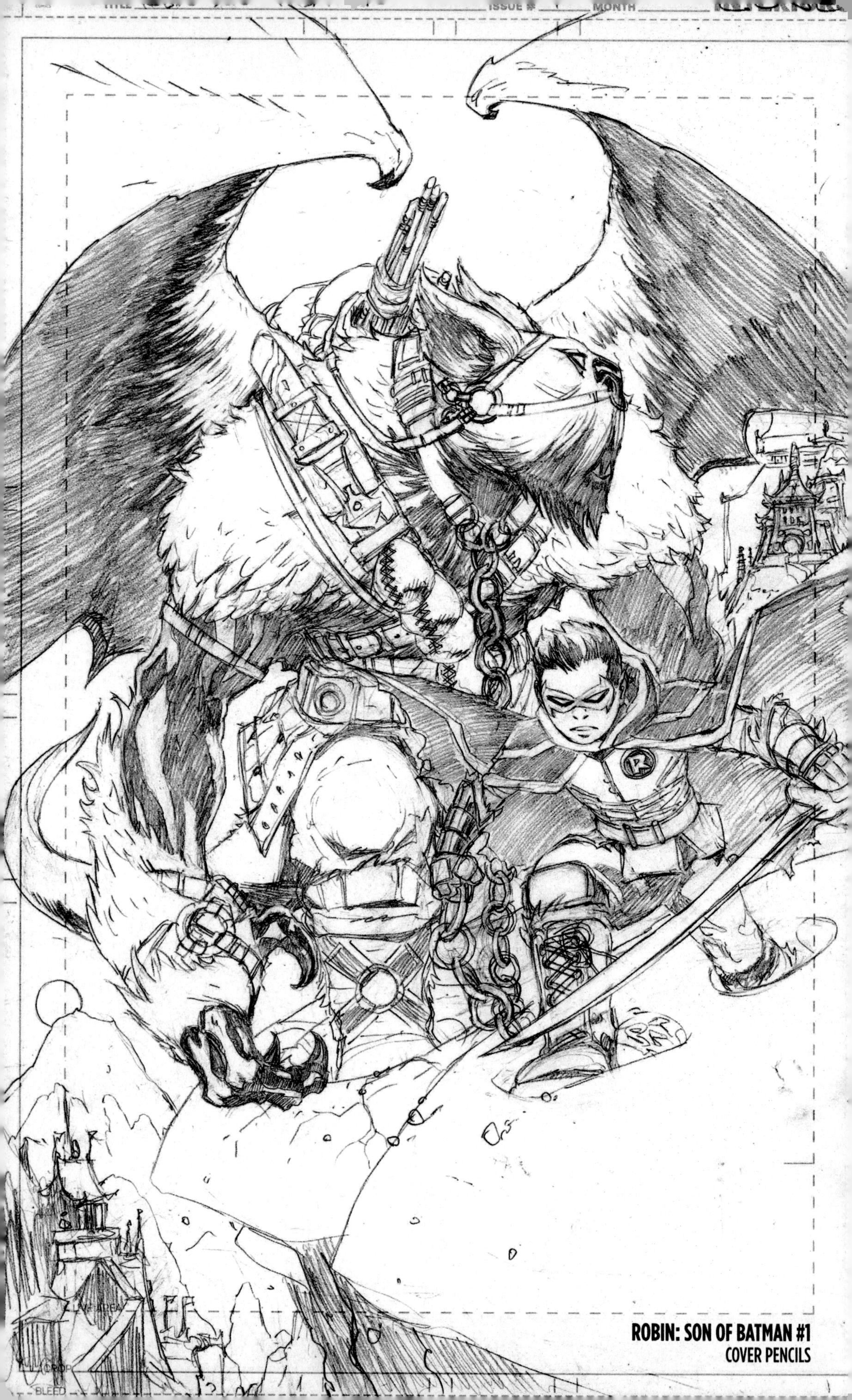

ROBIN: SON OF BATMAN #1
COVER PENCILS

ROBIN: SON OF BATMAN #6
UNUSED COVER SKETCH

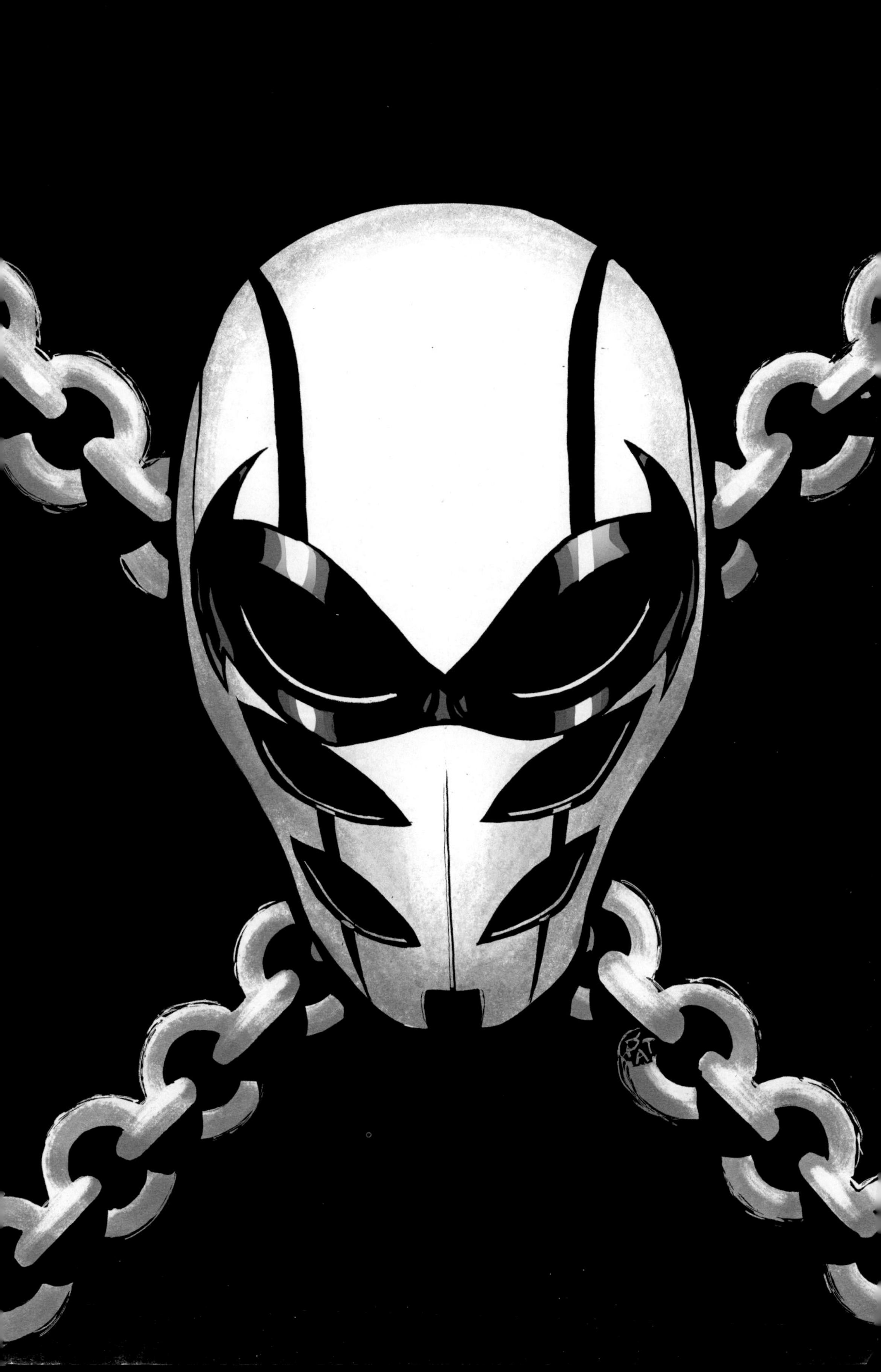

ROBIN: SON OF BATMAN #3
PAGE 10 PENCILS

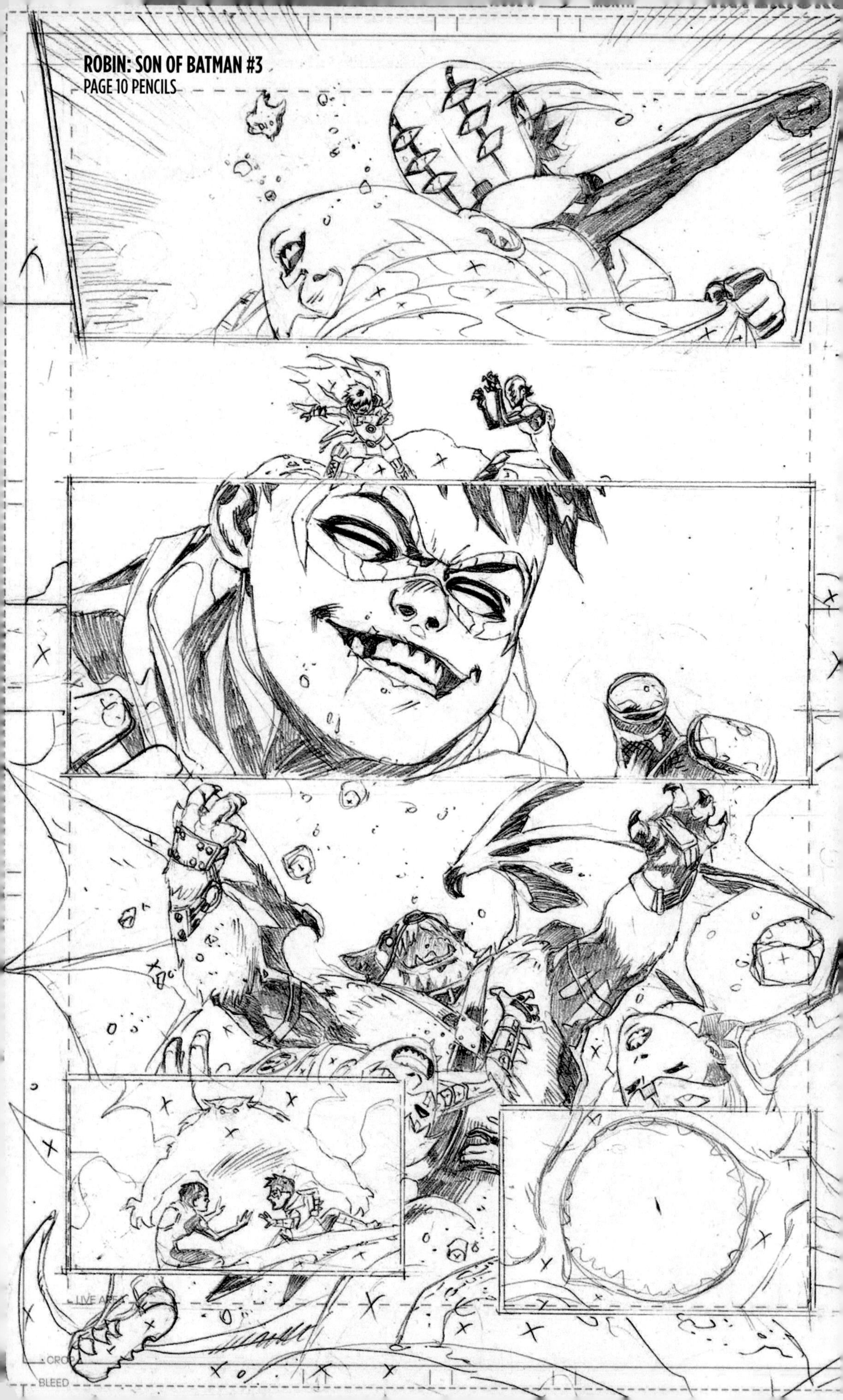

LIVE AREA
CROP
BLEED

ROBIN: SON OF BATMAN #4
PAGE 15 PENCILS

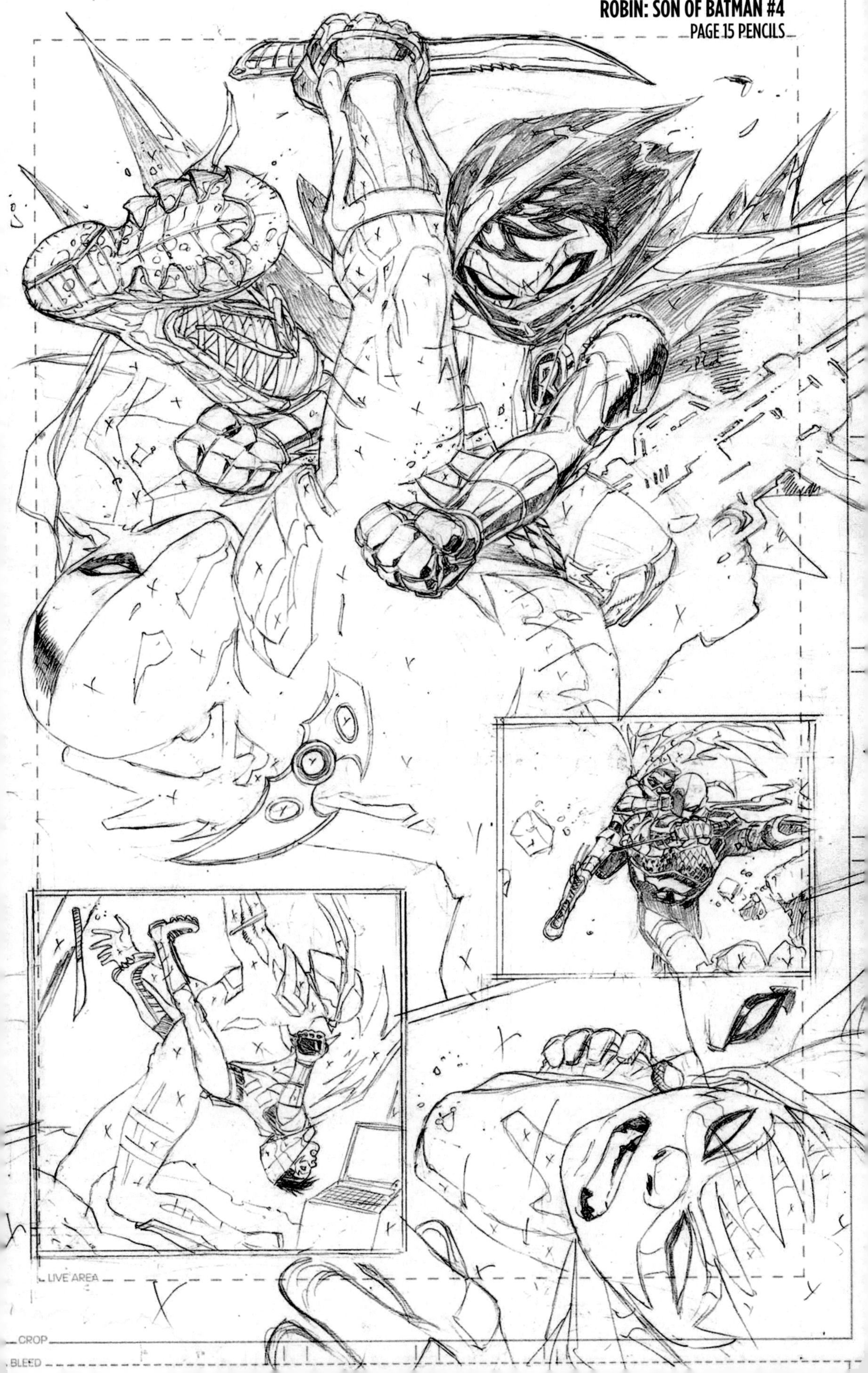
LIVE AREA
CROP
BLEED

ROBIN: SON OF BATMAN #5
PAGE 16 PENCILS

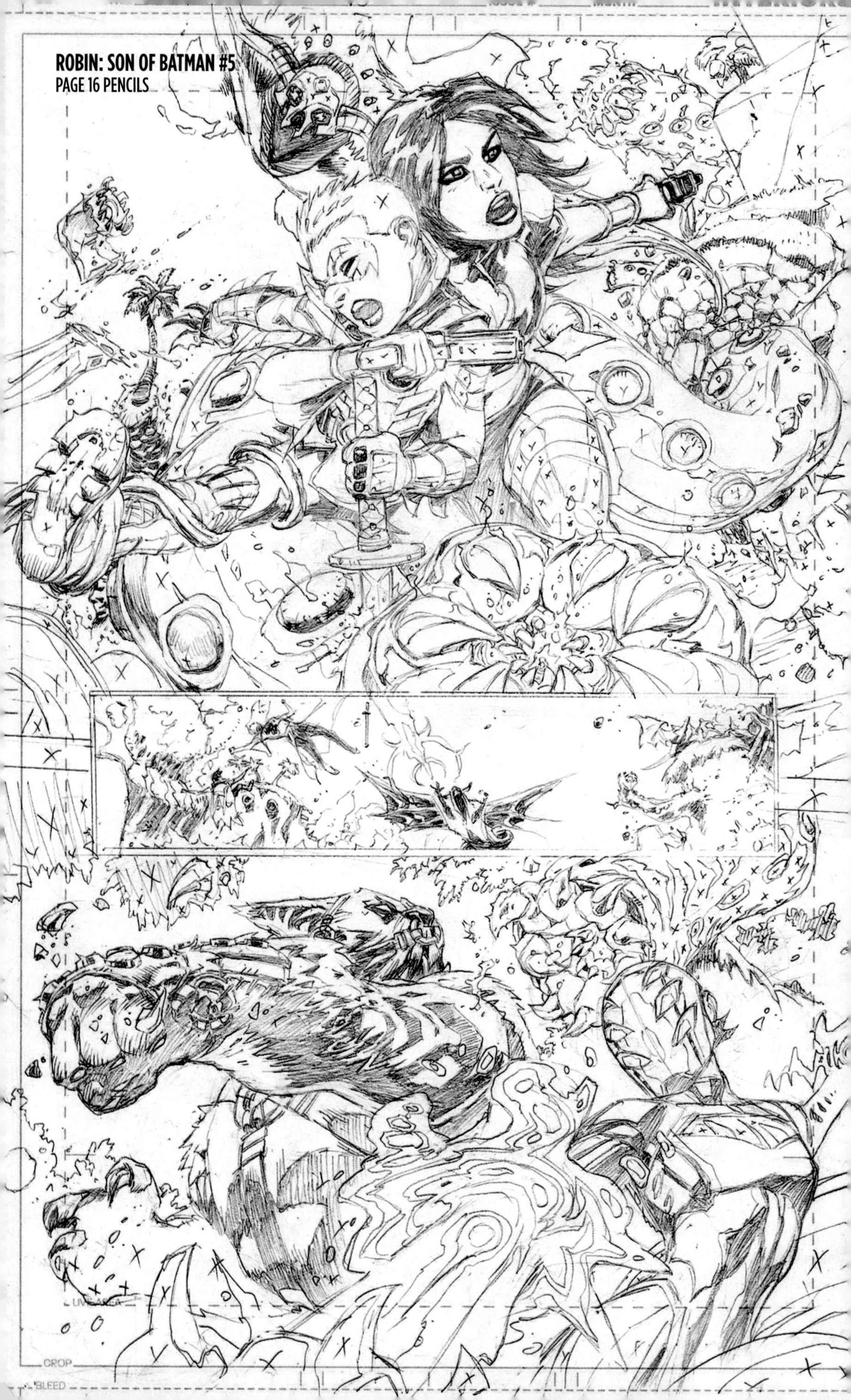

ROBIN: SON OF BATMAN #6
PAGE 15 PENCILS

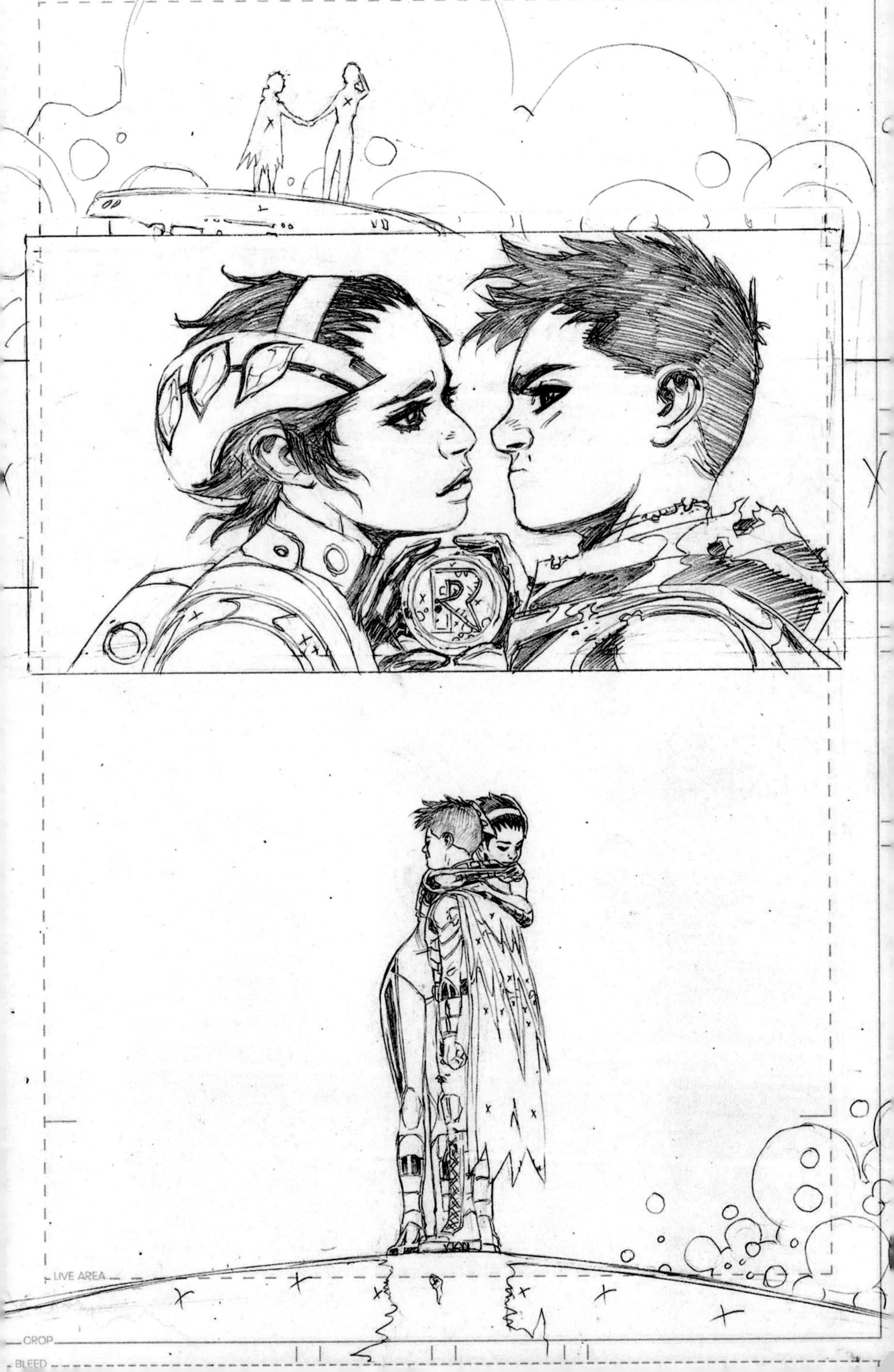
LIVE AREA
CROP
BLEED

DC COMICS™

GRANT MORRISON
with FRANK QUITELY & PHILIP TAN

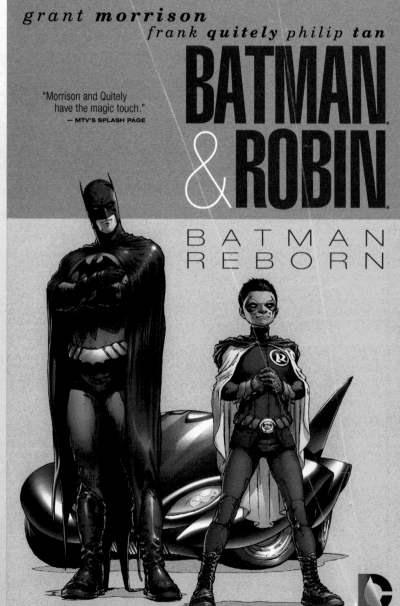

DC
COMICS™